THE ISSUE OF POLITICAL ETHNICITY IN AFRICA

Contemporary Perspectives on Developing Societies

JOHN MUKUM MBAKU, Series General Editor, Weber State University
MWANGI S. KIMENYI, Series Associate Editor, The University of Connecticut & KIPPRA, Kenya

Between 1989 and 1991, there were several changes in the global political economy that have had significant impact on policy reform in developing societies. The most important of these were the collapse of socialism in Eastern Europe, the subsequent disintegration of the Soviet Union, the cessation of superpower rivalry, and the demise of apartheid in South Africa. These events have provided scholars a new and challenging research agenda: To help the peoples of the Third World participate more effectively in the new global economy. Given existing conditions in these societies, the first line of business for researchers would be to help these countries establish and maintain transparent, accountable and participatory governance structures and, at the same time, provide themselves with more viable economic infrastructures. The *Contemporary Perspectives on Developing Societies* series was founded to serve as an outlet for such policy relevant research. It is expected that books published in this series will provide rigorous analyses of issues relevant to the peoples of the Third World and their efforts to improve their participation in the global economy.

Also in this series

Hope, K. R., Sr. (ed.) (1997), *Structural Adjustment, Reconstruction and Development in Africa.*
Mbaku, J. M. and Ihonvbere, J. O. (eds.) (1998), *Multiparty Democracy and Political Change: Constraints to democratization in Africa.*
Kimenyi, M. S., Wieland, R. C. and Von Pischke, J. D. (eds.) (1988), *Strategic Issues in Microfinance.*
Magnarella, P. J. (ed.) (1998), *Middle East and North Africa: Governance, democratization, human rights.*
Mbaku, J. M. (ed.) (1999), *Preparing Africa for the Twenty-First Century: Strategies for peaceful coexistence and sustainable development.*
Magnarella, P. J. (2000), *Justice in Africa: Rwanda's Genocide, It's Courts, and the UN Criminal Tribunal.*
Ngoh, V. J. (2001), *Southern Cameroons, 1922-1961: A Constitutional History.*

The Issue of Political Ethnicity in Africa

Edited by

E. IKE UDOGU
Department of Political Science
Francis Marion University
Florence, South Carolina, USA

LONDON AND NEW YORK

First published 2001 by Ashgate Publishing

Reissued 2018 by Routledge
2 Park Square, Milton Park, Abingdon, Oxon OX14 4RN
711 Third Avenue, New York, NY 10017, USA

Routledge is an imprint of the Taylor & Francis Group, an informa business

Copyright © E. Ike Udogu 2001

All rights reserved. No part of this book may be reprinted or reproduced or utilised in any form or by any electronic, mechanical, or other means, now known or hereafter invented, including photocopying and recording, or in any information storage or retrieval system, without permission in writing from the publishers.

Notice:
Product or corporate names may be trademarks or registered trademarks, and are used only for identification and explanation without intent to infringe.

Publisher's Note
The publisher has gone to great lengths to ensure the quality of this reprint but points out that some imperfections in the original copies may be apparent.

Disclaimer
The publisher has made every effort to trace copyright holders and welcomes correspondence from those they have been unable to contact.

A Library of Congress record exists under LC control number: 2014044164

ISBN 13: 978-1-138-73490-6 (hbk)
ISBN 13: 978-1-138-73488-3 (pbk)
ISBN 13: 978-1-315-18688-7 (ebk)

Contents

List of Tables   vii

List of Contributors   ix

Acknowledgments   xiii

1   General Introduction
     E. Ike Udogu   1

2   Ethnicity and Theory in African Politics
     E. Ike Udogu   13

3   Ethnicity and Political Economy of Africa: A
     Conceptual Analysis
     Kelechi A. Kalu   35

4   The State and Ethnicity in Africa
     Julius O. Ihonvbere   59

5   The Ethnic Dimensions of Nigeria's Post-
     Annulment Crisis: Case Studies from the South
     Olufemi Vaughan   79

6   Ethnic Politics and the Decay of the State in
     Kenya
     F. Wafula Okumu   99

7   The Ekutay: Ethnic Cabal and Politics in Sierra
     Leone
     Alfred B. Zack-Williams   125

8	The Limits and Possibilities of Conflict-Reduction Strategies in Africa's Polyethnic States *John Boye Ejobowah*	149
9	Western Discourse and the Socio-Political Pathology of Ethnicity in Contemporary Africa *Peyi Soyinka-Airewele*	167

Selected Bibliography   *187*

Index   *199*

List of Tables

3.1	Socio-economic and political indicators of selected sub-Saharan African states	49
3.2	Military expenditures for selected sub-Saharan African countries, 1998–1997 (in millions of local currency units)	51
3.3	Military expenditures for selected sub-Saharan African countries, 1988–1997 (in constant US dollars, millions)	52
7.1	Average rate of growth in per capita income, 1970–1995 in Sierra Leone	134
7.2	Demographic distribution and ethnic groups in Sierra Leone	136

List of Contributors

John Boye Ejobowah obtained his Ph.D. in political theory from the University of Toronto where he teaches African politics. His research interest is in late 20th century theory, constitutionalism and ethnic conflict-reduction. He has published in *Africa Today*, *Journal of Nationalism and Ethnic Politics* and *Journal of Third World Studies*.

Julius O. Ihonvbere is Professor of African politics in the Department of Government at the University of Texas at Austin, and currently serves as Program Officer, Governance and Civil Society Unit, The Ford Foundation, New York. His research interests focus on the state and democratization, human rights, the military and the new globalization. His prodigious works have appeared in such journals as *Africa Today*, *The Journal of Modern African Studies*, *Journal of Asian and African Studies*, *International Politics*, *The Journal of Political and Military Sociology*, just to list a few. He has published numerous books including *Nigeria: The Politics of Adjustment & Democracy* (Transaction Publishers, 1994); *Economic Crisis, Civil Society and Democratization: The Case of Zambia* (Africa World Press, 1996); and *Africa and the New World Order* (Peter Lang, 1998). He has also contributed numerous book chapters, including in the pages of this volume.

Kelechi A. Kalu is an Associate Professor of political science at the University of Northern Colorado, Greeley, Colorado. He was a Mellon Research Fellow in Government at Connecticut College, New London, Connecticut in 1994/1995. He is the current program chair of the International Studies Association-Southwest, 1999-2001. He is the author of *Economic Development and Nigerian Foreign Policy* (The Edwin Mellen Press, 2000). His publications and forthcoming works include articles in *International Journal of Politics, Culture and Society*, *Africa Today*, *Journal of Nigerian Affairs*, *Journal of Asian and African Studies*, *Journal of Third World Studies*, and several book chapters on African and Third World issues. He is currently working on a manuscript on international relations theory and conflict prevention in Africa.

F. Wafula Okumu is an Assistant Professor of political science. He teaches human rights issues in the Peace Studies Program, Department of Political Science, Chapman University, Orange, California. His research focuses on human rights and peace issues in Africa. He has written extensively on Kenya's contemporary politics in Kenyan newspapers. He has several forthcoming book chapters on African politics.

Peyi Soyinka-Airewele teaches African politics and international relations at Ithaca College, Ithaca, New York. Before joining the faculty at Ithaca College, Soyinka-Airewele taught at Colgate University, Hamilton, New York. Her research focuses on ethnic politics and ethnic minorities. Her works include *Ethnic Minorities in European Union: A Study of the Basques and Irish Republican Separatists* (Ile-Ife, Nigeria, 1988); and articles in several refereed journals.

E. Ike Udogu is a Professor of African and International Politics at Francis Marion University, Florence, South Carolina. He has published extensively on Nigerian and African politics. His research has been published in the *Makerere Political Science Review, Journal of Asian and African Studies, Journal of Developing Societies, IN DEPTH: A Journal for Values and Public Policy, Canadian Review of Studies in Nationalism, The Review of Black Political Economy, Journal of Black Studies, Journal of Political Science,* and *Journal of Third World Studies,* just to cite a few. He is the author of *Nigeria and the Politics of Survival as a Nation-state* (The Edwin Mellen Press, 1997); and editor of *Democracy and Democratization in Africa: Toward the 21st Century* (E. J. Brill, 1997). He has contributed numerous book chapters on African politics. He was a National Endowment for the Humanities Fellow, and serves on the editorial advisory board of Collegiate Press, San Diego, California. He is the Director of Research and Publication, African Studies and Research Forum (ASRF).

Olufemi Vaughan teaches history and political science at the State University of New York at Stony Brook, New York. He has published in *African Affairs, International Journal of Politics, Culture and Society, Journal of Asian and African Studies,* and *Journal of Commonwealth and Comparative Politics.* He is the author of *Nigerian Chiefs: Traditional Power in Modern Politics 1890s-1990s* (University of Rochester Press, 2000).

Alfred B. Zack-Williams is a Principal Lecturer in the Department of Sociology and Social Policy, University of Central Lancashire, Preston, England. He has written widely on Africa, and Sierra-Leone, in particular. He has published in the following journals: *Review of African Political Economy*, *Third World Quarterly*, *Journal of Black Studies* and *Africa Development*. He is the author of *Supporters, Tributors and Merchant Capital in Sierra-Leone* (Gower-Avebury Press, 1995). In addition, he has contributed several book chapters on African social and political issues. He is a member of the editorial board of the *Review of African Political Economy*.

Acknowledgments

The completion of this book, *The Issue of Political Ethnicity in Africa*, would have been impossible without the input and assistance of several institutions, colleagues and students. I am extremely grateful for their contribution to this work.

It is generally true, from human history, that the challenges that we face in different milieus help condition our very character. In this regard, I owe a depth of gratitude to Francis Marion University for creating the enabling environment that has nurtured, in a very special way, my scholarly drive, and made it possible for me to accomplish some of my major objectives. The school's support in granting me both release time and sabbatical leave to work on this book and other projects speaks highly of the University's support and commitment to furthering scholarship at this institution.

Additionally, I would like to extend my gratitude to members of the African Studies and Research Forum (ASRF) and the institutions and universities that support their tedious research efforts. In this respect, my special kudos go to the University of Toronto, Ford Foundation and the University of Texas at Austin, University of Northern Colorado, Chapman University, Ithaca College, State University of New York at Stony Brook, and the University of Central Lancashire, Preston, England. Let it suffice to say, however, that the views expressed in each chapter are those of the Africanist scholars who contributed to this volume.

There were others who contributed to this book by their encouragement, typing, critiquing, reviewing, offering computer assistance, and suggestions for improvement. In this regard, our special thanks go to Jimmy D. Kandeh, University of Richmond; David Black, University of Toronto; Amar Almasude, Francis Marion University; Katherine Mosely, Stony Brook, New York; Ed. Udogu, Lagos, Nigeria; Anthonia C. Kalu and Brook Blair, University of Northern Colorado; Kelette S. Foxworth, Francis Marion University and my research assistant; and Ora Harrison, Darlington, South Carolina.

Finally, the success of this project was made possible in part because of the unflinching support of the chairman of the ASRF, professor John Mukum Mbaku, of Weber State University, Ogden, Utah. He painstakingly formatted and reviewed some of these chapters. My colleagues and I are profoundly grateful to him, his research assistants, and institution for their contribution to this special volume, *The Issue of Political Ethnicity in Africa*.

E. Ike Udogu
Florence, South Carolina

1 General Introduction

E. IKE UDOGU

The study of political ethnicity, and its dysfunctional attributes in African politics, is of great concern to students of ethnicity especially on the dawn of the new millennium. It is not that its influence in the national life of the African people is novel; it is just that its centrifugal characteristics have become extremely vexing to Africa's policy makers. Thus, suggesting that the depth of this problem is likely to tax the wits of scholars concerned with governance and peaceful coexistence for some time to come.

In fact, students of ethnicity do acknowledge the peculiar impact of ethnic politics in Africa, and have attempted to proffer solutions to this phenomenon. Their efforts are yet to yield full result because of the sensitivity of the subject matter. Moreover, as a conflictive ideology in national and international politics, many political actors would rather avoid it. Such attitudes are due, of course, to the propaganda of nationalists and pan-Africanists, in pre- and post-independence Africa, that demonized ethnic tendencies and claims in national and international affairs (Udogu, 1999a, p. 151).

Although ethnic consciousness has existed throughout history, the analysis of its political impact did not receive sufficient attention. But as Hutchinson and Smith (1996, p. v) have noted: '[a] longer-term perspective reveals the significance of ethnic ties and sentiments in every period of recorded history, even when there are problems in interpreting, their meaning and diffusion in our often-fragmentary records... .'

In his illuminating volume, *Nation Against State: A New Approach to Ethnic Conflicts and the Decline of Sovereignty*, Gidon Gottlieb (1993), brought into sharp focus the increasing dilemma facing virtually every nation-state in contemporary politics. This development could be seen in Canada's Quebec province, United Kingdom's Scotland, Russian Federation's Chechnya, The Sudan's southern region, just to cite a few examples. Within these countries, important spokespersons rally members of their nationalities in pursuit of their claims for autonomy (Hall, 1979), ethnic self-determination and even secession.

Robert T. Gurr and Barbara Harff (1994, p. xiii) have contended that '... two years after the Cold War ended, twenty-two hot wars were still being fought around the world. Communal rivalries and ethnic challenges to states contributed to conflict in all but five of these episodes... The United Nations had thirteen peace-keeping operations under way, the most ever in its fifty-year history, and seven of these were aimed at separating the protagonists in communal conflicts. This evidence does not signal the end of history, rather, the early phase of a new era in world history, one that does not yet have a name.' In Africa, contends Larry Diamond, 'no issue has more seriously threatened political stability and national or sate cohesion than ethnic conflict' (Diamond, 1987, p. 117). Yet, scholars are divided as to whether the problem is ethnicity *per se* or its manipulation.

In any case, whereas in the past the nationalists have blamed ethnic chauvinists for fomenting and fanning the embers of ethnicity, many have come to realize that they underestimated its saliency in African politics. As they come to grasp its reality and attempt to comprehend its complexities, they are confronted with some of the pertinent queries articulated by R. N. Ismagilova (1978, p. 8):

- What effect do ethnic problems have on the socio-economic development and political life of African countries?
- What are the main trends in the ethnic development of African countries?
- What is the explanation of the intensification of inter-ethnic relations in a number of countries?
- What are the reasons for and the character of ethnic antagonisms?
- What are the social forces behind them?
- What are the ways to tackle ethnic problems?
- What is the ideology of tribalism or ethnicity?
- What effect does ethnicity or tribalism have on solving the most important problems of economic and social development?
- How is the problem of ethnic self-determination to be approached?
- How are questions of state structure, language, and so forth, to be solved?

In truth, these questions, *inter alia*, call for serious analysis and comprehension of ethnicity and its non-centripetal tendencies in this and other volumes.

It might be foolhardy, if not remiss, to ignore the central focus, i.e., the very theater on which ethnic politics are played out. In this regard, one is referring to the fragile African state whose very existence and sovereignty is under siege by ethnic cleavages in much of the continent. This is important since the essays that follow visualize the 'soft' states in Africa in a somewhat similar light. Put another way, the proceeding analysis augments the observations made by contributors to this work.

Over four decades ago, John Herz, in a somewhat identical context, wrote about the 'the rise and demise of the territorial state.' He noted that throughout history, that element or unit which afforded protection and security to its inhabitants has tended to become the basic political unit. He contended that people in the long run would recognize the authority which possessed the power of protection. The absence of authority or power to establish law and order would lead to anarchy.

Following developments which started in the nineteenth century, Herz observed that the territorial state was no longer in the position to perform this basic function. These occurrences included the following:

- the rapid loss of their self-sufficiency or autarky by the territorial states and their vulnerability to economic blockade;
- the emergence of super-national belief systems which made it possible for states to be undermined from within by means of psychological warfare; and
- military developments such as the increasing resort to large scale warfare and the advent of nuclear weapons.

He then affirmed that as a result of these factors, territorial states had lost their 'impermeability', the central significance which had made it possible for them to perform their protective function. Suffice it to say that Herz did not mean that the territorial state had physically collapsed out of existence, but he did imply, to some extent, that the rationale for organizing the world on the basis of territorial states had become problematic (cited in Rosenau, 1961, pp. 81–85). Indeed, in very few regions of the world could one find more 'collapsed' or 'failed' states than in Africa due to conflicts and overwhelming claims made by nations on the nation-state system.

It is against this backdrop that this book, *The Issue of Political Ethnicity in Africa*, rests on three pillars. The first pillar, which is made up of three chapters, provide the analytical foundation of the volume by synthesizing and synchronizing theories and practice. In the process, they shed some light on the role of ethnic politics and the state in Africa's political equation or calculus. The second pillar is also made up of three chapters. These chapters discuss case studies which illuminate the ethnic characteristics of various cleavages, and the extent to which they have been able to render some of the states 'irrelevant' in their citizen's daily lives. The third pillar consists of two chapters, which, among other things, suggest ways for solving and reconceptualizing the ethnicity paradox in African politics.

For example, in Chapter 2, E. Ike Udogu provides a theoretical superstructure on which the entire volume might be situated. In doing so, he borrowed a number of theoretical analyses across disciplines—in particular, political science and sociology. His study shed some light on a terminological 'controversy' which has continually troubled Africanist scholars. The issue has been based on nomenclature. That is, should African collectivities be referred to as 'tribes' or 'ethnic' groups? His position, like that of most students of African politics, is the substitution of ethnic for tribe when referring to the Kikuyus of Kenya, Igbos of Nigeria, Tutsis of Rwanda and Burundi, Shonas of Zimbabwe, Zulus of South Africa, and so on. Indeed, he recommends that ethnic and ethnicity should be superimposed over tribe and tribalism in their conceptualization of the interactions between these groups in Africa. But the centrality of this chapter is the discussion of theories and how they relate to the behavior patterns of ethnic groups. Indeed, such dogmas as ethnic boundaries, social closure, ethnic competition and others were explored using Kenya, Sierra Leone, Rwanda-Burundi and Cameroon as test cases.

Inter-ethnic rivalries and claims are generally made within a wider context and terrain—the state. So, Chapter 2 examines this complex turf and the political pulls of the ethnic leaders in their claims for self-determination on the state. In the end, the state only derives its legitimacy from those dominant groups that successfully extract substantial reward from it. The consequence of this competition is that the state finds itself under constant attack and stress from the marginalized cleavages—hence there exist constant instability in the continent from exploited and secessionist movements (e.g., the Sudan, Rwanda, Kenya, Nigeria, Cameroon, South Africa, etc.). To assuage these problems, the chapter suggests power-sharing, federalism and economic revitalization as possible strategies for effectively tackling these problems and meeting the needs of the various factions.

In his contribution, Kelechi A. Kalu (in Chapter 3) situates his essay on the political economy of Africa and examines the extent to which economic sentiments as an aspect of colonial experience help shed light on the problems of conflicts and underdevelopment in the continent on the eve and dawn of the twenty-first century. In order to accomplish this task, Kalu traces the historical developments of ethnicity from an international relations perspective, using as his springboard, the famous Westphalian treaty of 1648 which ended the 30 years religious war in Europe and saw the emergence of the modern nation-state system (Snow and Brown, 1996, pp. 93–94; Papp, 1984, pp. 13–14; Kegley and Witkopf, 1977, pp. 39–40). Ethnic consciousness existed in the European state system as is the case in Africa. Ethnic group character and interests were (and are) similar in both situations in spite of their different levels of 'sophistication.'

Also, Kalu analyzes the role of the state in Weberian and Marxist terms. But one issue remains: How do African policy makers view the state? Kalu attempts to answer this query within the framework of stability, especially since ethnicity as a social event and basis for social formation in a polity is essentially conflictual. Therefore, in Africa, the quest to centralize state authority to minimize ethnic conflicts was considered desirable, especially shortly after independence, and pursued vigorously. This assumption or solution to ameliorating economic crisis and ethnic clashes has not worked. Kalu concludes by stressing the need for the enlargement of the political space to allow for the participation of all collectivities within the context of a constitutional democratic framework.

In Chapter 4, Julius O. Ihonvbere underscores the significance of the state in the whole political calculus of ethnicity and other formations in Africa. Historically, this has always been the case. He finds the actions of multinational corporations and other agents to 'de-nationalize' the state dangerous. In spite of this trend, however, the state in much of Africa remains vibrant because of its ability to maintain itself through violence, and to silence ethnic cleavages and other factions agitating for greater liberalization in the political system. In the practice of this act, the state creates a problem of legitimacy, and it is therefore weakened by its own draconian policies. If the state is not hegemonic, it cannot effectively solve external and internal problems. In particular, it might not be able to resolve inter-ethnic conflicts and discrepancies between it and micro-national units. This condition is exacerbated by the state's capricious redistributive policies. In the distribution of the proceeds from the exploitation of the country's natural resources, few or no benefits accrue to the geo-ethnic entities that house these resources. Instead, the income generated by the exploitation of natural resources is siphoned off to support an unproductive and parasitic bureaucracy and the entities (e.g., the military) that enhance the incumbent's ability to maintain a monopoly on political power. The result is the politicization of the ethnic group for the purpose of waging war against the state. This was the situation among the Ogonis of Nigeria and the revival of the Hobbesian state of nature in Ogoniland (Grossman, 1996). But how are these contradictions between the state and the ethnic factions to be resolved in African politics since their saliency cannot be wished away? Ihonvbere suggests, among other things, a careful review of the Ethiopian model, in which the regime took into account the uniqueness and interests of the ethnic identity groups in crafting its new constitution (see also Kimenyi, 1998).

The three chapters that follow are case studies. They provide poignant illustrations of the battle between 'nation and state' in Africa. Thus, Olufemi Vaughan, in Chapter 5, notes with clarity the vortex of ethnicity in Nigerian politics. He asserts that the period from 1960–1966 were critical years in the republic's democratic metamorphoses, and that the failure of democracy to germinate in that country is attributable to the mobilization of ethnicity in the struggle for power and control of natural resources. Indeed, to understand the Nigerian state and what makes it tick, one must first comprehend its ethnic complexions. It is not that ethnicity is 'evil.' In fact, it has, in some occasions, been a force for 'good governance.' It has also, on other instances, been the source of the republic's Achilles' heel, as for example, the civil war of 1967–1970. Vaughan cites examples of numerous internal demands and claims on the state by a number of ethnic groups such as the Ogonis, Ijaws and others, but situates his study on the activities of some Yoruba ethnic groups in the period following the annulment of the presidential election of June 12, 1993, believed to have been won by the late Moshood Abiola (a Yoruba entrepreneur). The coalescence of two powerful Yoruba ethnic groups—Afenifere and Egbe Omo Yoruba, to do battle with the military junta of General Sani Abacha formed the bases of his lucid analysis. The rationales for the formation of these groups were to dislocate the Abacha administration and to thwart his ambition to succeed himself in an election scheduled for August 1998.

The impact of ethnicity in Kenyan politics and its ruination of the state is the central focus of F. Wafula Okumu's analysis in Chapter 6. There is a paradox in the Kenyan situation in that the problem of ethnicity in its politics was identified and condemned as long ago as the early 1960s shortly after independence. Indeed, noting its dysfunctional and conflictual characteristics in Kenyan politics in a debate in Parliament in 1967, Masinde Muliro affirmed emphatically as follows:

> We do not want a malady to overtake Kenya, we do not want a Congo in Kenya, we do not want another Nigeria in Kenya, we would like to see Kenya as a perfect example of an African developing nation. ...We can only do that today if we accept the facts of Kenya to be what they are, accept that there are different tribes in Kenya [...which] must be welded into one nation (Ismagilova, 1978, p. 137; also see Udogu, 1999a, pp. 151–152).

If the state in Kenya is 'decaying,' it must be that the Kenyans failed to pay heed to Muliro's admonition. In fact, Okumu's analysis is informed by this dilemma. The issue of poor leadership aside, the internal political dynamics of Kenya can best be understood within the context of the interaction of Kenya's ethnic mosaic. The manipulation of ethnicity by political entrepreneurs is the norm and any wayward actor in this political chess game could be liquidated if he or she does not play the game right. Such was the fate of Tom Mboya. Politics in this kind of setting becomes a zero-sum game. Okumu chafes at the fact that the politics of intimidation and violence for which the states in much of Africa (Nigeria, Algeria, Egypt, the Sudan, Cameroon, etc.) are notorious for, are methodically used by the custodians of the Kenyan state. Witness, for example, the ethnic cleansing in the Rift Valley of villages made up of Kikuyu, Luo and Luhya ethnic groups in 1992 (Nowrojee and Manby, 1993; Udogu, 1999a, p. 169). The politics of succession has not only sharpened the politics of ethnicity, but has also led to political prostitution of competing ethnic groups who claim that it is their turn to accede to power. President Daniel arap Moi is being courted, like never before, as the various ethnic groups spread out their plumage like a peahen before a peacock. So far, President arap Moi is playing the card of his possible successor so close to his chest and in so doing, has raised the ante for any would-be political leader of Kenya.

The above metaphor aside, the politics of anxiety is killing the Kenyan people, particularly the politicians who find the president to be too mercurial on this subject. President arap Moi cannot succeed himself, constitutionally, and he had said that he would not run for a third term. But who says he cannot use extra-constitutional powers to extend his stay in office when the time for his abdication draws nearer. The apprehension that there is no eminent successor and the possible chaos that might ensue should he pass away without an anointed leader, notes Okumu, has led, among other things, to the clamor for a new political dispensation likely to ameliorate political instability in the republic. This system of governance is dubbed *Majimboism* alias ethnic federalism (Kimenyi, 1998, pp. 43–63).

In Chapter 7, A. B. Zack-Williams addresses the complex politics of Sierra Leone within the framework of that country's ethnic and regional political alliances. The political intrigues in that republic are exacerbated by military incursion into national politics. Zack-Williams centers his analysis on the *Ekutay*, a fraternal Order whose *raison d'être*, especially during the leadership of Siaka Stevens, was to use the Weberian doctrine of social closure to retain power among the Limba ethnic group. But the Limbas constitute only about 8.4 percent of the total population of the country. In fact, the Mende (30.9 percent) and Temne (29.8 percent) over-whelm the Limbas. The question, therefore, is how do the Limbas with their 'lilliputian' population 'overpower' the majority ethnic groups politically? Zack-Williams elucidates the internal political dynamics of the *Ekutay* and how this ethnic fraternity lodged in the Limba ethnic group perfected its strategy for political dominance in spite of its numerical inferiority to the Mende and Temne ethnic groups.

John B. Ejobowah's disquisition in Chapter 8 sheds light on the enduring global intra-state ethnic conflicts. In Africa, ethnic conflicts increased markedly as the state-system came under major stress following the innumerable ethnic claims on it. In some cases such as Burundi, Rwanda, Somalia and Sierra Leone, these states simply 'collapsed.' Indeed, the phrase or terminology 'collapsed or failed' states is used often in the literature on the politics of developing nations to describe this phenomenon. The centrality of Ejobowah's thesis is how to concoct strategies that might help African states to assuage ethnic conflicts. This is particularly germane since the major activity of any (political) community is politics, and politics is by its very nature conflictual. Ejobowah offers a sensible guidance for mitigating or reducing ethnic conflict in African politics. His submission of liberal democratic genre as a possible panacea to the reduction of ethnic conflict in Africa is borne out by the assumption that liberal democracy espouses the rule of law, constitution and constitutionalism, human equality, *inter alia*. He argues that the efficacy of this theory rests on the assumption and existence of ethnic homogeneity. Its limitations, however, flow from the fact that in 'plural' societies there exist numerous ethnic groups with their diverse and conflicting interests. Therefore, in order to reduce tensions, the contradictory ethnic claims have to be reconciled. But the crux of the chapter is his attempts to 'pay dues' to some of the outstanding pioneers in the field of ethnic politics, and to use their works to buttress his arguments for conflict reduction in African politics. In particular, he paid homage to such scholars as the late Sir Arthur Lewis,

Donald Horowitz, Eric Nordlinger and Arend Lijphart. These scholars and others[1] have in their scholarships offered guidelines and strategies for conflict amelioration in 'divided' societies.

Peyi Soyinka-Airewele in Chapter 9 encapsulates one of the major dilemmas which African states are confronted with in terms of perceptions and nomenclature. This is particularly the case given the manner in which African political, social, and religious developments are portrayed in the Western media. In this regard, the image of Africa as the 'Dark' continent comes to the fore. Thanks to the superb works of such scholars as Basil Davidson,[2] and others, whose prodigious writings on African history have, in many ways, debunked some of the negative perceptions of African history. Soyinka-Airewele, like many Africanists, chafes at the depictions of African ethnicity in Western media. The colonial expeditions into Africa and their powers of inscriptions and labeling of African societies have afflicted the psychology of the indigenes of the continent which persists in post-colonial Africa. Thus, Africans who had historically traded with each other, and even married across ethnic groups, find themselves to be political 'enemies' in the 'reconstructed' modern state-system. Such animosities issued from the manner in which one ethnic group was played against the other by the colonial powers in attempts to control a 'stubborn' group. But what is particularly vexing to Africanists, contends, Soyinka-Airewele, is why ethnicity as a social, anthropological, political concept can be applied to some regions of the world in their inscriptions, and not to Africa where they are often referred to as 'tribes' with all the associated negative attributes. In effect, Soyinka-Airewele in her analysis in this chapter attempts to challenge scholars to apply uniform language in describing European and African 'tribes.' Most importantly, she urges African academies to offer courses on ethnicity and diversity in attempts to expunge the negative imputations issuing from the intellectual discourse and policy formulations in the continent. Contrary to the views espoused by nationalists and, indeed, pan-Africanists, Soyinka-Airewele suggests that ethnicity in Africa should be celebrated not shunned.

Notes

1. Within this context, our intellectual patrimony is extended to this brief selection of scholars: Ake, C. (1967), *A Theory of Political Integration*, The Dorsey Press: Homewood, IL.; Nnoli, O. (1978), *Ethnic Politics in Nigeria*, Fourth Dimension Publishers: Enugu, Nigeria; Kofele-Kale, N. (1981), *Tribesmen and Patriots:*

Political Culture in a Polyethnic State, University Press of America: Washington, DC.; Young, C. (1979), *The Politics of Cultural Pluralism*, The University of Wisconsin Press: Madison, WI.; Sklar, R. and Whitaker, C. S. (1966), 'The Federal Republic of Nigeria', in Carter, G. (ed.), *National Unity and Regionalism in Eight African States*, Cornell University Press: Ithaka, NY.; Hutchinson, J. and Smith A. D. (1996) (eds), *Ethnicity*, Oxford University Press: Oxford and New York. Glazer, N. and Moynihan, D. P. (1975) (eds.), *Ethnicity: Theory and Experience*, Harvard University Press: Cambridge, MA.; Ismagilova, R. N. (1978), *Ethnic Problems of the Tropical Africa*, Progress Press: Moscow; Geertz, C. (1963) (ed.), *Old Societies and New States*, Free Press: New York and Oxford; Connor, W. (1994), *Ethnonationalism: The Quest for Understanding*, Princeton University Press: Princeton, NJ.; Weber, M. (1978), 'The Origin of Ethnic Groups', in Roth, G. and Wittich, C. (eds.), *Economy and Society, Vol. 1*, University of California Press: Berkeley and Los Angeles, CA.; Barth, F. (1969), *Ethnic Groups and Boundaries*, Little, Brown and CO.: Boston, MA.; Scaritt, J. R. and Safran, W. (1983), 'The Relationship of Ethnicity to Modernization and Democracy: A Restatement of the Issue', *International Studies Notes of the International Studies Association*, Vol. 10, No. 2, pp. 16–21.

2. See Davidson, B. (1974), *Africa in History: Themes and Outlines*, Macmillan Publishing Company, Inc.: New York; Davidson, B. (1970), *The African Genius: An Introduction to Social and Cultural History*, Little, Brown and Company, Boston, MA.; Davidson, B. (1992), *Africa in History*, Free Press: New York.

References

Diamond, L. (1987), 'Ethnicity and Ethnic Conflict', *Journal of Modern African Studies*, Vol. 25, No. 1, pp. 117–128.
Gottlieb, G. (1993), *Nation Against State: A New Approach to Ethnic Conflicts and the Decline of Sovereignty*, Council on Foreign Relations Press: New York.
Grossman, J. (1996), *Hanged: Ken Saro-Wiwa in the American Print Media*, Inner Image Ink Publishers: Santa Cruz, CA.
Gurr, T. R. and Harff, B. (1994), *Ethnic Conflict in World Politics*, Westview Press: Boulder, CO.
Hall, R. L. (1979) (ed.), *Ethnic Autonomy-Comparative Dynamics: The Americas, Europe and the Developing World*, Pergamon Press: New York.
Herz, J. H. (1981), 'The Rise and Demise of the Territorial State', in Rosenau, J. M. (ed.), *International Politics and Foreign Policy*, The Free Press: Glencoe, IL.
Hutchinson, J. and Smith, A. D. (1996) (eds.), *Ethnicity*, Oxford University Press: Oxford and New York.
Ismagilova, R. N. (1978), *Ethnic Problems of the Tropical Africa: Can they be Solved?*, Progress Publishers: Moscow.
Kegley, C. W. and Witkopf, E. R. (1997), *World Politics: Trends and Transformation*, St. Martin's Press: New York.
Kimenyi, M. S. (1998), 'Harmonizing Ethnic Claims in Africa: A Proposal for Ethnic-based Federalism', *Cato Journal*, Vol. 18, No. 1, pp. 43–63.
Nowroje, B. and Manby, B. (1993), 'Divide and Rule', *Africa Report*, Vol. 38, No. 5, p. 35.

Papp, D. S. (1984), *Contemporary International Relations: Framework for Understanding*, Macmillan Publishing Company: New York.

Snow, D. M. and Brown, E. (1996), *The Contours of Power: An Introduction to Contemporary International Relations*, St. Martin's Press: New York.

Udogu, E. I (1999a), 'Ethnicity and Democracy in sub-Saharan Africa', in Mbaku, J. M. (ed.), *Preparing Africa for the Twenty-First Century: Strategies for Peaceful Coexistence and Sustainable Development*, Ashgate: Aldershot, UK.

Udogu, E. I. (1999b), 'The Issue of Ethnicity and Democratization in Africa: Toward the Millennium', *Journal of Black Studies*, Vol. 29, No. 6, pp. 790–808.

2 Ethnicity and Theory in African Politics

E. IKE UDOGU

The belief in group affinity, regardless of whether it has any objective foundation, can have important consequences especially for the formation of a *political community*. We shall call 'ethnic groups' those human groups that entertain a subjective belief in their common descent because of similarities of physical type or customs or both, or because of memories of colonization and migration; this belief must be important for the propagation of group formation... (Weber, 1996, p. 35).

It is around the preceding conjectures that we seek to do the following: (1) review part of the literature on ethnicity; (2) examine concisely some theories of ethnicity; (3) summarize the impact of ethnicity in selected African countries to illuminate some of the theoretical constructs; and (4) conclude with brief possible strategies for mollifying the powerful effect of political ethnicity in the African context.

The term ethnicity is a relatively novel or new concept, contended Glazer and Monynihan in 1975. Its usage and appearance in major dictionaries occurred in the 1950s and after. It was defined as the condition of belonging to a particular ethnic group, and characterized by a very special sense of pride (Glazer and Monynihan, 1975, p. 1). This definition has since metamorphosed into a much broader concept whose fuller meaning will be explored later on in this disquisition. When juxtaposed, however, against the concept 'tribe' often attributable to similar groups in Africa and elsewhere, the rationale for applying the concept 'ethnic' to supersede 'tribe,' in certain geographic areas, becomes more salient. The nomenclature, tribe, whose derivation is Roman is described in Webster's *Ninth New Collegiate Dictionary* as 'a social group comprising numerous families, clans, or generations together with slaves, dependents, or adopted strangers; a group of persons having a common character, occupation, or interest...' Some of these imputations are unflattering. And because its attributions sometimes denote or connote savagery in modern interpretation, many Africanists have argued for the expunction of 'tribe' from the political lexicon of African politics, its socio-anthropological usage or applications notwithstanding. Therefore, the words 'tribe' and 'tribalism' will be used synonymously with 'ethnic' and 'ethnicity' in this chapter.

In a broader sense, ethnicity is defined as

> a collectivity within a larger society having real or putative common ancestry, memories of a shared historical past, and a cultural focus on one or more symbolic elements defined as the epitome of their peoplehood. Examples of such symbolic elements are: kinship patterns, physical contiguity (as in localism or sectionalism), religious affiliation, language or dialect forms, tribal affiliation, nationality, phenotypical features, or any combination of these. A necessary accompaniment is some consciousness of kind among members of the group (Schermerhorn, 1978, p. 12; also cited in Hutchinson and Smith, 1996, p. 6).

Within this context, Hutchinson and Smith (1996, pp. 6–7) attempted to elaborate and shed more light on the above definition. To perform this task, they developed a concept dubbed 'ethnie.' Ethnie refers to a 'named human population with myths of common ancestry, shared historical memories, one or more elements of common culture, a link with a homeland and a sense of solidarity among at least some of its members.' In a way, their conceptual views of the invented terminology, ethnie, appears to be somewhat analogous and complementary to Shermerhorn's definition.

Manning Nash (1989, pp. 10–15) contends that

> cultural categories with social and group referents are the focus of ethnic inquiry. Where there is a group, there is some sort of boundary, and where there are boundaries, there are some mechanisms to maintain them. ...cultural markers of kinship, commensuality, and religious cult are, from the point of view of the analyst, a single recursive metaphor. This metaphor of blood, substance, and deity symbolize the existence of the group... This

trinity of boundary markers and mechanisms is the deep or basic structure on ethnic group differentiation. [They] separate ethnic groupings from other kinds of social aggregates, groups, and entities.

Okwudiba Nnoli has noted four salient characteristics of ethnicity:

- It is a social phenomenon associated with interactions among members of different ethnic groups. Ethnic groups are social formations distinguished by the communal character of their boundaries. The relevant communal factor may be language, culture, or both. In Africa, language has clearly been the most crucial variable. As social formation, however, ethnic groups are not necessarily homogeneous entities even linguistically and culturally...
- Much more than ethnocentricism, ethnicity is characterized by a common consciousness of being one in relation to the other relevant ethnic groups. This factor more than any other defines the boundary of the group that is relevant for understanding ethnicity at any historical point in time...
- Exclusiveness is an attribute of ethnicity. Ingroup-outgroup boundaries emerge with it and, in time, become marked, more distinct than before, and jealously guarded by the various ethnic groups...
- Conflict is an important aspect of ethnicity. This is inevitable under conditions of interethnic competition for scarce valuable resources, particularly in societies where inequality is accepted as natural, and wealth is greatly esteemed (Nnoli, 1980, pp. 5–8; see also Udogu, 1994, pp. 160–161).

Additionally, Crawford Young contends that the definition of groups is in constant flux. Indeed, any theory of ethnic conflict, he further argues, must take cognizance of the element of change as a central and critical factor. This is important since political phenomena are significant independent variables in determining the saliency of cultural conflict at any given point in time. He concludes that 'at any moment, ethnic conflict may appear to eclipse all other factors in the equation; a few years later, the same cleavage may appear entirely muted, and quite irrelevant to explication of the political process' (Young, 1979, p. 5).

Ethnicity, contends Daniel Bell (1975, p. 169), has become so relevant because it has a propensity for combining an interest with an affective tie. Ethnicity supplies a clear set of common identifications (language, food, music, names) when other social factors are more abstract. In political contestations for resources in a polity, ethnicity can provide the rallying cry for claiming recognition and advantage (Osaghae, 1991, pp. 237–258; 1995, pp. 325–344).

Ethnicity, as a concept, is both complex in its definition and disconcerting in its characteristics. Indeed, the preceding analyses bear these opinions out. Any wonder, then, that it has been noted that the application of ethnicity in sociological literature is inadequate, in fact, often confused. The concept may be defined in two ways: one static and descriptive, the other dynamic and analytic. Most explications of ethnicity have been descriptive and static in an endeavor to derive or isolate a set of characteristics or traits by which the concept may be delineated and comprehended. Herein lies much of the confusion, contends Orlando Patterson (1975, pp. 305–306). He infers that such 'definitions emphasize culture and tradition as the critical elements, and in so doing, are so descriptive that they become analytically useless, often so inclusive that they are not even worthwhile as heuristic devices' (Patterson, 1975, p. 306).

The foregoing conjectures and brief review of the literature were intended to provide the necessary springboard from which to comprehend the perplexities and difficulties in explaining the theoretical dimensions of ethnicity. Put another way, if scholars consider ethnicity to be a confounding concept, *a priori*, so are the theoretical explanations as to why its prominence and saliency in virtually all polities are of concern to students of ethnicity. The issue, here, is not ethnicity or ethnonationalism per se (Connor, 1973, pp. 1–23; see also Udogu, 1994, p. 159). The question, for a political scientist, is the extent to which its 'collateral' attributes impinge upon the conflictual politics of nation-states. Herein, then, lies the need to address some relevant theories of ethnicity with a view to illuminating some of the advantages and disadvantages of this subject matter in African politics.

Theoretical analysis

This brief theoretical discussion is grounded on two major seminal works on ethnicity, namely, *Ethnicity* (Hutchinson and Smith, 1996), and

Theories of Ethnicity (Stanfield, 1995). These sources supply a very rich texture of theoretical analyses that serve as the basis for the superstructure of this concise inquiry.

Clifford Geertz has argued that the emotionalism tied to one's membership in an ethnic group is so strong especially in traditional or modernizing societies that it becomes a very significant variable in the political character of a nation-state. Borrowing from the works of E. Shils (1975, pp. 113–145), he alludes to the dilemmas of the modern state system's abnormality and susceptibility to fundamental incongruencies rooted in the primordial attachments of various collectivities within a nation-state. In fact, Geertz notes:

> By a primordial attachment is meant one that stems from the 'givens'—or, more precisely, as culture is inevitably involved in such matters, the assumed 'givens'—of social existence: immediate contiguity and kin connection mainly, but beyond them the givenness that stems from being born into a particular religious community, speaking a particular language ...and following particular social practices...[Indeed], for virtually every person, in every society, at almost all times, some attachments seem to flow from a sense of natural—some would say spiritual—affinity than from social interaction. In modern societies the lifting of such ties to the level of political supremacy—though it has, of course, occurred and may again occur—has more and more come to be deplored as pathological (Geertz, 1963, pp. 103–113; 1996, pp. 41–42).

On the one hand, the theoretical basis of Geertz's contention flows from the assumption that individuals are born into an ethnic group (without a choice) which they may find difficult to 'disown or renounce' at least biologically or genetically. On the other hand, the state in which an individual resides, and in which one may claim an ethnic identity, could be renounced in spite of the state's demand for an individual's allegiance. Put another way, one finds it more 'problematical' to denounce one's primordial ties or sentiments to one's collectivity than the renouncement of the state to which one belongs (Kofele-Kale, 1981, p. 7).

For example, Ebino Babatope, minister of Transport and Aviation, in General Sani Abacha's administration, in an interview said:

...And if people think that because I am a minister that I have forgotten the fact that one, I'm an Ileshaman, two, I'm and Ijeshaman, and third, I'm a Yorubaman, then fourth, I am a Nigerian citizen, then such people should really go and examine themselves. I cannot divorce myself from the yearning and aspiration of the people of my roots (See Udogu, 1994, p. 160).

Indeed, as Steven Grosby (1996, p. 51) has noted, primordial sentiment is inexpungeable. N. Kofele-Kale (1981, p. 7) also echoed a similar sentiment when he asserted that primordial attachments applied to, educated and uneducated, rich or poor, individuals regardless of where they are domiciled. This sort of primordial attachment, it has been noted, created a serious destabilizing effect in Nigeria's political development. In truth, it has rendered attempts at political integration extremely perplexing (Udogu, 1990, pp. 157–175; Osaghae, 1991, pp. 237–258).

Fredrik Barth's (1969, pp. 10–19; Hutchinson and Smith, 1996, pp. 75–82) theoretical analyses, on ethnic boundaries within the framework of social and political interactions between ethnic cleavages in a nation-state, are informative on political ethnicity in Africa and elsewhere. Indeed, the theories of ethnic boundaries are nourished by primordial sentiment. Witness, for example, the politics of ethnonationalism within the British (Scotland), French (the Basque), and Spanish (also the Basque) polities. Ethnic boundaries could be visualized within the context of social, political and territorial limitations. Barth (1996, p. 79) notes that: 'ethnic boundary canalizes social life—it entails a frequently quite complex organization of behavior and social relations. The identification of another person as a fellow member of an ethnic group implies a sharing of criteria for evaluation and judgment.' In short, in this respect, the ingroup-outgroup dichotomy emerges but this division does not necessarily hamper interethnic relations based on mutual interests.

This theory is significant in much of Africa in which geoethnic boundaries are clearly demarcated—and in which social and political competitions take place. South Africa, Nigeria, the Sudan, Burundi, Rwanda, and Cameroon are some examples. In South Africa, Natal province is dominated by the ethnic Zulus, and is the nucleus of Mangosuthu Buthelezi's Inkatha Freedom Party (IFP) that contested the 1994 all-race elections (Udogu, 1999, pp. 151–176). Whereas these geoethnic boundaries are said to be relatively porous, among members of different ethnic groups, in the areas of social and cultural intercourse, the same might not be true in the area of political organizations or politics. In fact, these boundaries are sometimes politically impermeable. For example, the Alliance for Democracy (AD), a political party dominated by the Yorubas, a major geoethnic group in the southwest of Nigeria, demonstrated its political victory within its ethnic boundary in the local elections of December 1998, and gubernatorial elections of January 1999.

Within the framework of the foregoing discussion emerges the theory of 'social closure' coined by Max Weber (Cited in Stone, 1995, p. 397). Social closure applies to a strategy for group survival whereby social groups establish monopolies in order to avoid competition with rival groups that could be harmful to the group (the monopolizer) (Stone, 1995, p. 398; Udogu, 1999, pp. 151–176). This strategy, *inter alia*, might involve changing the rules of the game in favor of the monopolizer in order to eschew possible threats to the ingroup privileged position from the outgroup. Because this behavior pattern tends to smack at the notion of justice and fair play in a society, it heightens political tension and instability. Thus, it has been suggested that in contemporary political discourse, the philosophy and concept of 'social closure' governs the intellectual inquiry of many students of ethnicity in modern and traditional societies.

Ethnic competition theories, which flow from the 'theory of social closure,' emphasize the nature of resource competition as the basis for ethnic group formation, interethnic conflicts and the crystallization of ethnic political movements (Nagel, 1995, p. 445; Agbese, 1996, p. 146). These opinions approximate the ethnic organizational or mobilization paradigm within the context of constructivist paradigm. 'Constructivist paradigms tend to forsake primordial assumptions of ethnicity, insisting that modern ethnicity derives from political exigencies and the quest to adapt to novel political environment' (Gross, 1996, pp. 51 and 58). Gross contends that the organizational paradigm relies on rational, voluntary choice and the instrumentality of political association in pursuit of group interest(s) (Gross, 1996, p. 58; Bariagaber, 1998, pp. 1056–1057; see Yeros, 1999). To achieve group objectives, therefore, individuals and organizations sometimes concoct ideologies, slogans, and symbols which they use as rallying cries to whip up support from group members (Udogu, 1999, pp. 151–176).

The discussions so far have centered on ethnic groups and their peculiarities within a polity. But these various collectivities in modern and even traditional societies function in a society. Indeed, without the agglutination of various collectivities into a nation-state system, and the conflicting interactions which sometimes ensue as a result, the foregoing analyses would have been meaningless and, in fact, useless. It is to this end that the following brief discussion will center on the state and its place, or unique position, in the interactions between the various ethnic cleavages.

Ethnicity and the state: an overview

The analyses that follow suggest that the aforementioned theories—i.e., primordialism, ethnic boundaries, ethnic competition, social closure, *et cetera*, might be less useful without the existence of a territorial unit or entity. This politico-social and economic universe may be referred to, operationally, as the state. Jack Plano and Roy Olton (1982, pp. 286–287) defined a state as 'a legal concept describing a social group that occupies a defined territory and is organized under common political institutions and effective government.' Theodore A. Couloumbis and James Wolfe (1990, p. 60) affirmed that a state is a 'political unit defined in terms of territory, population, and autonomous government that exercises effective control of the territory and its inhabitants regardless of their ethnic homogeneity or heterogeneity.' It is within the framework of the sometimes mutual and sometimes antagonistic and conflicting interactions in a state that the very character of the nation-state could be discerned. In this vein, too, are the impacts on the nation-states of some of the ethnic theories already discussed. The political instability in much of Africa could be explained within this scope. One problem that these suppositions creates is the lack of commitment or allegiance to the nation-state by sub-national groups, particularly the minorities, whose interests are not always in sync, or congruent, with those of the state. This lack of commitment to the state, therefore, brings to the fore the question of political legitimacy of the state in many developing as well as some developed countries.

Probably, it was this reality that prompted Ladun Anise to contend that:

> ...There is a tendency to assume the primacy of the nation-state, and to assign universal legitimacy to its existence without ever elaborating the normative justifications for the validity of the nation-state. This is an inherited problem in Less Developed

Countries (LDCs), where the problems of development are usually analyzed almost exclusively in national terms. Essentially, it was the nationalism of the struggle for decolonization that gave the assumed legitimacy to the new nation-state. The new states are thus the children of the nationalism, except that it would be more analytically correct to treat the new political entities as state-nation rather than nation-state (Anise, 1979, p. 315).

In Africa, today, the critical issue is that ethnic groups within the post-colonial state are increasingly reverting to ethnonationalism due to alienation from the central government, especially minority groups who are peripheralized in the economic and political dispensations in their polities. They are construing their ethnic entities or nations to be the major level of analysis in matters that affect the lives of their collectivities. This is so because they view the state to be the source of their constant agony and therefore 'irrelevant' to their common interest. The subnationalist political fervor in Scotland within the United Kingdom is a good case in point. In Southern Africa, the attitude of the Afrikaner population in post-apartheid South Africa approximates this behavior pattern. And, in West Africa, the Ogoni ethnic minority group of Nigeria is perhaps the best example in the continent.

Moreover, Claude Ake (1985, p. 9) contends that 'the unique feature of the states in [Africa] and this is typical of periphery capitalist formations generally, is that the state has limited autonomy. That is, the state is institutionally constituted in such a way that it enjoys limited independence from the social classes, particularly the hegemonic class, and so is immersed in the struggle of the class [hence African states as constituted today are relatively weak because they lack the support of a majority of their populations].'

This political equation is made more complex by the fact that the key actors or the hegemonic class who press for ethnic claims on the state are themselves major players at the national level. For example, this in part was one of the dilemmas in Nigeria's First Republic as demonstrated in the geo-ethnic political actions of Sir Abubakar Tafawa Balewa, representing the interests of the Hausa-Fulani in the north, Dr. Nnamdi Azikiwe, protecting the interests of the Igbos in the east, and Chief Obafemi Awolowo, standing up for the Yorubas in the west (Udogu, 1997, pp. 1–28). The contradictions which emerge from the various loci (i.e., national and sub-national levels) in the political tussles flow from the center or locality of allegiance. That is, do political entrepreneurs representing micronational units declare their devotion to their ethnic groups or to the state? Indeed, it has become increasingly clear that some professed subnationalists are prepared to pursue their noncentripetal objectives if doing that consigned to their collectivities the power and resources for the groups' survival—and the state may be 'damned' in the process (Udogu, 1995, p. 3). This political attitude probably prompted Donald L. Horowitz (1985, pp. 100–101) to lament in the African situation that the contemporary political entrepreneurs, instead of playing the detribalizing role earlier assigned to them, often promoted their interests by invoking ethnic solidarity.

The foregoing theoretical and conceptual analyses on ethnicity, and their relations to the state might be hollow without a brief discussion of practical examples of ethnicity and their impact on the politics of Africa. It is to this end that the following summary on a few subjectively selected countries will suffice to shed some light on the intricacies of this subject matter. In pursuing this line of analyses, we have omitted the republics of Nigeria and South Africa, two key political players in sub-Saharan Africa, because they have been sufficiently dealt with elsewhere (Udogu, 1999, pp. 151–176). The proceeding concise discussions on political ethnicity will center on Kenya, Sierra Leone, Rwanda/Burundi and Cameroon.

Kenya

One of the political concerns expressed by some leaders in Africa is that if a multiparty system is allowed to flourish that could lead to the formation of many ethnically-based political parties with their virulent and centrifugal tendencies. Therefore to curb a possible plethora of such parties, it was deemed necessary to opt for a single-party system in order to avoid political chaos.

In Kenya, the dominant political philosophy and hypothesis, at least until 1992, was that a one-party system was or likely to further stability than a multiparty system. To encourage multi-partism, single-party advocates contend, could lead to deep ethnic crisis propagated by ethnically-based parties, social and economic malaise and political distemper. In short, in such a laissez-faire political system, electoral contests could result in a political Armageddon—the final battle for power that could lead to the balkanization of the nation-state.

This political gospel has been preached with some success until recently when the World Bank, the International Monetary Fund (IMF) and other multilateral lending organizations imposed their economic conditionalities on Kenya, linking multiparty democracy with international loans (Oakley, 1998, p.1). Besides the IMF and World Bank pressures and conditionalities on President Daniel arap Moi's regime to open up the political system, was the apprehension that in a free and fair election, he was likely to lose because of his unpopular policies. Perhaps more significantly was his fear that multiparty politics could lead to ethnic politics, and since he is a Kalenjin, an ethnic minority group, it was a foregone conclusion that he could be defeated by the majority groups, as for example, the Kikuyu.

In order to influence the outcome of the 1992 presidential election, some have alleged, a number of ethnically instigated clashes occurred in the area of the Rift Valley. Indeed, the Kalenjin (which constitute about 4 percent of the Kenyan population) launched an attack in late 1991 and early 1992 on villages made up of Kikuyu, Luo and Luhya ethnic groups with the loss of many lives (Nowrojee and Manby, 1993, p. 3). The strategy was intended to warn or admonish the republic of the impending 'tribal' chaos and doom that might befall the country should the nation be seduced by the notion of a multiparty democracy or further political liberalization.

It would seem that given the nature of the political prologue leading to the 1992 election and the policies of the regime that the opposition parties would be united in the single purpose of ousting arap Moi who has been in power since the death of the founding father, Jomo Kenyatta. But that was not to be the case. The union of the opposition politicians which was made up of the Forum for the Restoration of Democracy (FORD) could not hold the coalition together because of internal discrepancies flowing from irreconcilable ethnic interests and the hollowness or lack of concrete and solid programs to tackle the country's problems (Holmquist and Ford, 1994, p. 7). Little wonder, then, that in October 1992, the alliance collapsed and disintegrated into two ethnically-based political parties: FORD-Kenya and FORD-Asili. The leader of the former was the late Oginga Odinga, who drew his support from the Luo ethnic collectivity and that of the latter was Kenneth Matiba, with his political roots in the southern Kikuyu. A third opposition party was led by the erstwhile vice-president, Mwai Kibaki, whose political stronghold was among the northern Kikuyu (Oakley, 1998, p. 3). Indeed, not even the rage emanating from the 'ethnic cleansing' in the Rift Valley was sufficient to unite the opposition in the presidential election that ensued.

In the democratic election that pitted arap Moi's Kenyan African National Union (KANU) against the opposition parties, KANU won with 36 percent of the vote and maintained a majority of Members of Parliament (108 out of the 188 seats). In fact, it was noted that 'no Kikuyu, and only one Luo in KANU won their seats and as a result the regime nominated former MPs from those ethnic groups [as a consociational strategy to appease these collectivities]' (Oakley, 1998, p. 5).

In this political development there were three possible theoretical explanations, namely, ethnic competition, social closure and ethnic boundaries. Within the ethnic mix of FORD, itself, were two major ethnic groups, the Kikuyu and Luo. The assumption was that given the dominance of Kikuyus in terms of population, the Luos were going to be the 'junior' partners since they (i.e., the Luos) might not have been able to compete with the 'senior' partners—the Kikuyus, for plum posts. The issue, *inter alia*, for the Luos was why assist the Kikuyus to win political power only to be possibly marginalized in the party? In part, such an ethnic competition within FORD might have led to the collapse of the alliance into FORD-Asili and FORD-Kenya. Also, following the split, FORD-Asili, dominated by the southern Kikuyus, had hoped that a triumph in the electoral contestation could lead to the group's control of power and perks that came with political victory at the ballot box. On the other hand, FORD-Kenya which was controlled by the Luos, had a limited chance of winning on its own because it lacked the numerical strength to do so. Perhaps sensing an obvious defeat, the strategy of Oginga Odinga was clear: If FORD-Kenya could not win, then, let arap Moi, a Kalenjin, stay in power.

As to Max Weber's doctrine of social closure, it was obvious that the minority Kalenjins, to which the president belonged, would have liked to control power for its survival. After all, it lacks the numerical clout to withstand the more dominant ethnic groups, particularly the Kikuyus. Indeed, the Rift Valley imbroglio said to have been instigated by the Kalenjins, arguably, had its origins in this theory rather than 'animosity' toward the molested ethnic cleavages. In a real sense, therefore, the minority Kalenjins see their monopoly on political power as the major source of their survival in an ethnically-charged political system—a condition somewhat akin to the Tutsis in Burundi and Rwanda.

The theory of ethnic boundary in this context relates, among other factors, to the issue of resource distribution. So, the political struggle and competition in a multiethnic party democracy is for the authoritative allocation of values. Put another way, the duels in such a political drama are intended to decide the ethnic political cleavage who gets the spoils after a political battle. In this regard, who gets the pipe borne water, airport, highway, university, hospital, just to list a few of the major infrastructural projects. In politics, the party that is in control of the government generally makes these important decisions. The question within the framework of this discussion is why did Kenneth Matiba, leader of FORD-Asili (southern Kikuyu), not form an alliance with Mwai Kibaki, leader of an opposition party among the northern Kikuyus? It could be contended that one of the reasons stems from the assumption that if Matiba had won the presidential elections, development within his 'ethnic boundaries' probably would have escalated at the expense of the other ethnic groups. The reverse might have been the case if Kibaki had won.

Within the context of the foregoing brief analyses it should be noted, though, that there are other intangible variables other than those noted in determining the political character of these political entrepreneurs. In particular, the idiosyncratic variables or personality traits of the actors should be noted. This is the case since some of these politicians use political ethnicity as the instrumentality for pursuing their individual and group interests. But in the final analysis their leadership skills, or lack thereof, in handling ethnically motivated issues, in the political system, tend to bring into the limelight the very stuff of these theoretical constructs.

Sierra Leone

In the analysis of ethnic politicization in Sierra Leone, Jimmy D. Kandeh (1992, p. 81) noted that whereas the Creole dominated the political landscape in pre-colonial Sierra Leone, it did not take long in the post-colonial era for the other major ethnic groups, Mendes, Temnes and Limbas, to discover the power of ethnic solidarity in the struggle for political power. The lesson to be learned in the Sierra Leonean situation, as is the case elsewhere in Africa, is that the group that controlled political power also determined how the national resources are to be distributed. In this regard, it was noted that

> the linkage between competitive politics and the politicization of ethnic identities in Sierra Leone suggests, *inter alia*, that political ethnicity is primarily an instrumentalist phenomenon, its primordial underpinning notwithstanding. As an instrumentalist

construct, political ethnicity tends to collapse the distinction between ethnic identity, on the one hand, and political choices, affiliations and loyalties, on the other. It can express as well as distort common descent, expand as well as contract ethnic boundaries, benefit as well as neglect the mass of ethnically defined political groupings (Hayward and Kandeh, 1987, pp. 25–59; Kandeh, 1992, pp. 81–82).

Following the peripheralization and 'marginalization' of the hitherto dominant Creoles in the internal politics, the final battle (for the control of resources) was to be waged between the Mendes and Temnes. In the political duel or confrontation, Mendes (under the banner of the Sierra Leone People's Party—SLPP) had to lock political horns with the Temnes (under the aegis of the All People's Congress—APC) for control of the apparatus of government. For example, following the 1988 election, the ethnic composition of the cabinet was Mendes 5, Temne 12, Limba 4, Creole 3, and others 3 (Kandeh, 1992, p. 93). The allure and saliency of political ethnicity in the democratization enterprise in Africa issue in part from the expectations of the various ethnic groups at the grassroots level. In fact, G. M. Carew notes: 'The individual [or politician] is seen as an embodiment of the tribe, consequently his [or her] fortunes are strongly identified with the fortune of the tribe. If he or she succeeds it is the tribe that has progressed, and if he or she fails it is the tribe that has suffered a setback. ...[thus], each time a high office or post goes to someone in the community his or her tribesmen jubilate openly, culminating finally in a delegation to the Head of state [with special *kola nuts* and other forms of gifts] to thank him for the appointment of their son or daughter to the high office' (Carew, 1985, p. 6; cited also in Kandeh, 1992, p. 94).

Such jubilation could be taunting to the neighboring ethnic groups, who watch from the sideline because they are not so blessed with a similar fortune. Indeed, what this does is encourage ethnic competition as it whets the political appetite and sharpen the desire for ethnic solidarity in the next democratic competition. This is so because the newly appointed minister or high government appointee is likely to bring political goodies to his or her ethnic group at the seeming expense of the contiguous ethnic groups. This scenario brings into limelight the quest for political solidarity and active participation along ethnic lines in future political contestations to elect the 'big man' or 'big madam' who would bring home the bacon. Such political behavior pattern, in effect, nourishes the theory of ethnic boundaries, which, if not handled adequately, could result in ethnic political clashes.

Rwanda and Burundi

The proceeding analysis is predicated on the problematic politics in these countries. And, as elsewhere in the continent, the problems are rooted in the areas' colonial experience. Whereas journalistic narrations and interpretations of the crisis in these republics accentuate ethnicity as the causal factor of the carnage in Rwanda and Burundi, some scholars suggest that serious analytical interpretation of the crisis must shift the locus and rationale for the mayhem to the nation-state (Lemarchand, 1994, pp. 581–604; see also Mewbury, 1988; 1995, pp. 12–17). The issue and focus, these scholars contend, lie with the group that controls the state. Indeed, one scholar argues: 'When the assumption of the nation-state is taken away, the divide [or chasm] between the Hutu and Tutsi can at the same time be presented as trivial..., as the basis for [ethno]nationalist ideologies. ...In other words, there is nothing inherent to the nature of Hutuism or Tutsism which leads to fratricide...' (Walters, 1995, p. 345). Burundi has the same mix of majority Hutus and minority Tutsis as in Rwanda, but the Hutus are presently in political power, while Burundi's army and its judges are almost all Tutsi. Perceptually and realistically such a situation could be conflictive in many ways. First, how could the Hutus 'trust' the Tutsi judges to issue impartial judgments on litigations brought before the court by Hutu plaintiffs against Tutsis in this kind of political atmosphere? Second, if one were to subscribe to Mao Zeadong's dictum, that 'power comes from the barrel of the gun,' isn't it obvious that the Tutsis might be hell bent on controlling this instrument of coercion to the chagrin of the Hutus? In any case, the victory of the Tutsi-led Rwandan Patriotic Front in the political and military commotion in that republic bears the latter thesis out. Essentially, the doctrine propounded by a number of scholars to explain the phenomena in these countries is instrumentalist, nurtured by the theories of ethnic boundaries and competition. They contend that ethnicity is manipulated by the elite for political gains. But in the final analysis, it is the nation-state that suffers. Such was the case in the 'ethnic cleansing' in the Rwandan civil war of the 1990s (Newbury, 1995, pp. 12–17). Indeed, Julius O. Ihonvbere (1994, p. 54) in his lamentation with this kind of politics noted: '[The] politicization of ethnicity all over the continent has never been a basis for effective mobilization and national unity. It has generated deep-rooted suspicions, massacres, wastage of resources and general insecurity and confusion. In the end, the quest for nationhood suffers.'

It goes without saying, within the framework of the foregoing analyses, that the theories of social closure and ethnic competition are at play here. The competition for control of the state is one that has pitted the Hutus and Tutsis in what appears to be perennial pitch battles. The Hutus may control the political landscape only to the extent that they could use their numerical strength to win elections. But the true locus of power lies in the ethnic group that controls the military. Right now the Tutsis are in charge of the instrument of coercion. Not even the Hutu's 'strategy' of ethnic cleansing in Rwanda was able to undo the Tutsi's military advantage. So, in order to assure its survival, in a country in which its population is lilliputian when compared to that of the Hutus, the principle of social closure becomes, in effect, a *sine qua non*.

Cameroon

The discussion of ethnic politics in Cameroon presents a unique case from the perspective of its tripartite characteristics—i.e., anglophile, francophile and indigenous African complexions. In addition to the problematic marriage of French and English traditions in this multi-ethnic and multi-lingual state, political competition for power tends to sharpen the ethnic walls, interests and differences.

In the drive to amalgamate the two blocs in the Cameroonian polity, the late President Ahmadou Ahidjo opted for a great single unifying political party. In such a party, contended Ahidjo, democracy and freedom of expression would reign supreme, while simultaneously allowing 'contradictory' tendencies to flower and flourish within the party. This political attitude, it was contended, would serve as the springboard and, indeed, the hallmark for a truly democratic society (Le Vine, 1971, p. 107). But alas! this was not to be the case. Could this have been a set up?

In fact, Joseph Takougang (1996, pp. 52–53) has noted that it might be true that the one-party system mollified the threat to national unity and debarred the proliferation of ethnic political parties, but that recent developments in the republic suggest that after over three decades of one-party rule not much has changed to promote the spirit of nationhood that overrode or superseded ethnic and regional identities.

The political space enlargement in 1990 by the Paul Biya administration literally let the cat out of the bag, in a manner of speaking. The liberalization of the political system in the wake of political and economic pressures brought to bear on the system, by international lending organizations within the contest of the Structural Adjustment Program (SAP), led to the formation of political parties in 1992 for the multiparty legislative and presidential elections.

In this political contestation, the following parties were formed along ethnic and regional lines: (1) Cameroon People's Democratic Movement (CPDM) with its support among the Beti-Pahouin collectivity in the center, south, and east provinces; (2) the National Union for Democracy and Progress (NUDP), dominated by Foulbe and northern-Moslems; (3) the Social Democratic Front (SDF), which drew its support from the Bamiléké (mainly from the West province) and the Anglophone Cameroonians—primarily from the North West and South West provinces; (4) Union des Populations du Cameroun (UPC), which garnered its support from the Bassas in the littoral and west province; and (5) the Movement for the Defense of the Republic (MDR), which drew its support from the Kirdi ethnic group in the Far North province (Takougang, 1996, pp. 54–55).

The formation of these ethno-regional parties was not intended to further democracy *per se*. Rather, they were formed within the framework of resource competition theory for the control of amenities and scarce resources. This was important for the improvement of the ethnic constituencies. In such confrontations the nation-state is only relevant to the extent that it is being used to further group interest and advantage. It is within this context that a popular political discourse in the anglophone part of the country (that is, the former British Southern Cameroons which joined with *la république du Cameroun* to form the Federal Republic of Cameroon in 1961) today is the issue of independence. Some of its proponents argue that the inhabitants of this (English-speaking) area were not given the choice of possible sovereignty, by the UN, in the early 1960s when the area was decoupled from Nigeria and amalgamated with (French-speaking) Eastern Cameroon. The position of these advocates flows in part from the fact that this area is rich in crude oil, and has become the bread basket of the republic; yet, it does not see the benefit of its wealth in the form of development in the area (Konings and Nyamnjoh, 1997, pp. 207ff; Bayart, 1978, pp. 82–99). Their arguments are somewhat analogous to those of the Ijaw ethnic group in the oil producing areas of Nigeria. Such agitations based on economic marginalization tend to weaken the state. Again, the political behavior patterns in Cameroon fall within the framework of the tenets of ethnic competition, ethnic boundaries and social closure. It is probably this realization that prompted Ufo O. Uzodike (1996, p. 31) to write: 'Africa's current economic problems do not just betray a crisis of the state but also its problems of scarcity and management (of the economy and distribution). So while democracy or political liberalization can provide a more conducive environment for restructuring the state and management, it will not provide a palliative for the problems of scarcity in many countries. It is because of resource scarcity and the penalty that awaits [any ethnic political] losers that political [ethnicity and] control is accorded much importance throughout the continent.'

Conclusion

We have attempted to address the issues of ethnicity in African politics within the context of a few theoretical constructs. In applying these theories to brief case studies in sub-Saharan Africa, it is hoped that we have ever so slightly opened up the 'windows' to provide the reader with a glimpse, or perhaps a peek, into the influence of ethnicity in African politics. In so doing, we took cognizance of Nnoli's (1980, p. 9) conjectures that there are numerous pitfalls in attempts to explain the ethnic issues in Africa. First, such an effort may succeed in keeping ethnic emotions aflame by bringing their 'embers' to the fore of the consciousness of the informed public. Second, it may arouse or generate divisive inter-ethnic controversy—since ethnicity is a very sensitive question in national politics.

Indeed, it is a given that ethnicity does not matter much to a majority of Africans, as Richard Sklar and others have noted. This is so because in Africa, ethnic movements may be encouraged and incited to action by political entrepreneurs who use them to promote their individual and group interests (Sklar, 1967, pp. 6–7; 1979, pp. 531–552; Ismagilova, 1978, pp. 184–198; Rotberg, 1967, pp. 9–35).

But to mollify the dysfunctional characteristics of ethnicity may require the views enunciated by scholars concerned with political ethnicity. In this regard the views of David A. Lake and Donald Rothchild in their disquisition on how to manage ethnic conflict are instructive. They suggest four dimensions that might help mitigate ethnic conflict, and promote harmony. These are mutual respect, power-sharing, [genuine] elections, and regional autonomy and federalism (Lake and Rothchild, 1996, pp. 57–63). In the same vein, too, some Africanists (Udogu, 1994, p. 169; Uzodike 1996, pp. 21–38; Mbaku, 1998; Ihonvbere, 1999, pp. 45–59) have argued for the economic revitalization of the continent; in particular, they recommend the reformation of the economic and political institutions to create the enabling environment that could provide equality of opportunity, justice and fair play for all Africans.

References

Agbese, P. O. (1996), 'Ethnic Conflicts and Hometown Association', *Africa Today*, Vol. 43, No. 2, pp. 139–156.
Ake, C. (1995), 'The Nigerian State: Antinomies of a Periphery Formation', in Ake, C. (ed.), *Political Economy of Nigeria*, Longman Group Ltd: London.
Anise, L. (1979), 'Ethnicity and National Integration in West Africa: Some Theoretical Considerations', in Hall, R. L. (ed.), *Ethnic Autonomy Comparative Dynamics: The Americas, Europe and the Developing World*, Pergamon Press: New York.
Bariagaber, A. (1998), 'The Politics of Cultural Pluralism in Ethiopia and Eritrea: Trajectories of Ethnicity and Constitutional Experiments', *Ethnic and Racial Studies*, Vol. 21, No. 6, pp. 1056–1073.
Barth, F. (1969), *Ethnic Groups and Boundaries*, Little, Brown and Co.: Boston.
Barth, F. (1996), 'Ethnic Groups and Boundaries', in Hutchinson, J. and Smith, D. A. (eds.), *Ethnicity*, Oxford University Press: Oxford and New York.
Bayart, J.-F. (1978), 'The Neutralization of Anglophone Cameroon', in Joseph, R. A. (ed.), *Gaullist Africa: Cameroon Under Ahmadu Ahidjo*, Fourth Dimension Publishers: Enugu, Nigeria.
Bell, D. (1975), 'Ethnicity and Social Change', in Glazer, N. and Moynihan, D. P. (eds.), *Ethnicity: Theory and Experience*, Harvard University Press: Cambridge, MA.
Carew, G. M. (1985), 'The Multiethnic States and the Principle of Distributive Justice', Unpublished Mimeo.
Connor, W. (1973), 'The Politics of Ethnonationalism', *Journal of International Affairs*, Vol. 27, No. 1, pp. 1–23.
Couloumbis, T. A. and Wolfe, J. H. (1990), *Introduction to International Relations: Power and Justice*, Prentice-Hall: Englewood, Cliffs, NJ.
Geertz, C. (1963), 'The Integrative Revolution', in Geertz, C. (ed.), *Old Societies and New States*, Free Press: Oxford and New York.
Geertz, C. (1996), 'Primordial Ties', in Hutchinson, J. and Smith A. D. (eds.), *Ethnicity*, Oxford University Press: New York.
Glazer, N. and Monynihan, D. P. (eds.) (1975), *Ethnicity: Theory and Experience*, Harvard University Press: Cambridge, MA.

Grosby, S. (1996), 'The Inexpungeable Tie of Promordiality', in Hutchinson, J. and Smith, D. A. (eds.), *Ethnicity*, Oxford University Press: New York.

Hayward, F. M. and Kandeh, J. D. (1987), 'Perspectives of Twenty Five Years of Elections in Sierra Leone', in Hayward, F. M. (ed.), *Elections in Independent Africa*, Westview Press: Boulder, CO.

Holmquist, F. and Ford, M. (1994), 'Kenya: State and Civil Society the First Year after the Election', *Africa Today*, Vol. 41, No. 4, pp. 5–25.

Horowitz, D. L. (1985), *Ethnic Groups in Conflict*, University of California Press: Berkeley, CA.

Hutchinson, J. and Smith, A. D. (eds.) (1996), *Ethnicity*, Oxford University Press: New York.

Ihonvbere, J. O. (1994), 'The "Irrelevant" State, Ethnicity, and the Quest for Nationhood in Africa', *Ethnic and Racial Studies*, Vol. 17, No. 1, pp. 42–60.

Ihonvbere, J. O. (1999), 'Africa in the Twenty-first Century: The Challenges and Opportunities', in Mbaku, J. M. (ed.), *Preparing Africa for the Twenty-first Century: Strategies for Peaceful Coexistence and Sustainable Development*, Ashgate: Aldershot, UK.

Ismagilova, R. N. (1978), *Ethnic Problems of Tropical Africa: Can They Be Solved?*, Progress Publishers: Moscow.

Kandeh, J. D. (1992), 'Politicization of Ethnic Identities in Sierra Leone', *African Studies Review*, Vol. 35, No. 1, pp. 81–99.

Kofele-Kale, N. (1981), *Tribesmen and Patriots: Political Culture in a Polyethnic State*, University Press of America: Washington, DC.

Konings, P. and Nyamnjoh, F. B. (1997), 'Anglophone Problem in Cameroon', *The Journal of Modern African Studies*, Vol. 35, No. 2, pp. 207–229.

Lake, D. A. and Rothchild, D. (1996), 'Containing Fear: The Origin and Management of Ethnic Conflict', *International Security*, Vol. 21, No. 2, pp. 41–75.

Lemarchand, R. (1994), 'Managing Transition Anarchies: Rwanda, Burundi, and South Africa in Comparative Perspective', *The Journal of Modern African Studies*, Vol. 32, No. 4, pp. 581–604.

Le Vine, V. T. (1971), *The Cameroon Federal Republic*, Cornell University Press: Ithaca, NY.

Mbaku, J. M. (1998), *Corruption and the Crisis of Institutional Reforms in Africa*, The Edwin Mellen Press: Lewiston, NY.

Nagel, J. (1995), 'Resources Competition Theories', *American Behavioral Scientist*, Vol. 38, No. 3, pp. 442–457.

Nash, M. (1989), *The Cauldrum of Ethnicity in the Modern World*, University of Chicago Press: Chicago and London.

Newbury, C. (1988), *The Cohesion of Oppression: Clientship and Ethnicity in Rwanda, 1860–1960*, Columbia University Press: New York.

Newbury, C. (1995), 'Background To Genocide: Rwanda', *ISSUE: A Journal of Opinion*, Vol. XXIII, No. 2, pp. 12–17.

Nnoli, O. (1980), *Ethnic Politics in Nigeria*, Fourth Dimension Publishers: Enugu, Nigeria.

Nowrojee, B. and Manby, B. (1993), 'Divide and Rule', *Africa Report*, Vol. 38, No. 5, pp. 32–34.

Oakley, B. (1998), 'Democracy and the 1997 Elections in Kenya', A paper presented at the conference on 'Africa and Globalization: Towards the Millennium', at the University of Central Lancashire, UK.

Osaghae, E. E. (1991), 'Ethnic Minorities and Federalism in Nigeria', *African Affairs*, Vol. 90, No. 359, pp. 237-258.

Osaghae, E. E. (1995), 'The Ogoni Uprising: Oil Politics, Minority Agitation and the Future of the Nigerian State', *African Affairs*, Vol. 94, No. 376, pp. 325-344.

Patterson, O. (1975), 'Contest and Choice in Ethnic Allegiance', in Glazer, N. and Moynihan, D. P. (eds.), *Ethnicity: Theory and Experience*, Harvard University Press: Cambridge, MA.

Plano, J. and Olton, R. (1982), *The International Relations Dictionary*, Clio Press Ltd: Oxford.

Rotberg, R. (1967), 'Tribalism and Politics in Zambia', *Africa Report*, Vol. 12, No. 9, pp. 9-35.

Schermerhorn, R. A. (1978), *Comparative Ethnic Relations*, University of Chicago Press: Chicago, IL.

Shil, E. (1957), 'Primordial, Personal, Sacred and Civil Ties', *British Journal of Sociology*, Vol. 7, pp. 113-145.

Sklar, R. (1967), 'Political Science and National Integration: A Radical Approach', *Journal of Modern African Studies*, Vol. 5, No, 1, pp. 1-11.

Sklar, R. (1979), 'The Nature of Class Domination in Africa', *Journal of Modern African Studies*, Vol. 17, No. 4, pp. 531-552.

Stanfield, J. H. (1995) (ed.), 'Theories of Ethnicity', *American Behavioral Scientist*, Vol. 38, No. 3, pp. 389-390.

Stone, J. (1995), 'Race, Ethnicity, and the Weberian Legacy', *American Behavioral Scientist*, Vol.38, No. 3, pp. 391-406.

Takougang, J. (1996). 'The 1992 Multiparty Elections in Cameroon: Prospects for Democracy and Democratization', *Journal of Asian and African Studies*, Vol. XXXI, No. 1-2, pp. 52-65.

Udogu, E. I. (1990), 'National Integration Attempts in Nigerian Politics 1979-1984', *Canadian Review of Studies in Nationalism*, Vol. XVII, No. 1-2, pp. 157-175.

Udogu, E. I. (1994), The Allurement of Ethnonationalism in Nigerian Politics: The Contemporary Debate', *Journal of Asian and African Studies*, Vol. XXIX, No. 3-4, pp. 159-171.

Udogu, E. I. (1995), 'Ethnicity, the State and the Issue of Nation-building in Nigeria's Forthcoming Republic', a paper presented at the 13th annual meeting of the Association of Third World Studies, Jacksonville, FL.

Udogu, E. I. (1997), *Nigeria and the Politics of Survival as a Nation-state*, The Edwin Mellen Press: Lewiston, NY.

Udogu, E. I. (1999), 'Ethnicity and Democracy in Sub-Saharan Africa', in Mbaku, J. M. (ed.). *Preparing Africa for the Twenty-first Century: Strategies for Peaceful Coexistence and Sustainable Development*, Ashgate Publishers: Aldershot, UK.

Uzodike, U. O. (1996), 'Democracy and Economic Reforms: Developing Underdeveloped Political Economies', *Journal of Asian and African Studies*, Vol. XXXI, No. 1-2, pp. 21-38.

Walters, T. (1995), 'Tutsi Social Identity in Contemporary Africa', *The Journal of Modern African Studies*, Vol. 33, No. 2, pp. 343-347.

Weber, M. (1996), 'The Origin of Ethnic Groups', in Hutchinson, J. and Smith A. A. (eds.), *Ethnicity*, Oxford University Press: New York.
Yeros, P. (1999) (ed.), *Ethnicity and Nationalism in Africa: Constructivist Reflections and Contemporary Politics*, Macmillan Press: London and St. Martin Press: New York.
Young, C. (1979), *The Politics of Cultural Pluralism*, University of Wisconsin Press, Madison, WI.

3 Ethnicity and Political Economy of Africa: A Conceptual Analysis

KELECHI A. KALU

Introduction

Ethnicity, without politics and scarce economic resources, is atavistic and latent in nature. However, applied to multiethnic states in sub-Saharan Africa and other regions, ethnicity comes alive as the basis for a politicized search for redistribution of scarce resources. To be sure, in Africa, European expansionism encouraged ethnic sentiments among Africans, by nurturing the peoples' differences rather than their similarities; however, ethnicity is neither immutable nor inherently conflictual. Ethnicity is like a two-side sword—it tends to be the basis for communal identity and security; but it is also a basis for exclusionary practices, which sometimes result in conflict. Without the benefits of counterfactual insights, the extent to which ethnic manipulation and its impacts characterize much of political and economic discourse in sub-Saharan Africa at the end of the millennium will remain a puzzle. But, in the context of transnational developments in transportation and communications technology, and their integrating characteristics, politicized ethnicity is a part of the evolving social formation in many African states. Consequently, theoretical and methodological approaches will determine how well analysts provide explanations on the impact of ethnicity on political and economic development in Africa.

Adopting a political economy approach, this chapter examines the limit or degree to which ethnic sentiment as a component of the colonial legacy helps our understanding of issues of conflicts and underdevelopment in Africa at the end of the 20th century. It is also structured around three assumptions. First, that political decision determines the extent of ethnic accommodation or conflict. Second, in the context of scarce resources, ethnicity is politicized and therefore instrumental in political and economic decisions among the various groups. Third, a weak institutional framework gives rise to conflicts that may include ethnic, cultural and class differences, which are not necessarily specific to African states. Here, I argue that how Africans perceive their differences, rather than those differences, per se, determine whether or not ethnic differences are problematic. Furthermore, ethnic differences are heightened in the context of perceived weaknesses in the state's institutional framework. Analytical clarity on the nature of the state is *sine qua non* for understanding issues of ethnicity in Africa.

Conceptual clarification of ethnicity and nation-state

Don Handleman (1977) and Hutchinson and Smith (1996, p. 6) define ethnicity in broad and specific categories. First, *ethnic category* is characterized by perceived cultural differences between members and non-members of the ethnic group. Second, *ethnic network* involves interactions within member groups as well as distribution of resources to benefit members. Third, *ethnic association* is similar to ethnic network, but also includes a development of common interests in political organizations through which members' interests and goals are expressed. Lastly, ethnicity is characterized by the existence of an *ethnic community* which expresses all of the above in addition to the existence of a permanent, 'physically bounded territory' to which the group has political control. Thus, ethnic community as part of European social formation is the foundation of European State system. As a result, one of the consequences of several internecine wars fought by the Europeans was the breakdown of the imperial states system in Europe which, as a result, used ethno-linguistic and ethno-religious categories as the foundation to organize the centralizing power of the state between the 15th and 17th centuries.

Following the Westphalian Treaty in 1648, the state established its independence from the Church along nationalist (read ethnic) lines; consequently suggesting that people should organize around their own ethnic groups, which were usually equivalent to individual and sovereign nations. Thus, the concept of a *nation-state* derives from the Europeans' search for their ethnicities as the basis for social formation within the framework of the *state* as the most acceptable identity in the international order characterized by conflicts and conquests. As D. L. Sheth (1989, p. 619) observes, '...the state is not for all kinds of people, it is for a nation. The state exists not merely for maintaining law and order in the framework of which the ethnic pluralities live their own lives. It is a vehicle for ethnic aspirations, an engine of economic growth and development for an ethnically defined nation.' Thus, the *nation-state* is simply the congruence between the people/community (the nation) with the authority (i.e., the state) in the process of social formation. This differentiation is significant for understanding the impact of ethnic consciousness on the conflicts that seem inherent to political and economic development in Africa.

From the above, *ethnic consciousness* is an attachment and loyalty that one has in community with others either on the basis of language, religion, social, economic or cultural affinity or a combination of several or all of these. As evidenced in the social formation of the European states, ethnic consciousness is not necessarily detrimental to the economic and political development of the *state* or *nation*. However, as Elaigwu (1994, pp. 69–85) notes,

> ... ethnicity is ethnic consciousness transformed into a weapon of offence or defence in a competitive process in relation with other groups over desired scarce resources ... [which] could lead to the mobilization of ethnic bedfellows in order to maximize gains at the expense of the other competing group(s).

For Elaigwu, *ethnicity* as a social phenomenon and a basis for social formation is inherently conflictual. It is characterized by exclusivity in the process of interaction with non-members of the group, especially in multiethnic states such as those in sub-Saharan Africa where the existing modes of production and distribution are perceived to be skewed in favor of dominant ethnic and/or political groups.

The forgoing conceptualization is in congruence with the instrumentalist perspective on ethnicity, which argues that in the process of reconciling (re)distribution of resources those with cultural, language and/or religious similarities would tend to join together to gain the most of existing resources at the expense of out-groups. Given the absence of a familiar political organizing system in their encounters with the African continent, the puzzle for early European ethnographers was how to solve the perceived absence of a centralizing power in the modern

African state. For most of the pre-colonial encounter, European anthropologists categorized 'the non-state African systems' as products of 'primitive' societies. Consequently, advocates of modernization expected the imposed colonial states to solve problems of ethnicity in Africa. The nature of those imposed states and its relevance for understanding issues of ethnicity is discussed below.

Concept of statehood and its application to Africa

Examining the concept of *state* often evokes a dilemma: one may either accept a broad and therefore relatively insignificant definition of the state or agree that the state is '... not a universal concept but rather the product of a specific historical crisis...' that gave rise to the social formation and political organization of a given geopolitical experience (Ferguson and Mansbach, 1989, p. 18). The modern state is rooted in a specific Western experience. It came out of the 1648 Treaty of Westphalia that ended the thirty years war between Catholics and Protestants. However, the literature on the nature and functions of the state spans all theoretical and analytical positions.[1] From a sociological perspective (Max Weber), a state exists if it can exercise a monopoly on the use of force in a given territory. Consistent with the language and intent of the 1648 treaty, International Legal perspective (Ian Brownlie) sees the state as a 'legal person' characterized by a given geographical territory, population, government and political independence. Realists in international politics call this sovereignty. For Marxists (Karl Marx/Lenin), although it will eventually 'wither away,' the state reflects the economic interests of the ruling class. And Statists or Realists (Stephen Krasner) see the state as a composite of (1) politics more as a problem of rule and control, (2) state as an actor in its own right, (3) formal and informal institutional constraints on individual behavior, (4) a sense of history, and (5) as disjunctures and stress. Also, in contrast to a Marxist view of the state, Krasner (1978, p. 10) conceives of the state as 'a set of roles and institutions having peculiar drives, compulsions, and aims of their own that are separate from the interests of any particular societal group.' From that perspective, the state is an abstraction with no particular intent or design to reward any one individual or group in society. The state's generally agreed-on central function of ensuring the national security of its territory, maintaining law and order, and welfare is thus executed without regard to class, coalition and individual interests (Howard

Lentner, 1984, p. 368). From the Realist perspective, even though the existence of the state is dependent on efficient bureaucracy with the capacity to collect revenues (taxes) and use its natural and human resources, the state is apolitical. If we accept the abstract nature of the state from the Realist perspectives, we may conclude it is nothing but neutral in the game of politics where the players are real human beings with, sometimes, bitterly contested interests. It also follows that such a state is autonomous and unaffected by the different political machinations within it. However, if such a state is ineffective in its security functions, the likelihood exists that other states within the region or area, perhaps more efficient, will dominate it. But, such high abstract notions of the state have real and significant consequences for peaceful coexistence in a multiethnic social formation such as those found in sub-Saharan Africa.

If in popular sovereignty (the idea that government policies reflect the general wishes of the governed) citizens' choices impact government decisions, and given that the interest of the state is maintained by the government, we may equally conclude that states are anti-democratic,[2] and reject the Realist perspective as well as Western liberal prescriptions for Africa. Rejection of the foregoing perspectives leads to (a) the conclusion that the state as an abstract entity does not exist and (b) an acceptance (even if partially) of the Marxists' notion of the state as a reflection of the ruling class. Our choice notwithstanding, the question here is: which perspective gives a plausible road map for understanding the nature of the state and its consequences for ethnic conflicts in Africa?

Africa and the concept of state

Most scholars and policymakers in post-independence Africa promote *order* as a precondition for economic development. Centralized state authority in maintaining law and order is seen as essential, especially by policymakers concerned that political liberalization might result in anarchy and incapacity of the newly independent African states to unify the various nationalities within their territories. Post-independence experiences include central economic planning for national development and nation-building supported by the Western and African governments. However, as a number of African states like Uganda, Kenya,

Algeria, Sudan, Somalia, Congo, Ghana, Nigeria, Central African Republic, Benin, Tanzania, Ivory Coast, Zimbabwe, and Angola among others, went from hope to despair, from relative post-independence political stability to civil wars, coups and counter-coups, the general discussion on Africa shifted from economic growth to political liberalization. Bifurcation of political and economic analysis in international relations theory became applicable to Africa as the continent's problems began to be seen as either political or economic instead of studying them *pari passu*.

Such bifurcation not only served the interest of donor countries; the Cold-War-ideologically-structured international system facilitated maintenance of growing confusion about Africa. And, even though the continent is three and half times larger than the United States, analysts, policymakers and popular media houses tended to approach Africa as if it were a single country whose problems could easily be grasped. Post-independence African leaders were equally involved in the perceptual crisis in which external constituencies found themselves. For instance, military coups d'état and/or one-man rule became the norm in Africa. Equally significant, was the general acceptance by the leaders that individual countries needed economic aid from western governments in order to survive. Hence, aid donors in Daniel arap Moi's Kenya and the late Mobutu Sese Seko's Zaire, tried to outdo each other in the level of squandered aid from the West.

Most post-Cold War analysts generally acknowledge that the ongoing crisis in Africa is more than an economic or fiscal problem. It is sometimes seen as a *political* crisis which 'besides [being] the usual political instability or crisis of legitimacy' evidences 'the pervasive lack of democracy, which some perceive as a conflict between the state and people—a crisis arising from lack of popular participation in the development process.'[3] As I have argued elsewhere, the crisis in Africa is deeply rooted in the continent's historical experience, which goes beyond the ongoing democratization processes of African states, leadership crises and post-independence ethnic conflicts. The political and economic crisis in Africa in the 1990s is directly related to the crises of state and class formation before and during Africa's colonization (Kalu, 1995, pp. 10–22). To be sure, post-colonial alignments and realignments of socio-economic and political forces have reproduced inherited conflicts, coalitions, contradictions, and crises. But, these contradictions are directly related to the nature of Africa's forced incorporation into the western epistemological framework whose ignorance of extant African social formations maintained the puzzle because of a lack of serious solutions from modernization or Marxists theoretical perspectives.

Where the rain began to beat Africa[4]

At the birth of the contemporary international political system dating back to the 17th century, African nations were neither conceptually relevant as states nor were Africans seriously considered capable human beings to warrant a seat among the western colonial powers and, as such, were simply excluded (Jackson, 1993, p. 137). Following the Berlin Conference of 1884–85, the partition of Africa by the European powers had two main consequences for Africa—(a) the arbitrary merging of several ethnic groups which traditionally had little in common and, (b) the extension of European political and economic structures into Africa, incorporating the continent in a subordinate role to the European heartland. The forced incorporation of Africa into the international capitalist economic system whose rules privilege Africa's former colonizers remains the single most important aspect of the problem in the continent, whose solution may lie in the extent to which the colonial state is transformed consistent with geographical and ethnic realities.

While state formation in most other parts of the world, but especially in Europe, was a result of class conflicts in which early liberals denounced the 'divine rights' of Kings to rule, the process of state formation in Africa was stalled by the enforcement of the 'white man's burden.' The natural processes and class formation reflecting confrontations between communities and the emergence of larger political and administrative units were terminated through distortion by European colonization. New values, institutions, structures, and social relations were then imposed. More devastating for current political and class development in Africa, however, is the process of decolonization, which started at the conclusion of the First World War. According to Robert Jackson, the birth of African states contrasts with the usual pre-twentieth century sequential birth and death of states based on wars of conquest, colonization, or independence. The concurrent birthdays and uniform ex-colonial frontiers of African states are connected to a changed doctrine of international legitimacy, which occurred in the later half of the twentieth century and were based on the categorical and unrestricted right, colonial (as distinguished from national) self-determination of overseas colonies to become independent states without regard to preparedness or a need for institutional transformation. This is essentially a doctrine of birthright: territories formed by European colonialism are considered to have a right to become sovereign without regard to pre-colonial social formations of the different nationalities (Jackson, 1993, pp. 142–143).

Certainly, the implication from the above will seem to suggest that some states would have opted to remain extensions of the colonial empires, as was the case with a number of French colonies in West Africa. But, that misses the point. If European ethnographers and states decide when and how Africa participates in the international political and economic system whose rules are already established, then the tendency will be toward constraint on the ability of African states to design independent political and economic development strategies in an international system structured for exploitation and marginalization of peripheral and marginalized social formations. For example:

> The desire to retain sovereignty and not to surrender it or even share it ... is a powerful motive perpetuating the ex-colonial *status quo* in sub-Saharan Africa. Sovereignty gives a relatively small number of people control of State positions which confer enormous palpable advantages and privileges available to nobody else in the country.... [For example], management of foreign aid receipts; income from the movement of goods within jurisdictions and between them, ... through issuing tariffs and licenses; the ... unrivaled opportunities for corruption, and so forth (Jackson, 1993, p. 146).

Thus, and even though, sovereignty is a concept emerging from the 1648 Treaty, its empowering influence in Africa and elsewhere can be either positive or negative. While the concept of sovereignty recognizes every state in the world system of states as legal equals; the government of a state possesses sole legitimate right and power to use force. Consequently, for African states, the influence of sovereignty may be visualized in two ways. First, it may help to further the development of a constitutional democracy and therefore good governance in a political space characterized by differences in culture, ethnicity, class and region. Second, in the guise of national security, sovereignty may also be used to suffocate civil society and the democratic process, as has been the case for most of sub-Saharan Africa.

First, although every state is now politically independent in Africa, the fear of loss of power continues to constrain leadership transitions through the ballot boxes. For example, former autocrats in Ghana, Kenya, Zimbabwe, Nigeria, Benin and elsewhere have made attempts to transform themselves from autocrats to democrats, but few successes can be recorded in Ghana, Uganda and Benin. Political turmoil in Central African Republic, Nigeria, Congo, Algeria (irrespective of the election in 1999), Somalia, Angola, Guinea-Bissau continue because the autocrats, transformed or not, remain unwilling to preside over fair and openly contested elections. As the cases of Nigeria, Algeria, Sudan, Mozambique, Cameroon, Zambia and Kenya demonstrate, the few individuals who hold state power have enormous influence and access to the instrument of coercion necessary to silence their opposition. Also significant is the fact that power, conceptualized as the use of force, is employed for material accumulation, corruption, and the containment of presumed radicals, violations of human rights and silencing of the media. Moreover, one of the strategies of this intimidation is to make it difficult for rival political groups to participate in government. This was the case in countries like Ghana, Nigeria, Zambia, Algeria and Kenya, whose struggles for independence largely influenced other African nation's discourses on the impact of ethnic solidarity for the purposes of a new national unity or constructing a united polity.

At independence, the previously marginalized and underdeveloped local elites inherited the colonial state and foreign capital dominated all sectors of respective economies. In the settler colonies, conditions were worse as captured state power became the only institution within the control of the local elites to promote class and clan unity; encourage capitalist accumulation and defend themselves. To the bourgeoisie, the dictum was *'l'état c'est moi'* (which means, I'm the state)—hence the reluctance to give up power by those privileged to be the first to steer the ship of states in Africa since independence.

Ethnicity in Africa is therefore much deeper than existing theoretical frameworks explain. To the extent that ethnicity is perceived as a reflection of conditions of traditional society (primordialism); industrialization, as suggested by modernization theorists, will continue to be expected to shift the focus from communal to individual identities as a major strategy for solving the puzzle of ethnic conflicts in Africa. The logic of some modernization theorists is based on the argument that economic and political development within the framework of state formation will serve integrative functions of various differences, especially those characterized by ethnicity. The poverty of the modernization argument is in its historicity or lack thereof.

Analytical dimensions of ethnicity: a brief overview

For primordialists, especially Edward Shils (1957) and Clifford Geertz (1963), ethnic identity characterized by language, religion, region, blood, race and culture are inherent in all social formations and have a tendency to resist change. Thus, inspite of the evolutionary nature of historical change in the context of modernity, primordialists are of the view that ethnic identities are immutable and therefore present in modern states. As Robertson (1997, p. 267) notes, to the extent that 'ethnopolitics, social structures and political processes are trumped by individual identity,' ethnic groups act as a collective, thereby foregoing individual for collective interests. Thus, at the end of the Cold War and given a general decline in world conflicts, primordialists would point to increased conflicts in Africa and Eastern Europe—Czechoslovakia, Yugoslavia, etc., as an illustration of their argument.

However, modernization theorists do not see issues of ethnicity as a puzzle that necessarily has to be solved. Their focus is on economic and political development of African states—whose success continues to be expected to result in the increase in migration from rural to urban centers, increased higher education attendance, and thus a movement from 'primitive' to modern social formations that consequently will resolve ethnic issues. Initially, transport and information technological developments were supposed to increase interactions of individuals and communities moving them from communal to individual identities. However, the modernization perspective argues that a movement from authoritarian systems of government toward democracies will ensure that a democratic state will unify rather than fragment the different nationalities forced together in Africa by colonialism.

The modernists' argument suffers from the fallacy of a single alternative, especially with respect to the transformative imperative of democracy. Following the end of the Cold War, scholars and policymakers have learned that liberal democracy is not the only alternative to authoritarian governance, as military, as well as one-party regimes reign supreme in most African states, with serious life, political and economic implications for those the state defined as its 'enemies.' For now, at least, the assumption that democracy will cement the divisions between ethnic, cultural, religious, race and linguistics differences in the continent continues to yield negative results for most of post-independence Africa. From Nigeria, Sudan, Kenya, Democratic Republic of Congo, Liberia, Ethiopia to Rwanda and Burundi, ethnic sentiments flourish, becoming more politicized and intensely conflictual. As Benjamin Barber (1996) argues, even though there is a deep human need for community, factors essential to the survival of democracies present liberal democrats with a conundrum. Barber (1996, p. 298) opines that '... the great dilemma of community is that those forms of communal association that yield the highest degree of intimacy, membership, solidarity, and fraternity are those rooted in strong communal ties of the sort that arise out of blood, narrow belief, and hierarchy: the demonization of outsiders.' Consequently, an essential framework of modernization democracy is consistent in its impact on the European social formations whose organizing framework for state was largely ethnic based and ridden with conflict. This is not an argument against liberal democracy. My point here is that politicized ethnicity in sub-Saharan Africa is best understood in the context of scarce economic and political resources; a situation that is likely to continue into the foreseeable future, irrespective of the political system. However, as will be argued later, a hegemonic state whose powers are derived from a viable constitutional framework of governance is more likely to ensure (re)distribution of resources on the basis of a verifiable and just process of allocation.

However, instrumentalists such as Michael Banton (1994) and Michael Hechter (1995), argue that ethnic identities are not inherent in group or social formations of people. Rather, they see ethnic identities as social capital brought to bear on the political negotiation table by different groups and at different times. In a sense, ethnic identities are political resources just like money and/or votes. Hutchinson and Smith (1996, p. 8) also argue that ethnic identities are an important resource that political elites employ in securing the support of the masses as a strategy for gaining a desired good. These goods and/or goals are 'measured in terms of wealth, power, and status, and ... joining ethnic or national communities helps to secure these ends either by influencing the state or, in certain situations, through secession' (Hutchinson and Smith, 1996, p. 9). Seen in the foregoing light, and despite primordialists' claims to the contrary, ethnicity lacks boundary and/or an inherent quality. And, given that politics generally involves the process of redistribution of scarce economic resources on the basis of values, political actors are adept at using different strategies, including ethnic affinities, to their advantage. In that respect and consistent with the claims of this chapter, ethnicity is not necessarily conflictual. Rather, politicized ethnicity is characterized by competition for goods and services as evident in many sub-Saharan African states. However, there are some occasions, best exemplified by the conflict in Ethiopia, where ethnicity is not purely politics.[5] In such circumstances, the survival of the group (e.g. Eritrean struggle for independence) becomes more important than any political motive the leaders may have for organizing on the basis of ethnic affinity.

Understanding ethnicity in Africa

For Donald Horowitz (cited in Huntington, 1997, p. 70), 'An Ibo may be ... an Owerri Ibo or an Onitsha Ibo in what was the Eastern region of Nigeria. In Lagos, he is simply an Ibo. In London, he is a Nigerian. In New York, he is an African.' Thus, depending on the circumstance and situation, human interactions may breed primordial or instrumentalist tendencies. The question is: In what context and to what extent is primordial consciousness helpful for understanding the prevalence of ethnic-based conflicts in political, economic and social formation of most states in sub-Saharan Africa? The genesis, some would argue, is the colonial experience with its inherent policy of European power consolidation, which reached its apex in the Berlin Conference of 1884–85. However, analytical clarity of how European colonization is linked to widespread politicized ethnicity in Africa requires that those scholars interested in the topic examine the causal links carefully with the objective of providing a clear guide to predicting the future of ethnic conflicts and their resolution. Such a project should articulate the perceptual image the western cartographers, ethnographers and therefore policymakers had of 'primitive Africa' in their quest to dominate it.

In *Archeology of Violence* (1980, trans. 1994), Pierre Clastres argues that the European encounter with non-European social formations confronted the explorers with a radically different world from their own. Clastres (pp. 140–141) opines that:

> Explorers or missionaries, merchants or learned travelers, from the 16th century until the (recent) end of world conquest, all

agreed on one point: whether Americans (from Alaska to Tierra del Fuego) or Africans, Siberians from the steppes or Melanesians from the isles, nomads from the Australian deserts or sedentary farmers from the jungles of New Guinea, *primitive peoples were always presented as passionately devoted to war; it was their particularly bellicose character that struck European observers without exception.* From the enormous documentary accumulation gathered in chronicles, travel literature, reports from priests and pastors, soldiers or peddlers, one image continuously emerged from the infinite diversity of the cultures described: that of the warrior. An image dominant enough to induce a sociological observation: *primitive societies are violent societies; their social being is a being-for-war* (emphasis added).

Paradoxically, the 'European burden' became one of civilizing the primitive peoples by re-making those societies in the image familiar to Europeans. The civilization project took two forms. First, to Europeanize the primitive people and second, to restructure the primitive institutions, political spaces and economic formations such that they would become consistent with those of Europe. Within such frameworks, Europeans referred to premodern social groups lacking an institutionalized framework such as a state as *ethnies*, while similar social formations in Africa were referred to as *tribes*; thus, denoting European perception of early Africans and other non-Europeans as largely nomadic. Clastres' exploration of the rationale for the 'European burden' project is insightful and deserves further attention. He asks:

> What exactly do we mean by primitive society? The answer is furnished by the most classical anthropology when it aims to determine the specific being of these societies, when it aims to indicate what makes the irreducible social formations: primitive societies are societies without a State; they are societies whose bodies do not possess separate organs of political power. Based on the presence or absence of the State, one can initially classify these societies and divide them into two groups: *societies with a State and societies without a State.... All societies with a State are divided, in their being, into the dominating and the dominated* (Clastres, 1994, pp. 87–88; emphasis added).

Clastres argues that epistemologically, from Heraclitus, Plato to Aristotle, European social thought could not conceive of a society without a King. For the Europeans a 'society is unthinkable without its division between those who command and those who obey' (p. 88). As well, 'primitive societies are thus undivided societies ... classless societies—no rich exploiters of the poor; societies not divided into the dominating and the dominated—no separate organ of power' (p. 90). Likewise, 'the destiny of every society is to be divided, for power to be separated from society, for the State to be an organ that knows and says what is in everyone's best interest and puts itself in charge of imposing it,' (p. 90), irrespective of the social formation or the extent to which such command-obedience structure makes sense. The impact of such division on colonial Africa, was an institutionally weak political and economic structure. Its consequences for politicized ethnicity and the virulent costs to human lives and productivity in the post-independence African states is as yet unmeasurable.

However, as Frantz Fanon (1967, p. 35) argues, to the extent that the colonialists' strategy of domination did not allow for 'cultural confrontations,' the indigenous cultures were not destroyed. Rather, 'Exploitation, tortures, raids, racism, collective liquidations, rational oppression take turns at different levels in order literally to make of the native an object in the hands of the occupying nation. This object man, without means of existing, without a *raison d'être*, is broken in the very depth of his substance.' Fanon (1967, p. 38) also notes that, in an initial phase of institutionalizing European command-obedience structure, the occupying power legitimizes

> ... its domination by scientific arguments, ... [that denies] the 'inferior race' ... on the basis of race. Because no other solution is left it, the racialized social group tries to imitate the oppressor and thereby to deracialize itself. The 'inferior race' denies itself as a different race. It shares with the 'superior race' the convictions, doctrines, and other attitudes concerning it. Having witnessed the liquidation of its systems of reference, the collapse of its cultural patterns, the native can only recognize with the occupant that 'God is not on his side.' The oppressor, through the inclusive and frightening character of his authority, manages to impose on the native new ways of seeing [and thinking], and in particular a pejorative judgement with respect to his original forms of existing.

Table 3.1 Socio-economic and political indicators of selected sub-Saharan African states

	Burundi	Ethiopia	Kenya	Nigeria	Rwanda	Sierra Leone
% of population below poverty level	36.2%	..	42.0%	43.0%	51.2%	68.0%
Public expenditure on education as % of GNP	2.8% (1995)	4.7% (1995)	7.5% (1995)	6.4% (1980)	2.7% (1980)	3.8% (1980)
Public expenditure on health as % of GDP, 1990–95	1.9%	1.7%	1.9%	0.3%	0.9%	1.6%
Military expenditure as % of GDP	4.4%	2.2%	2.3%	0.8%	5.2%	6.1%
Total external debt in US $, millions	1,034	10,077	6,893	31,407	1,127	1,167
Total external debt as % of GNP	47%	149%	64%	114%	47%	78%

Sources: World Bank (1998), *World Development Report, 1998/99*, Oxford University Press: New York; *SIPRI Yearbook, 1998*.

Thus, while European domination and objectification of Africa was based on race and European perception of its role as that of showing Africans the path to civilization, the post-independence African leaders use ethnicity in its primordial and instrumental characteristics to maintain, dominate, suffocate and manipulate the citizens and the resources for their personal goals. Post-independence African leaders have resorted to violence reminiscent of colonialist violence against Africans. Both the colonial and post-independence autocracies have inflicted heavy cost on Africa in human and material resources. For example, the Economic Commission for Africa estimates that between 1980–88, war in Southern Africa cost the region between US $56 billion to $62.45 billion at 1988 prices. The human cost is estimated at 1.5 million deaths, including 925,000 infants and young children (Rimmer, 1995, pp. 300–301). These costs are largely attributed to apartheid South Africa's destabilization of the frontline states as well as wars in Angola and Mozambique.

The cost of wars attributed to ethnic 'differences' and clashes in other parts of Africa remain as debilitating as the foregoing figures. Perhaps Fanon was right in arguing that the impact of colonialism resulted in the Africans realizing that 'God is not on our side.' But, given political independence, perhaps, the appropriate phrase should be 'African leaders are not on their side.' This observation is derived from Table 3.1, which arguably, illuminates the priorities of most African governments.

The countries listed in Table 3.1 were selected on the basis of their involvement in interstate and/or intrastate conflicts largely seen by analysts to have ethnic and/or class implications. As the table shows, the costs in terms of political decisions that the governing elites make in many African countries is most obvious in the military and external debt data. Compared to its 1985 expenditure at 3.0%, Burundi's 1995 military expenditure of 4.4% represents an increase of 1.4%. However, the external debt rose dramatically from US $190 million in 1980 to $1,034 million in 1996, which represents 47% of its gross national product. For the same time period, Rwanda used 5.2% of its GNP in military expenditure, with its external debt rising from US $166 million in 1980 to $1,127 million in 1996, representing 47% of its GNP. Burundi's war with Rwanda presents a more visible impact of how manipulated ethnic identities is an open sore in Africa.

For Ethiopia, its military expenditure[6] is down from a 6.7% of GNP in 1985 to 2.2% in 1995. However, this decline in military expenditure is deceptive. As Tables 3.2 and 3.3 show, while Ethiopia's military expenditure in US dollars has declined, its value in local currency continues to rise. It is equally significant that Ethiopia's external debt, which stood at $824 million in 1980, increased to $10,077 million in 1996 representing 149% of its gross national product. However, it is plausible to conclude that the above figure (specifically from 1988–1990) illustrates the relationship between ethnic conflicts and military expenditure in Ethiopia. Likewise, we may conclude that (among other reasons), the decline in military expenditure from 1991 to 1996 may be attributed to the resolution of the Ethiopian-Eritrean conflict.

Table 3.2   Military expenditures for selected sub-Saharan African countries, 1988–1997 (in millions of local currency units)

State	1988	1990	1992	1994	1996	1997
Angola (kwanza)	44.0	52.4	388	31,100	—	78,200
Burundi (francs)	4,809	6,782	8,121	10,589	15,408	20,199
Ethiopia (birr)	1,508	1,740	667	710	762	—
Ghana (cedis)	4,603	9,006	23,242	36,147	72,644	93,148
Kenya (shillings)	4,090	5,240	4,290	6,570	—	—
Nigeria (naira)	1,720	2,286	4,822	6,608	15,500	17,450
Rwanda (francs)	2,800	7,964	11,863	5,700	—	—
Sierra Leone (leones)	230	1,369	10,081	15,546	17,119	9,315

Source: Stockholm International Peace Research Institute (SIPRI), (1998), *Armaments, Disarmament and International Security*, Oxford University Press: Oxford.

Note: The local currency is given in parentheses below each country.

Thus, while most African countries record a decline in military expenditure calculated in dollars, when calculated in local currency, all the countries given in Table 3.1 show significant increases in military expenditure as a percent of GNP. As shown in Tables 3.2 and 3.3, while Kenya's military expenditure appears constant at 2.3% of GDP, calculations in local currency show that the increase in Kenya's military expenditure is significant. Equally significant is its increased external debt from $3.3 billion in 1980 to about $7 billion in 1996.

Table 3.3   Military expenditures for selected sub-Saharan African countries, 1988–1997 (in constant US dollars, millions)

State	1988	1990	1992	1994	1996	1997
Angola	—	598	584	301	—	385
Burundi	38.4	45.3	48.8	50.6	48.8	50.0
Ethiopia	511	520	133	127	130	—
Ghana	23.3	26.5	52.7	52.5	45.2	45.5
Kenya	306	300	158	129	—	—
Nigeria	884	728	939	522	548	520
Rwanda	32.9	89.0	101	26.4	—	—
Sierra Leone	6.6	11.6	25.5	25.9	18.4	9.0
sub-Saharan Africa (billions)	10.4	9.9	7.9	6.4	6.2	5.6

Source: Stockholm International Peace Research Institute (SIPRI), (1998), *Armaments, Disarmament and International Security*, Oxford University Press: Oxford.

Also for Nigeria, although military expenditure is down from 1.5% in 1985 to 0.8% in 1996 calculated in dollars, this decrease is only relevant when calculated in terms of total expenditure in dollars. Based on local currency, the SIPRI data show a much higher increase in Nigeria's military expenditure (see Table 3.2).

Similar to other sub-Saharan African countries, Nigeria's external debt increased from $8.9 billion in 1980 to $31.4 billion in 1996, which represents 114% of its gross national product. Sierra Leone's military expenditure went from 0.8% in 1985 to 6.1% in 1996 with external debt of $1.2 billion representing 78% of its GNP.

As previously noted, Clastres (1989) argument that primitive societies are stateless societies is apt here for understanding the relevance of the above data to the political economy of ethnicity in Africa. Briefly, ethnic differences do not inhibit cooperation and collaboration on the basis of constitutional or a federal system of government. Rather, it is our perception of scarcity that has led those who inherited the mantle of the colonial state to recreate the colonial mode of domination and therefore conflict over scarce resources. Thus, in post-colonial Africa, *power* accorded the governing class rather than the traditional *prestige* accorded to elders—an essential aspect of most communal African social formation and the basis for the existence of the Council of Elders and/or Obas and Emirs—has become an instrument of domination. The expectation of future domination, assimilation, subordination and even enslavement (in the case of Sudan) helps to intensify ethnic politics and conflict. This is evident in the case of South Africa with its bureaucratic corruption and the challenge to the African National Congress by Chief Mangosuthu Buthelezi's Inkatha Freedom Party. Largely composed of members of the Zulu ethnic group, such a formation is likely to test the fragile democratic government in post-Mandela South Africa.

As David Welsh (1996, p. 489) has noted, '[c]ollapse of the state in Somalia, virtual implosion of the state in Liberia, horrific genocide in Rwanda, endemic conflict in Burundi, a seemingly never ending civil war in Sudan, and the failure of either democratic or military regimes in Nigeria all appear to point to a massive failure to cope with ethnicity.' The states that have succeeded in managing politicized ethnicity are either small island states like Mauritius or ethnically homogeneous states like Botswana. In both instances, economic indicators have largely been better when compared to the rest of sub-Saharan Africa. But, in the context of extensive waste of national resources evidenced by socioeconomic political indicators such as borrowing for non-productive, non-income earning projects, expenditure for arms which tends to reduce investments in economic and social infrastructure are likely to impede economic development in Africa. It is significant that public policies be based on merit rather than political ethnicity.

Conclusion

Clearly, there is a need for a constitutional democratic framework for governance in sub-Saharan African countries. However, such a system of government will not succeed in the context of declining investment in social and economic infrastructures. And, contrary to Mwangi S. Kimenyi (1998, p. 58), ethnic differences are not likely to be harmonized by '... relying upon the 'tribe' as a basis for organizing governments in Africa.' Although, ethnicity has territorial imperative, but, in the absence of an 'external enemy,' class may become a basis for acrimony. Furthermore, prisoner dilemma models[7] are largely relevant in the context of a democratic governance structure characterized by organized interests that compete for resources on the basis of group interests. Membership in such groups, though voluntary, requires dues payment if the benefits are not to be excludable. For, in situations where the benefits that accrue from organized interests' activities are characterized by non-excludability, such a group is faced with free rider problems. Also, in the case of ethnicity, contrary to Kimenyi, we do not inherently 'choose' what ethnic groups we belong to—even if some may do so for political expedience. Otherwise, we might have difficulty explaining why, especially in the colonists/colonized context, one might choose (not unusual in French West Africa) to be dominated rather than belong in the dominant group. On the domestic level, given that governments (including constitutional democracies) are necessarily based on the politicization of the command-obedience structure, those whose inclinations lead them to want to dominate others (as for instance, the military class) are unlikely to accede to ethnic based governments in Africa. Therefore, the objective of a viable constitutionally-based government should not be to further fragment the different but yet similarly situated social formations in Africa, but to seek their unity in the context of a just governance structure that promotes strength in diversity and unity in collective action.

Notes

1. For specific debates and definitions of the state, the following works should be helpful. Weber, M. (1964), *The Theory of Social and Economic Organization*, Free Press: New York. This edition edited by Talcot Parsons; Trimberger, E. K. (1978), *Revolution from Above: Military Bureaucratics and Development in Japan, Turkey, Egypt, and Peru*, Transaction Press: New Brunswick, NJ; Brownlie, I. (1979), *Principles of Public Law*, 3rd ed., Clarendon Press: Oxford; Nordlinger, E. (1981), *On the Autonomy of the Democratic State*, Harvard University Press: Cambridge, MA; Geertz, C. (1981), *Negara: The Theatre State in Nineteenth Century Bali*, Princeton University Press: Princeton, NJ; Skowronek, S. (1982), *Building a New American State: The Expansion of the National Administrative Capacities*, Cambridge University Press: New York; Tilly, C. (ed.) (1975), *The Formation of National States in Western Europe*, Princeton University Press: Princeton, NJ; Grew, R. (ed.) (1978), *Crises of Political Development in Europe and the United States*, Princeton University Press: Princeton, NJ; Laski, H. J. (1935), *The State as a Concept in Theory and Practice*, The Viking Press: London; Watkins, F. M. (1934), *The State as a Concept in Political Science*, Harper & Brothers Publishers: New York; Lubasz, H. (1974), *The Development of the Modern State*, Macmillan: New York; Krasner, S. (1984), 'Approaches to the State: Alternative Conceptions and Historical Dynamics', *Comparative Politics*, Vol. 16, No. 2 (January), pp. 223–246; Lentner, H. H. (1984), 'The Concept of the State: A Response to Stephen Krasner', *Comparative Politics*, Vol. 16, No. 3 (April), pp. 367–377; Kohli, A. (ed.) (1986), *The State and Development in the Third World*, Princeton University Press: Princeton, NJ; Lenin, I. (1932), *State and Revolution*, International Publishers: New York.

2. To the extent that realists are more concerned about international politics and its impact on national security, the nature or type of government at the domestic realm is irrelevant. What is emphasized is the extent states can rationally use their resources to achieve national security goals. Thus, realists would see a democratic process as a restraint if not a constraint on unitary rational decision making.

3. See, Adebayo Adedeji, 'Development and Ethics: Putting Africa on the Road to Self-Reliant and Self-Sustaining Process of Development.' Keynote address delivered at the first plenary session of the Thirty Third Annual Meeting of the African Studies Association, Baltimore, Maryland, November 1–4, 1990, p. 9. See *African Renewal*, a Report of a Conference on State, Conflict and Democracy in Africa, Convened March 6–9, 1997 at Massachusetts Institute of Technology. Hyden, G. and Bratton, M. (eds.) (1992), *Governance and Politics in Africa*, Lynne Rienner: Boulder, CO.

4. For the 'Rain' metaphor, see Achebe, C. (1967), *A Man of the People*, Anchor Books: New York, pp. 34–35.

5. I am not here suggesting that the 'Brown' and 'Black' issue or chasm in Sudan is not important. Rather, consistent with the argument in this chapter, to the

extent that resources are scarce, individuals in positions of authority are more likely to define the struggle and/or argument in its ethnic contexts. For example, the central question in Sudan is: should southern Sudan be independent from the north? A viable response to the question is unlikely without a serious consideration of the claims of the Sudanese Peoples' Liberation Army (SPLA). The SPLA rose to the defense of the southern Sudanese when it became clear that Numeiri's government intended to use the 'September Laws of 1983' to impose the Sharia judicial process on the non-Muslim southerners. See Tripp, C. (1997), 'The Sudanese Civil War in International Relations', in Hale, W. and Kienle, E. (eds.), *After the Cold War: Security and Democracy in Africa and Asia*, Tauris Academic Studies: London. In the foregoing example, the racial and resource dimensions of ethnicity go beyond politics to the question of civilizational struggle. However, in the long run, ethnic identities—both instrumental and primordial—are likely to be employed in resolving resource issues between and within ethnic groups.

6. The question here might be whether military expenditure is attributed to ethnic conflicts or civil wars. My response is, counterfactually, what if there were no civil or ethnic wars? And, given that most of the wars in African states are intrastate wars, marginally involving external actors and occurring in largely multiethnic states, they may be considered ethnic-conflict-induced expenditures (e.g., data on Ethiopia, 1988–1990) and therefore, opportunity costs to social and economic expenditures.

7. The Prisoner's Dilemma Model (PDM) is explained using the idea of a group of prisoners planning to escape. Each prisoner has the choice of being faithful to the group and benefiting from their plan, or betraying the group for what might be a considerable reward from the authorities. If each prisoner considers that these choices will have first occurred to the others, this means that each stands in danger of special retribution if first betrayed. In this situation, each one chooses secretly whether to keep faith or betray the group and then points are scored when the choices are revealed. When this situation is simulated in a game involving two players, the rules are such that if the two players keep faith with each other, then moderate benefits are earned by both. If both players betray each other, then there is a minimal benefit. But if one player can sucker the other into keeping faith while betraying him, he earns the maximum benefit while the victim gets nothing. The pay-off structure in a given PDM can be represented as defection/cooperation (DC), mutual cooperation (CC), mutual defection (DD), and cooperation/defection (CD). Assuming human rationality, the preference order is DC>CC>DD>CD. In contrast to the instrumental and primordial argument on ethnicity (DC), the preference order in Kimenyi's ethnic-based federalism argument presupposes that (CC) would be the dominant pay-off structure.

References

Banton, M. (1994), 'Modelling Ethnic and National Relations', *Ethnic and Racial Studies*, Vol. 17, pp. 2–19.
Barber, B. R. (1996), *Jihad vs. McWorld: How Globalism and Tribalism are Reshaping the World*, Ballantine Books: New York.
Caporaso, J. A. and Levine, D. P. (1992), *Theories of Political Economy*, Cambridge University Press: New York.
Clastres, P. (1989), *Society Against the State: Essays in Political Anthropology*, Zone Books: New York.
Clastres, P. (1994), *Archeology of Violence*, Semiotext(E): New York.
Elaigwu, J. I. (1994), 'Ethnicity and the Federal Option in Africa', *The Nigerian Journal of Federalism*, Vol. 1, pp. 69–85.
Fanon, F. (1967), *Toward the African Revolution*, Grove Press: New York.
Ferguson, Y. H. and Mansbach, R. W. (1989), *The State, Conceptual Chaos, and the Future of International Relations Theory*, Lynne Rienner Publishers: Boulder, CO.
Geertz, C. (1973), *The Interpretation of Cultures*, Basic Books: New York.
Gurr, T. R. and Harff, B. (1994), *Ethnic Conflict in World Politics*, Lynne Rienner Publishers: Boulder, CO.
Handleman, D. (1977), 'The Organization of Ethnicity', *Ethnic Groups*, Vol. 1, pp. 187–200.
Hechter, M. (1995), 'Explaining Nationalist Violence', *Nations and Nationalism*, Vol. 1, pp. 53–68.
Huntington, S. P. (1996), *The Clash of Civilizations and the Remaking of World Order*, Simon & Schuster: New York.
Hutchinson, J. and Smith, A. D. (eds.) (1996), *Ethnicity*, Oxford University Press: Oxford.
Ihonvbere, J. O. (1994), 'The "Irrelevant" State, Ethnicity and the Quest for Nationhood in Africa', *Ethnic and Racial Studies*, Vol. 17, pp. 42–60.
Ihonvbere, J. O. (1996), 'Evolving Sovereignty in an Interdependent World: The Challenge of Democratization in Sub-Saharan Africa', *International Politics*, Vol. 33, pp. 245–268.
Jackson, R. H. (1993), 'Sub-Saharan Africa', in Jackson, R. H. and James, A. (eds), (1993), *States in a Changing World: A Contemporary Analysis*, Oxford University Press: Oxford.
Jalali, R. and Lipset, S. M. (1993), 'Racial and Ethnic Conflicts: A Global Perspective', in Caraley, D. and Harris, C. (eds.), *New World Politics: Power, Ethnicity, and Democracy*, The Academy of Political Science: New York.
Kalu, K. A. (1995), 'Democratic Transitions in Africa and the 1993 Elections in Nigeria', *CONPO Review*, Vol. 4, pp. 10–22.
Kalu, K. A. (1996), 'Political Economy in Nigeria: The Military, Ethnic Politics and Development', *International Journal of Politics, Culture and Society*, Vol. 10, pp. 229–247.

Kimenyi, M. S. (1998), 'Harmonizing Ethnic Claims in Africa: A Proposal for Ethnic-Based Federalism', *Cato Journal*, Vol. 18, pp. 43–63.

Lentner, H. (1984), 'The Concept of the State: A Response to Stephen Krasner', *Comparative Politics*, Vol. 16, pp. 367–377.

Mazrui, A. A. (1990), *Cultural Forces in World Politics*, Heinemann Educational Books: Portsmouth, NH.

Rimmer, D. (1995), 'The Effects of Conflict, II: Economic Effects', in Furley, O. (ed.), *Conflict in Africa*, Tauris Academic Studies: London.

Robertson, L. R. (1997), 'The Constructed Nature of Ethnopolitics', *International Politics*, Vol. 34, pp. 265–283.

Sheth, D. L. (1989), 'State, Nation and Ethnicity: Experience of Third World Countries', *Economic and Political Weekly*, Vol. XXIV, No. 12 (March 25), pp. 619–626.

Shils, E. (1957), 'Primordial, Personal, Sacred and Civil Ties', *British Journal of Sociology*, Vol. 7, pp. 113–45.

SIPRI. (1998), *SIPRI Yearbook 1998: Armaments, Disarmament and International Security*, Oxford University Press: Oxford.

Udogu, E. I. (1994), 'The Allurement of Ethnonationalism in Nigerian Politics: The Contemporary Debate', *Journal of Asian and African Studies*, Vol. 29, pp. 159–171.

Welsh, D. (1996), 'Ethnicity in Sub-Saharan Africa', *International Affairs*, Vol. 72, pp. 477–491.

World Bank (1999), *World Development Report, 1998/99*, Oxford University Press: New York.

4 The State and Ethnicity in Africa

JULIUS O. IHONVBERE

African ruling classes, unlike their metropolitan counterparts, have no faith in the future of their respective nations, let alone in the future of the continent (Gana, 1985, p. 129).

Introduction

What has become clear in the last three decades is that the state remains central to the overall process of reconstruction and accumulation. In the struggle to rebuild the nation-state, construct identities, and build new platforms of inclusion, participation, and politics, the state remains a critical factor and actor. This is not unusual or peculiar to Africa (Ake, 1978, p. 65). Historically, the state has been central to the processes of class formation, growth, accumulation, and development. Thus, the project of unmediated *destatization* sponsored by the multilaterals in the 1970s through the 1980s was not only misguided but also dangerous to the enormous task of growth and development in Africa. Yet, the debate on the nature of the state in Africa seemed to have ended rather abruptly.[1] It is interesting to note that no clear political positions were adopted in terms of understanding the specifics of state power and their implications for growth, development, stability and progress in the continent. There is no doubting the fact that as a precipitate of the continent's historical experiences and the realities of dependence and underdevelopment, the state has come to play a major role in the political economy of African social formations. It should have been expected therefore, that in the struggle to reverse underdevelopment, mobilize the masses, lay a viable foundation for self-reliance and self-sustainment and provide for the basic human needs of the vast majority, the state would play a *positive* role.²

The African experience has been radically different from the experiences in Europe and North America. The state has become a tool in the hands of a largely decadent, unproductive, corrupt and dependent dominant class. The dominant elite has tried to use the state and its structures to build powerful political platforms to protect their own narrow interests but not to pursue what might be described as a *national* project. Even if this weakness and limited vision was the product of the colonial experience, over three decades of persistent struggles to survive attacks from fractions of the military, unions and their workers, students, and other opposition communities, ought to have dictated a new elite strategy for survival. On the contrary, the state is used by the governing elite for accumulation as against legitimation purposes. Its structures, institutions and instruments are easily employed by the dominant forces to repress, exploit, and marginalize non-bourgeois communities and interests. Overall, Africa's predicament is clearly evident in the absence of viable strategies for responding to critical questions of identity, nationality, citizenship, ethnicity, and gender.

While ethnic and nationality groups and constituencies are waxing stronger in the articulation of alternative overt and covert strategies of survival and resistance, the state is gradually being retrenched. Clearly, the limited autonomization of the state makes it not only non-hegemonic but also incapable of resisting penetration and manipulation by powerful external forces. As well, its limited autonomization contributes to its instability and inability to manage the contestations for dominance within and between social and political constituencies. The state not only relies on violence and intimidation to sustain itself, but also relies on a full or partial surrender to indigenous and foreign investors, donors, and lenders. These interests package a security agenda that often deepens existing conflicts culminating in coups and counter-coups, armed insurrections, violent protests, and at times criminal massacres. Thus, the masses in Africa relate to the state as an exploitative, coercive, and alien structure. Its custodians lack credibility and legitimacy and are thus incapable of mobilizing or leading the people. Given the violent nature of the state, the masses turn to ethnic, religious and philanthropic organizations for hope, leadership, self-expression and support. The state becomes largely 'irrelevant' in their consciousness and existential conditions. It is at this level that we speak of the 'irrelevant state' i.e., a state which has virtually lost its capacity to provide leadership and direction, mobilize human and material resources, and effectively mediate class contradictions and conflicts (Ihonvbere and Ekekwe, 1988; Ihonvbere, 1994).

This chapter makes the argument that the character of the state in Africa is what has encouraged ethnicity and ethnic politics. It is also what has encouraged the numerous violent conflicts in the continent that continue to mortgage opportunities for growth, development, and democracy.

Understanding the nature of state domination in Africa

It is important to understand why the state acts as a mediating and intrusive force in Africa. The state is everywhere in the lives of African peoples; yet, it cannot guarantee the basic necessities of life and cannot guarantee the safety of life and property. But it is there to extract resources, intimidate the powerless, silence the courageous, and strike all sorts of unequal and self-preserving relations with profit and hegemony-seeking external interests. Consequently, the state has been described by some critics as 'vampire', 'predatory', 'irrelevant', and 'impotent'. Why has this become the rule rather than the exception in Africa?

In Antonio Gramsci's (1981) discussion of hegemony in *Selections from Prison Notebooks,* he argued that a state could be dominant at two levels. The first is what he refers to as *political* domination. This is where a state relies on force, violence, coercion and other extra-legal methods to retain control or dominance over society. In this case, the state creates, services and relies heavily on a well-armed military machine (Thomas, 1984). Such a state is intolerant of opposition and spends quite heavily on security, especially internal security. The custodians of state power develop a siege mentality and see every form of disagreement as evidence of a plot to seize state power by force. Of course, it usually responds by force to such perceptions. To maintain control such an unsteady and violent state strikes very subservient, but extensive security pacts with foreign interests and this often enables it to unleash a reign of terror on its citizens. Finally, it does not matter whether such a state is military or civilian in character. As Daniel arap Moi in Kenya, Mobutu Sese Seko in Zaire, M. Nguema in Equatorial Guinea, Paul Biya in Cameroon, Generals Ibrahim Babangida and Sani Abacha in Nigeria, and Mohamed Siad Barre in Somalia have clearly demonstrated, civilian and military despots can close political spaces, suffocate civil society, eliminate opponents, and squander scarce resources on building personality cults.

The second level of state dominance is at the level of *civil society*. Here, the state does not rely on violence; at least, not in the first instance. Rather, it relies on moral, intellectual, spiritual and emotional manipulation and leadership. The prevalent ideas and consciousness are those 'sponsored' or 'released' into society by the state, its agents and agencies (Williams, 1960). The state in this situation of dominance appears to work for community and the general good. It is willing to utilize all available resources to build an impression of equality, justice, and fair play into which all citizens buy even if gross inequality, racism, injustice, and limited openings for the powerless characterize the system. While both levels of domination are what Gramsci calls *hegemony*, he notes that domination at the *political* level is tenuous while domination in civil society, tends to be more permanent. Political domination is tenuous because it is not constructed on consent but on terror, manipulation, and other extra-legal mechanisms.

If we apply this mode of analysis to Africa, we find that the state is not dominant in civil society. Rather, African states are only dominant at the political level. There is an extensive reliance on the police, secret service, foreign military bodies, and the armed forces to maintain order, discipline and control. There is also an extensive reliance on the use of threats, violence, repression and intimidation in order to contain popular pressures and retain control over social forces in society. The entire political landscape is constructed on a façade of unity: the idea of nationhood is forced on the people and not constructed with and by the people. The struggle for hegemony within the overall political culture is informed by the belief that the capture of power and the ability to deploy the instruments of coercion will guarantee security and safety. Even more, those who capture power assume that they would be safer if and only if their particular ethnic or religious, and at times, regional ethnic group dominate the commanding heights of the political economy. Since this has to be an undemocratic project, it relies on illegality to the core and builds the foundations of anger, disillusionment, opposition, and the erosion of state and elite legitimacy.

To be sure, there is a level at which we can contend that this steady construction of despotism and gradual closure of democratic openings is the direct precipitate of Africa's historical experiences i.e., the contact between the previously *pre-capitalist* societies and the forces of western imperialism (Rodney, 1974; Fanon, 1978; Brett, 1973; Ake, 1981). This contact culminated in the monetization of the economy; structural deformations, distortions and disarticulations; a partial revolutionization of pre-capitalist modes/relations of production and exchange; ruthless exploitation; underdevelopment and dependence and peripheralization in a highly exploitative world capitalist system. Of course, the contact with the forces and agents of imperialism specifically ensured that foreign capital gained a dominant foothold in Africa; that an unproductive, corrupt and dependent foster elite was created to service the colonial and neo-colonial societies; and that the state structure bequeathed at *political* independence had to rely on violence and force to reproduce itself. This is because of the limited commodification of production forces; the non-autonomization of the state; and the general degree of consciousness, organization and action amongst factions and fractions of non-bourgeois forces. Consequently, African elites, at political independence had to focus on building a democratic state, surviving new pressures from within, and resisting pressures from powerful external interests. Given that most elites had been created and nurtured by the imperialist powers, their struggles readily became struggles of limited objectives, opportunism, and ideological manipulation.

Perhaps, equally important in determining the weakness, instability and mediated hegemony of state structures in Africa is the fact that it is not used for legitimation or development purposes. Rather, the state and its institutions just like politics are consistently manipulated for accumulation and other extra-legal purposes (Ake, 1985). This, of course, creates the impression that the state is a class state; it caters for the privileged, it is manipulated by the privileged and its resources, especially its ideological apparatuses and instruments of coercion service the privileged with only occasional concessions to the poor to avoid possible rebellion from the latter. This is a development that should not be taken lightly in Africa. There is virtually no African country where non-bourgeois forces take the state seriously. Loyalty to the state is often superficial, only as required demonstration to avoid punishment. True, they can be seen on election day, after many have been compromised (with rice, salt, and other forms of bribe), voting for the 'unopposed' candidate, taking part in often staged rallies, and partaking in the usually noisy and robust celebration of 'independence.' The reality is that many communities have carefully exited from the state and see it as a dangerous force intent on containing their rights to self-expression, community organization, and the enjoyment of the basics of life. Taxes are paid reluctantly, if at all. Public institutions and public services are ridiculed and regarded as targets of attack whenever the opportunity to do so arises.

The combination of the tendencies, limitations, and contradictions highlighted above in the epoch of monopoly capital underscores the crisis, instability, and 'irrelevance' of the state in much of Africa. In reality, the euphoria about the purported benefits of globalization and structural adjustment notwithstanding, the African elite, overall, is still largely an unproductive, dependent, and very much divided one. Its tenuous relations to production and heavy dependence on the state and foreign capital for accumulation also increases its inability to understand the pressures from below much less reach accommodation with non-bourgeois communities. Moreover, since these indigenous forces dominate the state, they tend to use it to service the needs of foreign capital and their local agents at the expense of non-bourgeois forces (Ake, 1987).[3] Thus, politics, development (growth) planning, resource allocation, foreign trade, sources of foreign aid and military supplies and other policies aimed at systemic reproduction come under the direct and/or indirect influence of transnational forces (Ake, 1987). Under these conditions, the state virtually looses control of the social formation. Its structural coherence dissolves into ad-hoc and post-hoc responses to developments and crises and the character and accumulative bases of the dominant classes come to determine its role and relevance in society:

> In Africa, there are few social formations that are capitalist enough or socialist enough to be identifiable as clearly boasting the state form of domination. The unique feature of the socio-economic formations in post-colonial Africa is that the state, if we can properly talk of such an existence at all, has extremely limited autonomy. The state is composed in such a way that it enjoys limited independence from the social classes—particularly the hegemonic social class—and is immersed in the class struggle. Because autonomization is the essence of the state as a modality of domination, it is not clear whether we can properly talk of the state in post-colonial Africa. That is not to say that government does not exist (Ake, 1985, p. 108).

Of course, in the literature produced and extensively distributed worldwide by the multilaterals and bilaterals, even conservative Western scholars, the exploitative and unequal relations between the African state and its custodians on the one hand, and transnational capital on the other is good: it is helping Africa build a capitalist base, promote capital accumulation, infrastructural development, and technology. Ultimately, Africa would be best for it. This was the same claim in the 1940s and 1950s. Today, according to the World Bank itself and as confirmed by the Organization of African Unity (OAU) and the UN Economic Commission for Africa (ECA), Africa is much worse off on all indicators of development, ravaged by AIDS, debts and drought and ignored by the new forces of globalization. The ways in which this dependent and largely unproductive disposition curtails the ability of the state to respond to popular demands are often ignored. The fact that deepening pressures and resistance from marginalized interests increasingly force the elites to rely on violence and gross human rights abuses and that such state responses force the opposition underground and erodes state legitimacy are also ignored. As more and more citizens feel helpless and ignored, as more get brutalized, and as opportunities shrink at the public sphere, the resort to the ethnic base for survival becomes intensified.

This issue of 'limited independence' is very crucial to our analysis. Because the state is not hegemonic and lacks autonomy, its full immersion in the class struggle not only increases its vulnerability and manipulability but also marks it out as a biased and class state. The state is thus unable to plan effectively for development. It is unable to mobilize for self-reliance or to regulate the activities of profit and hegemony-seeking transnational corporations. It is unable to withstand or mediate the pressures and impact of the deepening crisis of world capitalism and it is unable to effectively mediate intra-and inter-class contradictions and conflicts. Social forces, in their struggle for dominance, accumulation and survival, challenge and confront each other with little or no restraint. Politics loses all its rules and values. The major preoccupation of the state and its custodians become survival; not the provision of basic needs to the various collectivities in the polity. This preoccupation deepens with increasing systemic crisis culminating in border clashes, civil wars, coups and counter coups and the ruthless implementation of harsh IMF and World Bank inspired monetarist programs. Claude Ake explains the context and implications of these conditions thus:

> Non-autonomization of class domination means among other things that the state is immersed in class struggle and cannot mediate it, that the rule of law is not properly instituted with the result that political competition is without norms and unrestrained.

> All this places a high premium on political power and makes the struggle for power Hobbesian. The state of affairs in turn tends to block the development of productive forces generally and economic development in particular... because the power struggle is so intense, politics becomes an absorbing pursuit to the detriment of everything else including economic development (Ake, 1985, p. 112).

The general result of this unfortunate development or condition in which the development of society is sacrificed on the altar of personal political interests and expediency is that:

> Those in power develop a siege mentality and see everything in terms of increasing their power. A tradition of authoritarianism and brutality has made mobilization for development impossible. Repression is such a prominent feature of the social formations of Africa that there can now be no question of the people being the end of development: there is now no question of any meaningful pursuit of self-reliant strategy of development that is so badly needed... (Ake, 1985, p. 112).

Moreover, a crisis-ridden social formation abandons development and self-reliance as priority areas. The confrontation within and between social classes creates hostile conditions for the attainment of people-centered goals, then anarchy, alienation, ethnic conflicts and class contradictions and struggles are bound to become dominant features of society and social relations. Ironically, all over Africa, the responses by the state and bourgeoisie to such situations have been increased repression, human rights abuses, depoliticization, ideological containment, divide-and-rule tactics, intimidation and bribery (Ake, 1978; Thomas, 1984). These in themselves only make the state relevant *politically* but not in civil society. Indeed, it has been asserted that:

> Because of the non-autonomization of class domination, the ruling class is undisciplined and vulnerable despite its political authoritarianism. One expression of this lack of discipline is the unrestrained exploitation of the subordinate classes. Sometimes the exploitation is so extreme that the working class is not really able to reproduce itself... Exploiting the subordinate classes can

neither be in the interest of social capital or the development of the productive forces (Ake, 1985, p. 113).

Clearly, opportunities for building bridges and platforms of inclusion, tolerance, and good governance have been negated or subverted by the character and politics of the state and its custodians. In fact, in contemporary Africa, the state is constituted to work against the interests of the people. This condition is exarcebated by external influence and interests. Business with foreigners tends to increase in periods of crisis. America's trade with Nigeria increased under the regime of the country's most diabolical dictator, General Sani Abacha. As well, during the Liberian civil war in which hundreds of women and children were being killed, Western businesses were doing lucrative business with then rebel leader Charles Taylor. Finally, the brutality and inhumanity of apartheid did not stop business interests, again, mostly from the West and Japan, from trading with South Africa in spite of UN and OAU sanctions. Yet, these unholy business relations with dictators in Africa have precipitated very deep conflicts and divisions within African states by increasing the power of the despots over those of civil society (Gana, 1985, p. 120).

The state is able to perform the role of maintaining inherited conditions of poverty, corruption, ethnic antagonisms, foreign domination and instability because, according to Gana,

> The state in contemporary Africa... remains primarily the instrument of the metropolitan bourgeoisie for the reason that the internal process of capital accumulation is subordinated to the requirements of external, primarily metropolitan interest... The state has functioned as the conduit for the transfer of Africa's surplus abroad, generating the crisis of underdevelopment with few historical parallels (Gana, 1985, p. 129).

It is not only the conditions above that make the state 'irrelevant' in Africa. In fact, in some cases, the conditions above make the state the more 'relevant' albeit, politically to special groups within the nation-state. It seems that the more 'politically relevant' a state is, the less relevant it becomes at the level of civil society. This is because individuals and communities that are subjected to violent repression and all sorts of social, economic and cultural abuses and deprivations easily become alienated from the state, even the society. It means that reliance on force subverts the goals of civil society, for example, political and economic inclusion of the various publics within the political system. However, it is more the interplay of power and politics within African states that makes the state 'irrelevant'.

The legitimacy of the bourgeoisie, the stability of the state, and the expectations that the post-colonial state and its custodians will make a substantial difference from the colonial period were dashed by increasing poverty, disease, illiteracy and repression (Hutch, 1974). The reality of Africa is that contradictions and conflicts arising from ethnic, nationality, and identity claims also have a direct relationship to poverty and forms of deprivation. It is quite common to see conflicts arising from elite and state strategies to appropriate resources from a particular community without any concern for the living conditions of the people. In Zaire, South Africa, and Nigeria this has been the case. The Ogonis of Nigeria for instance responded to environmental degradation, impoverishment, and marginalization by organizing along sub-ethnic lines and making critical demands on the state. The response from the state included violence, intimidation, military occupation of Ogoniland, and the execution by hanging of nine Ogoni leaders. The situation gets worse where a few ethnic groups dominate the state. In this case, ethnic groups in the resource-rich portions of the country see the extraction of resources and neglect as a deliberate strategy by the dominant ethnic groups to appropriate their resources and consolidate their marginality. For an elite that controls the state and the instrument of coercion, desperate poverty can compel it to develop an unpopular agenda for *enbourgeoisment* through primitive accumulation at the expense of other classes or groups. If the society is already riddled with cleavages, contradictions, distrust, and instability, such an agenda easily expresses itself in ethnic, religious or other primordial terms for the purpose of survival. The resulting conflicts and violence can be devastating to the quest for nationhood, democracy or development.

As we have seen in much of Africa, while the 1970s represented a period of fair economic growth despite the oil price crisis, the 1980s and 1990s witnessed unprecedented deterioration of economic conditions. Pressures from inflation, divestment and deindustrialization as well as unemployment, rising debts and debt-servicing obligations simply weakened the state, its institutions, and agents. The crisis moved from being just national in character to being local as villages were ravaged by all forms of problems that the state could not respond to. This condition has led to deteriorating quality of education, starvation, even child abuse and marital breakdowns not only in the cities but also in the villages.

The inability of the state to respond to the crisis of economic stagnation or underdevelopment compelled non-bourgeois forces to seek alternative legal and extra-legal means for survival. They turned to churches, mosques, ethnic organizations and so on for their identities and strength.

The material basis of ethnic consciousness and politics[4]

The very high degree of human suffering, disillusionment, anger, alienation, rural decay, and urban dislocation that have accompanied monetarist responses to the African economic crisis, hold major implications for the potency of ethnicity and the subversion of the goals of nationhood. The point is that the poor majority, have no option but to find solace, support and security in ethnic or communal associations where the state has failed woefully. Such conditions where loyalty and support for the state are mediated by loyalty to and support for ethnic associations, social clubs and other interests, mean that it is important that we re-examine the foundations of ethnic politics in Africa. It is all too convenient to dismiss ethnic identity and politics as indicators of commitment to rabid tribalism and some form of uncivilized carry over from the past. But every African, in fact human being, with some loyalty to identity form(s) knows that this is a false and pretentious attack on ethnic identity.

In Africa, the ethnic identity by itself has never posed a problem to human survival. Even where such identity has been recently constructed, it has only become necessary in the context of state failure and the search for accommodation in a complex and difficult political environment. Indeed, it is only the *activation* of such identity in the struggle to expand political spaces, displace others, appropriate resources, monopolize power, or engage in extra-legal agendas that has given ethnicity and ethnic politics its negative connotation. When such identity claims are ignored, suppressed or marginalized, communities have been forced to design alternative strategies to engage the repressive state. A look at the independence constitutions of African states would reveal a deliberate effort to ignore or trivialize questions of identity, nationality, even citizenship and language. A top-down political agenda was initiated by some regimes to 'force' nationhood and citizenship on the people at the expense of their respective cultural histories and loyalties. As we have seen (even in communist states), these projects failed one after the other irrespective of ideological rationalizations.

African leaders have reified the nation-building project, placing it above all other goals. This is done because it helps those in power to lay claims to authority and remain relevant in the political web they have constructed. In the process of constructing this web made up of identities, ethnicities, and nationalities, the political leaders simply poured scorn on ethnicity or tribalism. Because the leaders and their experts 'failed' to appreciate peoples' loyalties to their ethnic identities, in the context of failed states and mortgaged economies, often policy failures were blamed on ethnicity and ethnic politics. The truth is that all Africans necessarily belong to ethnic groups (Nnoli, 1978, p. 5). In fact, within this context Nnoli notes:

> Ethnic groups are social formations distinguished by the communal character of their boundaries. The relevant communal factor may be language, culture or both. In Africa, language has clearly been the most crucial variable. As social formations, however, ethnic groups are not necessarily homogeneous entities even linguistically or culturally (Nnoli, 1978, p. 9).

Thus, there is nothing intrinsically bad in belonging to an ethnic group. In fact, prior to the advent of colonial domination, ethnic groups in Africa fought violently between and within themselves. They also coexisted peacefully, traded and intermarried among themselves. However, with colonialism, religion, region and ethnic identity took completely new forms. They were manipulated as part of the divide-and-rule tactics of the colonial powers. Certain ethnic groups were favored at the expense of others. Some were barred completely from holding certain positions, enjoying certain facilities, cultivating certain crops and so on. The ethnic groups were instigated against one another and emerging leaders were given ethnic labels and regarded as ethnic leaders. These measures were taken as part of the grand imperialist program of subjugation, domination and exploitation of the colony. It is precisely for this reason that ethnicity cannot be 'made a decisive independent variable' (Nnoli, 1978, p. 9). It is also based on the points above that we can make the argument that it is in fact the state, as represented by its custodians, that has created and promoted ethnicity in Africa. Left on its own, it poses no problem to the quest for nationhood in Africa. But ethnic consciousness is carried by social actors with varying social, economic and political interests and aspirations. It is therefore the socio-economic and political purposes for which ethnicity is activated and deployed that hold implications for the quest for rational politics, stability and national unity in Africa.

It is important that we always bear in mind therefore that the politics of ethnicity was promoted in the colonial period. The proto-bourgeoisie in the early periods of colonialism imbibed this as part of the politics of resource generation and allocation and it became a very useful tool in the post-independence period for mobilizing regional (ethnic) support for personal or class based ambitions and goals. This became the more important in view of the marginalization of indigenous elites from the production process and the dominant role of foreign capital. The local elites found ethnicity a very potent force in their competition for favored positions in transnational corporations. As well, given their largely unproductive location in the social formation, the state became the means to rapid capital accumulation and power. Again, ethnicity, just like religion was an available tool employed to whip up support, antagonism, suspicion and emotions in the struggles to win access to the state and preside over the collection and allocation of scarce resources. As Eme Ekekwe points out:

> It is in the competition for control of and/or access to the state that a ... component of the ideology of development comes in. This component is ethnicity. Conflict between ethnic groups can be manifestations of class struggles and competitions. In the Nigerian situation this appears to have been the case; explanations of ethnic conflict there would be incomplete without references to the class situation. As Amilcar Cabral pointed out, it is usually those persons who are detribalized and well off-such as those who comprise the governing class-who resort to an appeal to ethnicity. There exists a certain dialectic between ethnicity and class that has to be appreciated in the search to understand politics in many post-colonial societies (Ekekwe, 1986, p. 109).

Furthermore, the ethnic factor is so strong and effective not only because of the poverty of the masses who are the easy victims of ethnic manipulations especially within a patron-client context but also because of the limited development of production relations. This is well explained by Claude Ake:

> The bulk of the subordinate classes consist of peasants, workers and petty-commodity producers but mainly of peasants. The

> peasants are still deeply involved in the production of use value and their involvement in commodity relations is limited. In the essential pre-capitalist social relations in which they find themselves there is little social atomization and individualism, and the differentiation of interests is rudimentary. In short, the legal form is as underdeveloped as the commodity form, the person has not yet fully emerged as a legal subject (Ake, n. d., p. 6).

The above is very crucial for it continues to provide a fertile ground for the elite to play ethnic politics by manipulating the fears of the peasants, capitalizing on their largely pre-capitalist environment and manipulating their aspirations.

Thus, ethnicity within the context of neo-colonial politics and production relations subverts the goals of nationhood at two main levels. The first is that the dominant elites exploit the ethnic factor to carve out and retain spheres of interest while advancing their personal, class and occasionally community interests. In this case, 'ethnicity becomes a mask for class privileges (Nnoli, 1978, p. 10). In addition, Nnoli (1978, p. 13) notes that:

> By diverting attention away from imperialist exploitation and the resultant distortion of African economic and social structures, ethnicity performs the function of mystification and obscurantism. Consequently, it helps to perpetuate imperialism, and militate against the imperative of revolutionary struggle by hampering the development of a high level of political consciousness by its victims.

Thus, it is the politicization of ethnicity by the bourgeoisie in furtherance of their respective inter-and intra-class struggles that has generated contradictions that subvert the goals of democracy and development in Africa. Ekekwe (1986, p. 110) supports this position when he notes that the pattern of ethnic politics 'is directly related to the struggle within the (petty) bourgeois class for control of state apparatuses.' But, of course, this politicization of ethnicity all over the continent has never been a basis for effective mobilization and national unity. It has generated deep-rooted suspicions, massacres, wastage of resources and general insecurity and confusion. At the end of it all, the larger democratic project and the autonomization or unity of the nation-state suffers.

The other level at which the ethnic factor subverts the goal of nationhood arises from the economic crisis discussed earlier on. Either at the national or continental levels, deep-rooted economic crisis, desperate poverty, repression and harassment lead people to rely less on the state, its institutions and agents and leads to the transfer of loyalty from the state to ethnic and other associations. Thus, most Africans confront the state as a wicked, exploitative and coercive force. Claude Ake (n. d., pp. 7–8) explains this in the Nigerian case:

> Most Nigerians confront the state not as a public force but as an alien and hostile coercive power. This is all the more so because the Nigerian state, lacking autonomy, is immersed in the class struggle and is conspicuously a state for the few against the many, because the Nigerian state tendentially appears as irrelevant or hostile, a critical condition for the transfer of loyalties to ecumenical levels is removed. Nigerians embraced ethnic identity all the more. *The ethnic groups have been emotionally and materially supportive of their members, and do not rely on coercion* (emphasis added).

The above then is the crux of the matter. Ethnic or community unions all over Africa do not often rely on coercion in pursuing their objectives; they generally provide 'entry points' into, and support in, the urban systems. For example, ethnic associations and communities run scholarship schemes, serve as sources of information and provide refuge and hope in times of crisis. They also have political functions. Quite often, ethnic groups serve as the platform where politically ambitious individuals may test the political waters. In most of these areas, especially to the less dominant or ethnic minority groups, the state in Africa has proved irrelevant.

It is obvious, therefore, that where the post-colonial state had failed to provide hope, support and direction to the masses, ethnic associations have tended to succeed. To be sure, these associations are easily 'captured' by ethnic notables, ethnic opportunists, and ethnic entrepreneurs and used to advance parochial self-interests. This is, of course, largely due to the 'limited development of commodity relations and on a more fundamental level, ... the (limited) development of productive forces' (Ake, 1985, p. 11). In any case, the ability of ethnic notables to manipulate ethnic associations also reflects the degree to which the members of the association have transferred their loyalties to the notables via the association.

Under the conditions described thus far, how can we expect the goals of national integration, unity, stability, growth and development to be attained? Clearly, it is a struggle between the state and the ethnic group or community: the former relying on violence and unable to protect or provide for the poor; and the latter, relying on accommodation, support, dialogue, and the emphasis on a collective destiny anchored on the ethnic group. So far, it is a battle that the state is losing.

Conclusion

From our discussion so far, we have identified four major factors in the continuing strength and relevance of ethnicity and ethnic identity in Africa: (i) the character of the non-hegemonic, 'irrelevant' and unstable post-colonial state; (ii) the highly factionalized nature of the largely unproductive and subservient dominant classes; (iii) the conditions of poverty, marginalization, exploitation and repression of the poor majority; and (iv) the continuing power and relevance of ethnic communities and associations that have steadily replaced a collapsed, collapsing, stagnant or 'irrelevant' state. The contradictions and conditions identified above have combined at various levels to generate insecurity, tensions, wars, conflicts, the transfer of resources abroad, and underdevelopment. The insecurity of the elites who dominate the state and control the means of coercion has compelled them to rely on violence, human rights abuses, intimidation and depoliticization. This way, they promote alienation, distrust, and subvert possibilities for growth, development and democracy. As well, the mismanagement of scarce resources, flirtations with monetarist policies, commitment to the indigenization of unequal exchange and emphasis on exchange or distribution as against production, have made life worse for non-bourgeois forces. Thus, they too have been compelled, especially with increasing repression to withdraw their loyalties from the state that they see as biased (in favor of the privileged), exploitative and coercive. They now seek support, refuge and direction from ethnic and religious associations.

It would appear therefore that existing internal and external relations of power, production and exchange in Africa cannot support the quest for stability, democracy and development in the continent. Ethnicity, as well, cannot be 'the basis for explaining and changing society' (Nnoli,

1978, p. 12). Ethnic positions, consciousness and actions have to be confronted with class-consciousness. With increasing commodification of labor and the integration of rural producers into world capitalism, the stranglehold of ethnic consciousness is withering away in some quarters as evidenced in the cross-ethnic alliances and programs of action in human rights and prodemocracy movements as well as in the trade unions. But we cannot be absolute about this since these organizations are still very vulnerable to ethnic politics. In fact, there are deep cleavages and contestations within ethnic communities and ethnic entreprenures that fail to deliver or protect the interests of the group are generally sidelined. As A. B. C. Ocholla-Ayayo (1988, p. 86) has correctly observed: 'While nearly every ethnic group may demand a degree of autonomy, they also want a place at the center of the state and a share of the national cake, to the extent that if their leaders choose to ignore the center, they are likely to get discarded.' The elite, preoccupied with looting the public treasury has also failed to recognize the emergence of a new class of citizens, bourgeois and non-bourgeois, that is committed to operating politically and accumulating economically across ethnic boundaries. This class could constitute the core of a new national agenda. As Martin Doornbos (1998, pp. 22–23) has noted, '...one of the most significant long-term transformations affecting the nature and focus of ethnic articulations in various parts of Africa has been the emergence and manifestation of a protonational bourgeoisie. Members of these strata may themselves selectively downplay ethnic backgrounds, identifying more strongly instead with national characteristics and points of orientation-from which they have often benefited a good deal.' Fortunately or unfortunately, the weak post-colonial state has been incapable of recognizing this fact and taking advantage of opportunities to increase its relevance in ethnic constituencies in order to weaken ethnic warlords.

Given the continued 'irrelevance' of the state, ethnicity remains a potent force. The quest for democracy in Africa has to be sought in a popular and collective resolution of the African crisis (Ake, 1978, p. 107). Critical questions of constitution making and constitutionalism must be taken more seriously. Constitution-making to the extent that the process involves the people and their communities and constituencies so that issues that are important to them are considered; constitutionalism, in terms of the establishment of important institutions in civil society to take the document to the people. This way, it becomes a *living* document, accessible to the people so that they can use it to defend their democratic rights. Recent constitutions in Uganda, South Africa, Ethiopia, Ghana, and Eritrea are moving in this direction. These constitutions openly take positions against military coups, emphasize the sovereignty of the people, and clearly articulate the centrality of nationality, language, identity, and ethnicity. Although their efficacy are still to be measured, it is critical that we continue to search for political arrangements that will take ethnic configurations and demands into consideration rather than ignore or trivaliaze their importance. As Ethiopia has recently demonstrated, it is possible to organize national political platforms along ethnic or nationality lines. As Fasil Nahum (1997, p. 51) has noted in relation to the Ethiopian experiment:

> One feature of great import throughout the Constitution and one that places this constitution on a pedestal of its own, more or less, is the utmost significance given to the ethno-linguistic components of the society. The preamble of the Constitution does not open with the familiar 'We the People...', it is 'We, the Nations, Nationalities and Peoples of Ethiopia...'. This is not a constitution of the Ethiopian citizens simply lumped together as a people. The Ethiopian citizens are first categorized in their different ethno-linguistic groupings and then these groupings come together as authors of, and beneficiaries from, the Constitution of 1994.

Finally, the opening up of democratic spaces, strengthening of civil society, and the acknowledgement of pluralism in the political process are unavoidable if the ethnic issue in Africa is to be addressed in any way in the next millennium. Emphasis on human rights and civic education hold out promises for building new networks and relationships that transcend ethnic particularity without excluding them. In fact, a homogenization project is antithetical to a true human rights and prodemocracy agenda. It is the sort of inherent democratic culture of give-and-take that drives the work of environmental, women's, prodemocracy, human rights, and other grassroots movements that can also generate the much needed momentum for understanding and effectively responding to ethnic disarticulations in Africa. As Martin Doornbos (1998, p. 27) has concluded:

> ...ethnic pluralism and coexistence-as Africa has in fact known for most of remembered time in most of its regions-requires and

presupposes a give-and-take attitude on the part of all the social groupings and strata concerned. In its absence, insistence on conformity to the emerging cultural standards of the new national elites is likely to engender increasingly embittered articulations of ethnic consciousness and the expressed need for cultural survival on the part of peripheralized groups (Doornbos, 1998, p. 27).

Acknowledgments

An earlier version of this chapter appeared in *Ethnic and Racial Studies*, Vol. 17, No. 1 (1994), pp. 42–60.

Notes

1. See the works of Issa Shivji, M. Mamdani, Colin Leys, John Saul, Terisa Turner, Michela von Freyhold, R. Kaplinski, S. Langdon and a host of others who made useful contributions to the initial debate on the post-colonial state.
2. By 'positive role' we assume that the role a state plays in any social formation can either be 'negative' or 'positive'. If it is a popular state i.e., one which acts in the specific and general interest of the majority, then such a role is positive and vice versa.
3. Ake has argued that the African bourgeoisie and the respective state structures they dominate, are obstacles to development in the continent. See his *Revolutionary Pressures in Africa*, Zed Press: London, 1978, pp. 65–77.
4. For other works that have dealt with the problem of ethnicity see Nnoli, O. (1978), *Ethnic Politics in Nigeria*, Fourth Dimension: Enugu; Mamdani, M. (1976), *Politics and Class Formation in Uganda*, Monthly Review Press: New York; Mafeje, A. (1971), 'The Ideology of Tribalism', *Journal of Modern African Studies*, Vol. 9, No. 2; Magubane, B. M. (1969), 'Pluralism and Conflict Situations in Africa: A New Look', *African Social Research*, Vol. 7, No. 2 (June).

References

Ake, C. (1978), *Revolutionary Pressures in Africa*, Zed Press: London.
Ake, C. (1985), 'The Future of the State in Africa', *International Political Science Review*, Vol. 6, No. 1, pp. 105–114.
Ake, C. (ed.) (1985), *The Political Economy of Nigeria*, Longman Group Ltd: London.

Ake, C. (n.d.) *Theoretical Notes in the National Question in Nigeria*, University of Port Harcourt Press: Port Harcout, Nigeria.

Brett, E. A. (1973), *Colonialism and Underdevelopment in East Africa*, Heinemann Press: London.

Doornbos, M. (1998), 'Linking the Future to the Past-Ethnicity and Pluralism', in Ocholla-Ayayo (ed.), *Ethnicity and the State in Eastern Africa*, Nordiska Afrikainstitutet: Uppsala.

Ekekwe, E. (1986), *Class and State in Nigeria*, Longman Group Ltd: Lagos and London.

Fanon, F. (1978), *The Wretched of the Earth*, Grove Press: New York.

Gana, A. T. (1985), The State in Africa: Yesterday, Today and Tomorrow', *International Political Science Review*, Vol. 6, No. 1, pp. 129–135.

Gramsci, A. (1981), *Selection from Prison Notebook*, International Publishers: New York.

Ihonvbere, J. O. (1994), 'The "Irrelevant" State, Ethnicity and the Quest for Nationhood in Africa', *Ethnic and Racial Studies*, Vol. 17, No, 1, pp. 42–60.

Ihonvbere, J. O. and Ekekwe, E. N. (1988), 'The Irrelevant State, the National Question and the Future of Dependent Capitalism in Nigeria', in Ihonvbere, J. O. (ed.), *Dependent Capitalism and Crisis in Nigeria*, Jodah Publishers: Benin City, Nigeria.

Mafeje, A. (1971), 'The Ideology of Tribalism', *Journal of Modern African Studies*, Vol. 9, No 2, pp. 253–262.

Magubane, B. M. (1969), Pluralism and Conflict Situations in Africa; A New Look', *African Social Research*, Vol. 7, No. 2 (June), pp. 529–554.

Mamdani, M. (1976), *Politics and Class Formation in Uganda*, Monthly Review Press: New York.

Nahum, F. (1997), *Constitution for a Nation of Nations-The Ethiopian Prospect*, Africa World Press: Lawrenceville, NJ. and Asmara, Eritrea

Nnoli, O. (1978), *Ethnic Politics in Nigeria*, Fourth Dimension Press: Enugu, Nigeria.

Ocholla-Ayayo, A. B. C. (1998), 'Ethnicity as a Mode of Conflict Regulation', in Salih, M. and Markakis, J. (eds.), *Ethnicity and the State in Eastern Africa*, Nordiska Afrikainstitutet: Uppsala.

Rodney, W. (1974), *How Europe Underdeveloped Africa*, Howard University Press: Washington, D.C.

Thomas, C. (1984), *The Rise of Authoritarian State in Peripheral Societies*, Monthly Review Press: New York and London.

Williams, G. A. (1960), 'The Concept of 'Egemonia' in the Thought of Antonio Gramsci: Some Notes on Interpretation', *Journal of the History of Ideas*, Vol. 21, No. 4, pp. 586–599.

5 The Ethnic Dimensions of Nigeria's Post-Annulment Crisis: Case Studies from the South

OLUFEMI VAUGHAN

Nigerian postcolonial politics cannot be understood without stressing the significance of ethnicity in the process of power configuration at every level of government. The complex ethno-regional negotiations that dominated the decolonization process foretold the role that communal ideologies would play in the postcolonial period. Students of Nigerian politics agree that the country's two attempts at liberal democracy (1960–66 and 1979–83) failed because of the overwhelming preoccupation of the political class with capturing the distributive agencies of the state through the mobilization of ethnicity (Post and Vickers, 1973; Falola and Ihonvbere, 1985; Joseph, 1987; Diamond, 1988). They also suggest that persistent manipulations of ethno-regional identities contributed significantly to a tragic civil war (1966–70) that claimed the lives of at least a million people. These developments, in turn, entrenched the military as a major player in the recurrent ethno-regional struggles for state power. These exigencies have progressively reduced Nigeria's diverse cultural communities to fortresses of political ethnicity (Ihonvbere, 1994a; Udogu, 1994).

Thus, ethnicity does not simply matter in Nigeria; it provides the critical platform through which other salient sociopolitical variables—such as class, religion, gender, and region—are expressed. Yet, while ethnicity remains the critical medium for the manipulation of power by the dominant classes and constituencies, ethnic structures have also emerged as the critical rallying point of resistance to oppressive and corrupt regimes. The present chapter will seek to integrate these two perspectives: the conventional instrumentalist view, which underscores the centrifugal impact of political ethnicity on the postcolonial state, and a progressive trend, in which communal groups serve as fronts for movements of resistance to repressive regimes. Thus, while political ethnicity remains the critical medium of elite consolidation, new social movements are embracing these local communal structures as a resource of progressive change.

The southern Nigerian brief case studies analyzed here exemplify this Janus-faced character of ethnicity—both as an instrument of accumulation (and its ideological veil), and a critical domain for the articulation of mass resistance. The instrumentalist perspective tended to dismiss ethnicity as mainly mediums in which the political class seek refuge behind communal themes and symbols. In such a context of narrow class domination, ethnic doctrines simply function to consolidate the structures of the neo-patrimonial or rentier states (Ibrahim, 1997; Lewis, 1997). I will argue that, confronted with the rapid decay of the Nigeria state in the 1990s, a new generation of civic leaders are reconstructing ethnic themes as the medium for the articulation of not only communal but democratic aspirations.

The national political context: military rule and ethnicity in the 1990s

The complex interaction between ethnicity and the Nigerian state in the 1990s has featured in the rapid consolidation of military rule, increasingly centered on the Hausa-speaking northern states, and, conversely, the erosion of the pre-existing arrangement resting on fragile alliances of ethno-regional political classes, that sustained Nigerian politics after decolonization. This re-organization entailed a growing gap between the moral authority of local communities, on the one hand, and, on the other, the patently amoral and predatory activities of the holders of state power (Hyden and Williams, 1994; Vaughan, 1995). The ethno-regional foundations of the state—centered on regional politicians, military cliques, communal powerbrokers, senior civil servants, and contractors—reflects both the colonial legacy and the structural imbalances and acrimonious partisanship that have only intensified since decolonization.

Yet as a central part in the prevailing culture of politics, ethnicity has not always undermined the collective aspirations of Nigeria's diverse communities, but has on many occasions been a force for 'good governance'. These dual manifestations of ethnicity—the instrumentalist perspective whereby ethnicity initially reinforces but eventually undermines the state, and a positive element, where ethnicity assists in the revitalization of civil society—were steadily expressed in dominant political themes, notably the ethno-regional character of partisan politics, the Civil War, the ethnic makeup of the military, the rationale for the creation of states, and the allocation of state revenue. The formal perspective—the instrumentalist—has a distinguished tradition in Africanist social science scholarship. Similarly, while the latter has enjoyed little attention in studies of the postcolonial African state, Africanist historians have noted the significance of ethnic-based movements as critical agents in the revitalization of communal aspirations in the colonial era. Furthermore, during the decolonization process for instance, the Yoruba-dominated political party, the Action Group (AG), implemented progressive policies that were committed to the sociopolitical transformation of the Yoruba region. And, in the tumultuous years following independence, a faction of the AG leadership struggled to link progressive communal aspirations to overarching national ideologies. It was thus a tragedy for Nigerian progressives that the more critical elements in the AG, NCNC (National Conference of Nigerian Citizens) and NEPU (Northern Elements Progressive Union) failed to transcend their dominant ethnic base in the immediate post-independence years (Post and Vickers, 1973; Diamond, 1988). This failure to forge progressive coalitions steadily entrenched the distributive tendencies of ethnicity, consolidating the power base of political elites as ethno-regional powerbrokers. What is new now—and which gives this old issue relevance—is that ethnicity is not just simply penetrating and corrupting the state. Rather, its more progressive tendencies have not been harnessed as mediums of communal interdependence and compromise.

These trends were particularly apparent during the severe economic downturn and the recurrent consolidation of military power in recent years (Ihonvbere, 1994b; Soyinka, 1995). This development has exacerbated the internal contradictions within beleaguered communities, at the same time throwing up new forms of resistance, aimed against successive military regimes and contentious programs of political and economic liberalization.

This situation reached crisis level when Nigeria's military ruler, General Babangida (a Hausa-speaking northern officer) annulled the presidential election of June 1993, decisively won by M. K. O. Abiola, a popular Egba-Yoruba businessman and philanthropist.[1] This brazen act proved to be a colossal blunder, not just ending a cynical attempt to impose 'democracy' from above, but assaulting Nigeria's fragile ethno-regional balance of power. The annulment led to resistance in Abiola's Yoruba stronghold, ultimately forcing General Babangida to surrender power to a weak interim government headed by an ally, Ernest Shonekan (a Yoruba). The political impasse that persisted under the interim government led to the coup that brought another Hausa-speaking officer, General Sani Abacha (Babangida's deputy) to power in November 1993. And when Abacha grew more intransigent, targeting Abiola's Yoruba stronghold, the crisis took on an even greater ethnic character as a pro-democracy movement, centered on the Yoruba region, mounted fierce resistance to the clearly illegitimate regime. This ethnic alignment eroded the traditional tripartite struggles between the dominant regional political classes—Hausa-Fulani to the north, the Igbo to the southeast, and the Yoruba to the southwest.[2]

This disequilibrium was further complicated by the intense resistance mounted by ethnic minority communities of the petroleum-producing region of the Niger Delta. Confronted by mass poverty, political repression, and severe environmental degradation, the opposition of these communal groups to both the Babangida and Abacha regimes and to the multinational oil corporations, had gained national and global prominence by the early 1990s. Their courageous resistance added a new element to Africa's post-Cold War debates on democratization, human rights, and neo-liberal economic reform. Ironically, it was the spirited resistance of one of Nigeria's smallest ethnic groups, the Ogoni—led by the Movement For the Survival of the Ogoni People (MOSOP)—that first brought the crisis to global attention (Naanen, 1995; Ihonvbere and Shaw, 1997).

Because of their pre-occupation with narrow, but vital economic issues, these organizations deepened the political morass in the republic. By failing to build cross-cutting regional coalitions that could sustain effective resistance, however, they were easily suppressed by the Babangida and Abacha regimes. These factors, at least in the short term, explain the abrupt suspension of MOSOP's radical opposition when Ken Saro-Wiwa and his eight Ogoni compatriots were tragically executed by the Abacha regime in November 1995. Nevertheless, their 'martyrdom' became a rallying cry for the struggles of other ethnic minorities of the Delta against the excessive concentration of power and resources in the hands of the dominant ethno-regional military/civilian elite. In the context of a deepening state crisis, oil minorities have emerged as the focal-point of Nigeria's highly-charged debate on the national question in the 1990s. Throughout the south, popular reactions against military rule took on profoundly communal dimensions during this period. We will now examine the role of ethnicity in the critical south-western region—where, following the annulment of the presidential elections in 1993, (widely believed to have been won by Abiola, a Yoruba), opposition to military rule was most effectively sustained.

Yoruba resistance to the post-annulment regimes

As south-western communities became the focal point of resistance against military rule, General Abacha systematically isolated Yoruba leaders from the prevailing tripartite arrangement that had dominated Nigerian politics since decolonization. He appointed trusted allies, mostly northerners, to important military and government positions. The Yoruba presence in the new government was limited to a clique of Abacha loyalists who promptly lost support in their own beleaguered region. In addition, while leaders of opinion and political activists of diverse backgrounds suffered from the repression of the Abacha regime, the Yoruba region became particularly targeted. Yoruba leaders of various interests and perspectives thus joined in projecting the Abacha regime as the common enemy, intent on marginalizing the Yoruba from power and the distributive resources of the state. Prominent Yoruba allies of General Abacha were targeted as self-serving sycophants who had betrayed their communities to a Hausa-speaking military oligarchy. As in earlier Yoruba political conflicts (Mackintosh, 1962 and 1963; Peel, 1983; Laitin, 1986; Apter, 1992; Vaughan, 1994; Pemberton and Afolayan, 1996), a pan-ethnic notion of Yoruba solidarity crystallized to ward off the assault of the Abacha regime. This had a significant impact on the tripartite rivalries between the Hausa-Fulani, the Igbo, and the Yoruba.

Reviewing the climate of communal suspicion fueled earlier by the Civil War, the Abacha crisis deepened the division between the political classes of the major southern groups—the Igbo and the Yoruba. It also encouraged open confrontations between Yoruba and Hausa-Fulani political elites, and intensified the suspicion of the oil minorities with respect to all three dominant groups. But it was in the historical rift between the Igbo and Yoruba political classes (of Southern Nigeria) that Yoruba resistance to the Abacha regime would have its most significant implications.

Although most Igbo communities had supported Abiola's presidential election, the subsequent rejection of the election results by prominent Igbo allies of General Abacha was interpreted by pro-democracy activists (most of them Yoruba) as the abandonment of a common cause against a northern-dominated military regime. The paradoxical (Udogu, 1995, p. 217) public embrace of General Abacha by former secessionist leader Odumegwu Ojukwu, following the imprisonment of Abiola, was a striking example of this development. While it would be wrong to suggest that Ojukwu was representative of the Igbo in general, his vocal campaign against the June presidential election (*New York Times*, June 6, 1998), was conveniently projected by Yoruba nationalists as a stereotypical Igbo betrayal. Prominent Igbo leaders, in turn, were sensitive to the irony of the Yoruba-Abacha confrontation given the key Yoruba role in the federal alliance that had crushed the Biafra secession. Thus, it was hardly difficult to portray this attitude as typical of the Igbo as a whole. A *Washington Post* report eloquently captures this sentiment:

> Igbos remember, often with bitterness, the war that broke out when their region seceded from Nigeria in 1966 as the state of Biafra. After four years of grinding warfare, Nigeria won largely by imposing a food blockade that starved hundreds of thousands of civilians—perhaps the majority of the estimated 1 million people who died in the war (*Washington Post*, June 6, 1998).

Despite Abiola's electoral success in the northern states, ethno-regional tensions were also apparent between Yoruba and Hausa-Fulani elites. Responding primarily to the annulment of the elections, Yoruba resistance to military rule was mounted by pan-ethnic organizations such as *Afenifere* and the Washington, D. C.-based *Egbe Omo Yoruba* that sought to unite Yorubas abroad against the Abacha regime. Aggrieved Yoruba leaders presented the annulment as an assault on their communities as a whole, contending that the northern-dominated regime was bent on marginalizing the Yoruba from power. In fact, the antagonism toward Abacha was exacerbated by his self-succession bid. A press release by the influential *Egbe*, illustrates this sentiment following the sudden death of Abiola in July 1998:

> Are there still Nigerians who are truly driven by gimmickry, that the long awaited broadcast of General Abdulsalam Abubakar will help resolve the fundamental political problems currently plaguing the country. The answer simply is NO from the perspective of the over 30 million Yoruba people in the eight states of Kwara, Kogi, Lagos, Ondo, Ogun, Osun, Ekiti and Oyo...It is a special tribute to the spirit of Yoruba tolerance that in spite of all the abuse, we still forge ahead in the hope of building a democratic and federal dispensation. Tragically, these expectations have gone with the wind as the hegemonic Hausa-Fulani power elite returns at every point to insist on power, a control which is always assured through the manipulation of the military and the various security agencies (*Egbe*

Omo Yoruba, Press Release, July 19, 1998).

But despite such embellished portrayals of the Yoruba as the principal victims of a Hausa-Fulani oligarchy, Yoruba sentiments were not simply irrational nor merely a smokescreen for narrow parochial objectives. While the Yoruba as such were not the real victims of the Abacha regime, organizations such as the *Egbe* and *Afenifere* did reflect real frustrations during these years. And since Yoruba communities were the major centers of resistance to military rule, Yoruba activists were particularly victimized by state security agents. This sense of vulnerability was intensified when the regime announced an alleged coup plot by dissident officers in December 1997. Of the twelve alleged plotters who were subsequently sentenced to death or life imprisonment in April 1998, ten were prominent Yoruba officers, including Deputy Head of State Lieutenant General Oladipo Diya, and federal ministers Major Generals Tunji Olanrewaju and Abdulkarim Adisa. More importantly, the removal of these officers not only brought an end to any Yoruba presence in the Provisional Ruling Council, but also further diminished the already marginal Yoruba involvement in critical military formations such as armory, infantry, signals, and intelligence where Hausa-speaking officers retained a commanding role. The role of Yoruba officers, like their other southern counterparts, was now limited to the professional ranks of the medical, legal, and educational corps. Thus, while most Yoruba leaders saw the alleged coup plotters as prodigal sons who had betrayed the Yoruba cause, they still felt compelled to rally to their defense given the ongoing marginalization of the Yoruba in state affairs (*Africa Confidential*, January 9, 1998). This incident thus brought Yoruba vulnerability and discontent to a head.

In reaction to this development, Yoruba communities and spokesmen mounted open resistance to General Abacha's proposed transition program to a democratic government slated for August 1998. In May 1998, for instance, violent demonstrations occurred in response to a pro-Abacha demonstration in Ibadan. Appealing to a wider pan-Yoruba solidarity, the Ibadan rebellion was a clear departure from the narrow, Ibadan-centered communal identity that had confronted the modernist project of the Yoruba political class during decolonization (Post and Jenkins, 1973). More importantly, it figured in a wider wave of violence, sparked by the annulment of the 1993 election and erupting again with the sudden death of Abiola in July 1998—when irate Yoruba mobs attacked Hausa migrant communities in several south-western towns (*Washington Post*, August 10, 1998). What prevented these ethnic clashes from reaching a dangerous level was the more accommodating attitude of Abacha's successor, General Abubakar, who succeeded General Abacha after the latter's sudden death in June 1998. Abubakar terminated Abacha's transition program, and promised fresh elections that would usher in a civilian government in May 1999.

When General Abdulsalami Abubakar assumed the position of Head of State and Commander of the Nigerian Armed Forces, he was confronted with an atomized civil society, and a deeply divided officer corps that had clearly lost the confidence of Nigerians. General Abubakar also had to contend with persistent pressure against military rule by Nigerians in Western countries and by international human rights organizations. These developments encouraged General Abubakar to introduce a transition program to democratic rule which struck a balance between the interests of the ruling military clique and those of the ethno-regional political elites that had been marginalized by Abacha. This entailed rejection of pro-democracy demands for the restructuring of the state through an independent constitutional conference of diverse constituencies.

While insisting on a transformation of the distributive resources of the state, Yoruba leaders responded to Abubakar's initiative. Significantly, with the presidential annulment as the rallying point for the mobilization of ethnic constituencies, these leaders had failed to forge alliances with even more marginalized communities, especially those from the Delta.

Expressed through *Afenifere*, the platform of the Yoruba political class was coordinated by leading obas, elders, chiefs and politicians. At the organization's 1998 summit, the conference chairman, eminent historian Saburi Biobaku noted:

> Nigeria is yet again at a political crossroads, but this time, we, the Yorubas must not loose our bearing...We have been treated like a political punching bag, to be battered at will by those who have successfully directed the affairs of the country since independence. To ensure a stop to this, all our people, young and old irrespective of their callings, political persuasions, or affiliations, must come together to take a common position, set out common goals, work out appropriate strategies and lay down *modus operandi* for the attainment of salvation for our people (*Nigerian Vanguard*, July 31, 1998).

Later in the year, the organization endorsed a pan-Yoruba political party, the Alliance for Democracy (AD), to contest the forthcoming local, state, and federal government elections. By early 1999, AD had recorded resounding victories in the Yoruba states of Oyo, Ogun, Oshun, Ondo, Lagos, and Ekiti. However, with the exception of Kwara and Kogi states, with their significant Yoruba populations, the AD failed to garner support in any other states of the federation.

The spirit of resistance was now left to the pre-dominantly Yoruba pro-democracy umbrella groups, the Campaign for Democracy, the United Action for Democracy, and the Joint Action Committee for Nigeria. While maintaining their opposition to Abubakar's transition program, to ongoing abuses of human rights, and to corruption within the governing military clique, these organizations cautioned against a retreat to purely ethnic constituencies. While their leaders recognized the role of ethnic mobilization in the resistance to military rule, they were also mindful of the need for cross-cutting alliances with civil libertarians and with pro-democracy and human rights activists in other regions of the country. Thus, though dominated by Yoruba leaders, the pro-democracy groups also included prominent non-Yoruba, who helped lend broader regional and national appeal. Furthermore, along with the militant Yoruba nationalist organization, the Odua People's Congress, these pro-democracy groups repeatedly called attention to the plight of the oil-producing communities of the Delta.

However, General Abubakar's conciliatory gestures to the ethno-regional leadership rapidly eroded the political influence of the pro-democracy movement. As politicians were drawn back to the old ethno-regional alignments, the progressives' call for a sovereign national conference that would restructure the Nigerian state was predictably rejected. Thus, pro-democracy activists—such as Beko Kuti, Gani Fawehinmi, Femi Falana, Olisa Agbakoba, Wole Soyinka, and Julius Ihonvbere, who had mounted a courageous opposition to military rule in the 1990s—gradually lost ground. At least for the moment, the politics of protest was superseded by the pragmatism of the dominant Yoruba political class and its counterparts in other regions. This trend was also exemplified in the reaction of the Igbo leaders to the transition program of the interim regime. In this development, one important unifying factor was the determination to see an end to military regimes in Nigeria.

Igbo reactions to the Abubakar interim regime

As is usually the case in Nigeria, ethno-regionalism emerged as a formidable organizing base for Igbo leaders during General Abubakar's interim regime. As the political space expanded to accommodate the old ethno-regional leadership, Igbo powerbrokers held a series of consultative meetings of leaders of opinion from the pre-dominantly Igbo states of Enugu, Abia, Anambra, Imo, and Ebonyi. In a landmark summit meeting, following General Abubakar's announcement of the transition program, prominent Igbo politicians, traditional rulers, chiefs, and elders met in Enugu in July, to forge 'a common front that would advance Igbo interest in the evolving political dispensation' (*Nigerian Vanguard*, July 31, 1998). Led by Second Republic[3] Vice-President Alex Ekwueme, the conference identified 'a four-point agenda' for 'meaningful' Igbo participation in Abubakar's political initiative. First, like other southern constituencies that decried the political ascendancy of Hausa-speaking elites, Igbo leaders called for the restructuring of the federation into six geo-political zones (a return to the political arrangement of the First Republic,[4] centered on the regional governments). Second, they demanded the restructuring of the armed forces, state security agencies, and law enforcement institutions so that they would reflect the makeup of these zones. Third, they insisted that the federal government guarantee the basic constitutional rights—especially residency, citizenship, and minority rights—of all Nigerians irrespective of their ethnic origin. Finally, they called for the implementation of a revenue allocation formula that would privilege the 'principle of derivation'[5] over all other criteria.

Thus, as in the case of the Yoruba, the Igbo political class was mindful of the extent to which the domination of the Hausa-speaking officer corps had altered the balance of power in the favor of the north. Their far-reaching demands reflect the widespread discontent of the south with this arrangement—and also foreshadowed the severe centrifugal ethnic pressures that were likely to unfold after the military handed power to a civilian government in 1999.

Not surprisingly, the military government rejected the Igbo leaders' demands. Such changes, in any case will not be granted on mere request; their realization would require strong popular pressures from below. This, in turn, would certainly benefit from a rapprochement between the Igbo and Yoruba political leadership. As it is, in the geo-political universe of Nigeria, 'northern hegemony' thrives because of the oppositional political strategies that divide the south, animated and legitimated by historical memories that date back to the ethno-regional struggles of decolonization, the AG crisis of 1962–1966, (Diamond, 1987) and most importantly, the Civil War of 1967–1970.

In the Niger Delta, however, demands for reform were not confined to words; they were expressed through the real life experiences and struggles of marginalized communities. This development, the subject of our final concise case study, suggests how marginal ethnic minorities—ravaged by poverty, repression, and environmental degradation—were able to mobilize resistance against the military regime and the oil multinationals.

Oil minorities and the Abubakar interim regime

The opposition of Niger Delta minorities to the Babangida, Abacha, and Abubakar regimes, as well as the multinational petroleum corporations, provides compelling evidence of the potential role of communal groups as bases for resistance and change. This wave of ethnic resistance, centered on Ogoni and Ijaw communities, was articulated by local civil libertarians and environmentalists, and by human rights, women, and youth organizations, throughout the 1990s. Expressing varying ideologies, the opposition of these groups was primarily sustained by ethnic and communal appeals—that have dominated Nigerian politics since the colonial period. Their oppositional stance stems from communal conflicts that date back to the nineteenth century and the political struggles of colonial and postcolonial Nigerian politics (Ikime, 1968). More recently, this resistant stance was expressed through the resistance of MOSOP to the Babangida and Abacha regimes. This militancy spread to other oil producing communities, notably the Ijaw, assuming even greater intensity after the death of General Abacha in June 1998.

In two historic pronouncements, the Kaiama Declaration, and the Port Harcourt Resolution, the Ijaw Youth Council (IYC) and the Pan Niger Delta Conference, in December 1998 and January 1999 respectively, formally declared their opposition to the Abubakar regime and oil multinationals. In the case of the Kaiama Declaration, a new generation of Ijaw leaders, utilizing local historical accounts of domination by the major ethnic groups sought to mobilize the support of the Ijaw people. History is thus employed as an instrument of resistance against repressive postcolonial regimes. Following this historical statement, the IYC declared:

- All land and natural resources (including mineral resources) within Ijaw territory belong to Ijaw communities and are the basis of our survival...

- We cease to recognize all undemocratic decrees that rob our communities of the right to ownership and control of our lives and resources...

- We demand the immediate withdrawal from Ijawland of all military forces of occupation and repression by the Nigerian state. Any oil company that employs the services of the armed forces of the Nigerian state to 'protect' its operations will be viewed as an enemy of the Ijaw people...

- We, therefore, demand that all oil companies stop exploration and exploitation activities in the Ijaw area. We are tired of gas flaring, oil spillages, blowouts and being labeled saboteurs and terrorists...

- Ijaw youths and peoples will promote the principle of peaceful coexistence between all Ijaw communities and with our immediate neighbors, despite the provocation and divisive actions of the Nigerian state, transnational oil companies and their contractors... We offer a hand of friendship and comradeship to our neighbors: the Itsekiri, Ilage, Urhobo, Isoko, Edo, Ibibio, Ogoni, Ekpeye, Ikwerre, etc. We affirm our commitment to joint struggle with the other nationalities in the Niger Delta area for self-determination (*The Kaiama Declaration*, 1998).

By presenting this radical blueprint, the IYC, claiming to represent the largest ethnic group in the region, threw down the gauntlet against the Nigerian state, and the operation of oil multinationals in the Delta Region. But when the organization attempted to translate its strong words into actions, it was ruthlessly crushed by Nigerian troops.

This, however, did not prevent another radical minority group in the Delta, the Chikoko Movement, from organizing a broad, multi-ethnic alliance in Port Harcourt in January 1999. Drafted at a meeting of delegates from various 'ethnic nationalities' on January 26, 'the Port Harcourt Resolutions of the Peoples of the Niger Delta' identified a *modus operandi* for a diverse group of discontented communities in the Niger Delta Region. Noting the long record of manipulation of local leaders by the federal government and oil companies, and the history of acrimonious conflict among these communal groups, the resolution sought to develop a pan-Delta political consciousness based on a shared experience of domination and exploitation. More importantly, tracing the historical anomalies of the double exploitation by 'neocolonialism and internal colonialism,' the delegates endorsed the Kaiama declaration and the positions taken by other ethnic groups, notably the Aklake Declaration of the Egi Peoples, the Ogoni Bill of Rights, the Moreto Charter of Demands of the Ogbia people, the Resolutions of the Urhobo Economic Summit, and the Resolutions of the Isoko National Youth Movement. More specifically, delegates called for:

- the restructuring of the Nigerian Federal Government through the institutional framework of a Sovereign National Conference (SNC) convened independently through mass democratic action;

- a mechanism to resolve 'the inter and intra ethnic squabbles among the peoples' of the Niger Delta Region;

- considerable control by 'federating units' over their land, natural resources, environment and culture;

- the establishment of 'a financial arrangement of fiscal federalism' which will allow for a universally enforced formula of revenue derivation and revenue sharing over all resources and with specified power sharing arrangements between the central government and federating units;

- the establishment of a trust fund for unpaid dues and allocations to Niger Delta communities;

- the establishment of a Niger Delta Survival Fund (NDSF) 'to prosecute the struggle' of local communities for 'self determination';

- empowerment of local government authorities to marshall resources for the re-generation of the region; and

- priority for Niger Delta indigenes in employment, social welfare, public utilities, and community services in the oil *industry (The Port Harcourt Resolution,* 1999).

Finally, another blueprint for ethnic self-determination was issued by the Toru-Ibe Forum in January 1999. In a document that called for the creation of a state for Ijaw minority communities, Ijaw leaders petitioned the Federal Military Government for a Toru-Ibe Zone of culturally cohesive Ijaw local government authorities and for the creation of the Toru-Ibe State, bringing together the fragments of the Ijaw people still scattered between Ondo, Edo, and Delta States. Furthermore, they claimed that while the relatively well-paying jobs from oil companies had become a major source of patronage for dominant ethno-regional elites, Ijaw communities were subjected to abject poverty, neglect, and environmental degradation. It also demanded an aggressive training program for Ijaw youths so that they could secure employment with oil corporations; the provision of public infrastructure, education, and health care facilities for the Ijaw communities; payment of adequate compensation to individuals and communities that have lost their properties due to the authoritarian policies of previous regimes; and enactment of laws that would protect the environment in oil-producing areas (*Nigerian Vanguard*, January 21, 1999).

These demands for self-determination, social justice, and democracy immediately attracted the attention of oil-producing communities. For the first time, diverse constituencies, linked by well-organized institutions that cross-cut communal boundaries (and that also had strong ties to their co-ethnics in other parts of Nigeria and overseas) were mobilized on an unprecedented scale. Ijaws, Ogoni, Urhobo, Ogbia, Egi, Isoko, etc., despite varying ideological orientations, mounted resistance against the Abubakar regime and oil companies, notably Shell, Chevron, Elf, and Agip. In turn, the government and the multinationals resorted to strategies of co-optation, containment, and coercion.

The Abubakar regime reacted swiftly, manipulating age-old animosities between the Ijaw, Itsekeri, Urhobo, Edo, and Yoruba communities of Delta, Ondo, and Edo states. Furthermore, borrowing a leaf from its predecessors (especially the Abacha regime in the tragic case of MOSOP), the Abubakar regime branded the leaders of the new organizations as 'militant rebel-rousers' who lacked grassroots appeal. At the same time, the regime sought to co-opt its own 'legitimate' intermediaries in the local communities—the chiefs and elders. But when the regime insisted that traditional notables pay courtesy calls on state and federal military governments to pledge their loyalty, most of them fearing reprisals from militants, tactfully avoided state officials (*Daily Champion*, January 10, 1999).

With logistical support from Chevron, the regime also took military action against the opposition groups and the communities with which they were involved. In two tragic incidents, government forces fired live ammunition and tear gas at peaceful demonstrators in Kaiama and Port Harcourt (in December 1998 and January 1999, respectively), killing several people. Women, who had also become visible in the resistance movement, were also subjected to the brutality of state security forces. In a peaceful demonstration in support of the Kaiama Declaration in January 1999, for instance, women and children were particularly subjected to the repression of the security forces. The personal account of a spokeswoman for the Niger Delta Women for Justice, Aniemeseigha Brisibe is instructive here:

> We cannot afford to fold our hands and watch our sons killed, our women raped and our lands polluted by oil companies. As mothers, sisters and daughters of Ijawland, we are the sanctuaries of continuity. We came out to march peacefully in support of the Kaiama Declaration and the forces of occupation rolled out their carpet of brutality to welcome us. They embraced us with violence (*Bulletin of the Ijaw Youth Council*, No. 2).

And of the approximately one thousand women reported to have demonstrated in Port Harcourt in January, Nimi Asei's testimony was poignant:

> They tore my dress to pieces. They flogged me. They threw me on the ground and sprayed their poisonous tear gas on us. I refused to cry. I refused to run. I told them to kill me. You can see the bruises all over my body. I now ache all over. This struggle must continue. We must control our resources and use [them] for our benefit.

Another woman who had experienced similar brutality from the combined team of Mobile police, army and navy, Ebi Kalaowei observed: 'they kicked me with their heavy boots; they flogged me with Koboko (horse whip). But they can never, never kill the Izon spirit, which is the spirit of justice and truth. We are fighting a just cause we will never lose' (*Bulletin of the Ijaw Youth Council*, No. 2).

For their part, the oil corporations, despite evidence that they had given support to state security forces, simply retorted that they were caught in the middle of unfortunate events. Shell's and Chevron's responses to internal and external pressures were at one and the same time defiant and conciliatory: we are the victims of a state and society in crisis; we have done so much to alleviate the plight of the masses of Niger Delta communities; and besides, these militants lack grassroots support; we have the support of the chiefs and elders, the legitimate representatives of local communities (The Ijaw National Congress, USA, January 22, 1999).

In any case, at least in the short term, state repression has succeeded in stemming the activities of these organizations. Given the ongoing economic crisis, however, the organizations are likely to resurface along with their grassroots appeal, when a civilian government emerges in the Fourth Republic. The discontent that started with Ogoni resistance to the Babangida and Abacha regimes, and proliferated under Abubakar's interim government, would be difficult to contain in a more open and democratic setting—that is, if far-reaching reforms are not instituted with respect to the exploitation of oil and the distribution of its revenues.[6]

In short, the struggle of the minorities of the oil-producing regions goes beyond the simple constitutional and electoral questions that had hitherto consumed the attention of the ethno-regional leadership. Because of their profound structural disadvantage in the geo-political configuration of power, combined with their strategic location in oil producing areas, Niger Delta minorities pose a difficult challenge to the state. Even as others embraced Abubakar's transition program, these groups continued to underscore the need to transform the distributive practices of the state. For these vulnerable communities, a legitimate democratization project must confer full rights of citizenship on individuals and address the severe economic exploitation and environmental degradation of these communal groups.

Conclusion

The conventional instrumentalist perspective on African communal consciousness and collective action has often obscured the complex role of ethnicity in contemporary Nigerian politics. We have tried to show that a greater appreciation of sociopolitical and historical realities, especially when analyzed in the context of the economic crisis and state decay of the 1990s, provides a more nuanced understanding of the shifting roles of ethnicity. Analyzed with an eye to the dialectical relationships of ethnicity and structures of power, we can see how communal groups may emerge as agents of grassroots resistance to repressive regimes, even as the state faces rapid decay.

These southern Nigerian case studies (rooted in group interests) reveal a confluence of sociopolitical circumstances, with different strands of local reaction to the excesses of military rule, conflicting patterns of elite consolidation and grassroots resistance, increasingly coming to center on a critical—but vulnerable—Hausa-speaking officer corps. In this complex universe of diverse, reactive ethnic communities and a state in crisis, collective action, entrenched in communal values, may take different forms. On the one hand, it might only strengthen the extractive impulses of ethno-regional political classes. Conversely, communally based action, allied with, and reappropriated by a new generation of pro-democracy and human rights activists, has emerged as an effective agent of resistance and progressive change. The critical challenge is whether these civic groups, along with their counterparts in the northern states, can engage in a sustained process of collaboration and compromise. The mutual accommodation of these voices of discontent, not to speak of their active alliances, would not only prove a formidable opposition to authoritarian regimes, but even more importantly, may help revitalize Nigeria's severely fractured civil society.

Notes

1. There is a growing scholarly literature on the enigmatic military regime of General Ibrahim Babangida, 1985–1993. The regime's cynical response to the severe economic downturn and popular pressures for democracy and human rights set the stage for the crisis that engulfed Nigeria throughout the 1990s. For authoritative analyses see Forrest, T. (1993), *Politics and Economic Development in Nigeria*, Westview Press: Boulder, CO; Ihonvbere, J. O. (1994b), *Nigeria: The Politics of Adjustment & Democracy*, Transaction Publishers: New Brunswick, NJ; Beckett, P. A. and Young, C. (eds.) (1997), *Dilemmas of Democracy in Nigeria*, University of Rochester Press: Rochester, NY; Diamond, L., Kirk-Greene, A. and Oyediran, O. (eds.) (1997), *Transition Without End: Nigerian Politics and Civil Society Under Babangida*, Lynne Rienner: Boulder, CO; Ihonvbere, J. O. and Shaw, T. (1998), *Illusions of Power: Nigeria in Transition*, Africa World Press: Lawrenceville, NJ.
2. This trend has dominated Nigerian politics since the decolonization process. With the Hausa-speaking political class holding the trump card, one of the two major southern ethnic groups—the Igbo and the Yoruba—have often been co-opted into a coalition at the national level of government. These alliances have generally resulted in the isolation of one of these major southern groups.
3. Students of Nigerian political studies generally refer to Nigeria's second failed attempt at a liberal democratic system (1979–1983) as the Second Republic.
4. With a Federal democratic structure that recognized three (later four) fairly autonomous regional governments (North, East, West and Midwest) from 1960–1966, the First Republic is a widely used term for this initial attempt in liberal democracy.
5. In an economy that relies mainly on the collection of oil rent from petroleum multinationals, revenue allocation is a fiercely contested issue by ethnic power-brokers. Because of their declining political influence, southern communities (especially the Niger Delta Region) where the bulk of Nigeria's economic resources are derived, have insisted on a special distributive system that would allocate revenue on the basis of the resources generated by each state. This revenue allocation formula is known as the 'principle of derivation.'
6. It is important to underscore the implications of these agitations for the viability of a democratic system in Nigeria. The renewal of a progressive ethnicity that fails to

articulate communal aspirations within broader national notions of democracy and development may only further undermine Nigeria's fractious federation. This trend complicated the Western-imposed perspective of civil society, human rights, and democratization that dominated Africanist political science scholarship in the immediate post-Cold War years.

References

Apter, A. (1992), *Black Critics and Kings: The Hermeneutics of Power in Yoruba Society*, University of Chicago Press: Chicago, IL.

Diamond, L. (1988), *Class, Ethnicity and Democracy in Nigeria: The Failure of the First Republic*, Macmillan Press: London.

Falola, T. and Ihonvbere, J. (1985), *The Rise and Fall of Nigeria's Second Republic*, Zed Press: London.

Hyden, G. and William, D. C. (1994), 'A Community Model of African Politics: Illustrations from Nigeria and Tanzania', *Comparative Studies in Society and History*, Vol. 36, No. 1, pp. 68–96.

Ihonvbere, J. O. (1994a), 'The "Irrelevant" State: Ethnicity and the Quest for Nationhood in Africa', *Ethnic and Racial Studies*, Vol. 17, No. 1, pp. 42–60.

Ihonvbere, J. O. (1994b), *Nigeria: The Politics of Adjustment & Democracy*, Transaction Publishers: New Brunswick, NJ.

Ihonvbere, J. O. (1996), 'Are Things Falling Apart? The Military and the Crisis of Democratization in Nigeria', *Journal of Modern African Studies*, Vol. 34, No. 2, pp. 193–225.

Ihonvbere, J. O. and Shaw, T (1998), *Illusion of Power: Nigeria in Transition*, Africa World Press: Lawrenceville, NJ.

Ikime, O. (1968), 'Reconsidering Colonial Rule: The Nigerian Example', *Journal of the Historical Society of Nigeria*, Vol. 4, pp. 421–438.

Jibrin, I. (1997), 'Obstacle to Democracy in Nigeria', in Beckett, P. and Young, C. (eds.), *Dilemmas of Democracy in Nigeria*, Rochester University Press: Rochester, NY.

Joseph, R. A. (1987), *Democracy and Prebendal Politics in Nigeria*, Cambridge University Press: Cambridge.

Laitin, D. (1986), *Hegemony and Culture: Politics and Religious Change Among the Yoruba*, University of Chicago Press: Chicago, IL.

Lewis, P. (1997), 'Politics and the Economy', in Beckett, P. and Young, C. (eds.), *Dilemmas of Democracy in Nigeria*, Rochester University Press, Rochester, NY.

Mackintosh, J. (1962), 'Electoral Trends and the Tendency to a One-party System in Nigeria', *Journal of Commonwealth Political Studies*, Vol. 1, pp. 194–210.

Mackintosh, J. (1963), 'Politics in Nigeria: The Action Group Crisis of 1962', *Political Studies*, Vol. 11, pp. 126–155.

Naanen, B. (1995), 'Oil-Producing Minorities and the Restructuring of Nigerian Federation: The Case of the Ogoni People', *Journal of Commonwealth and Comparative Politics*, Vol. 33, No. 1, pp. 46–78.

Peel, P. D. Y. (1983), *Ijeshas and Nigerians: The Incorporation of a Yoruba Kingdom, 1890s–1970s*, Cambridge University Press: Cambridge.

Pemberton, J. and Afolayan, F. (1996), *Yoruba Sacred Kingship: A Power Like the Gods,*

Smithsonian Institution Press: Washington, DC.
Post, K. and Jenkins, G. (1973), *The Price of Liberty: Personality and Politics in Colonial Nigeria*, Cambridge University Press: Cambridge.
Post, K. and Vickers, M. (1973), *Structure and Conflict in Nigeria, 1960–1966*, Heinemann Press: London.
Ranger, T. and Vaughan, O. (eds.) (1993), *Legitimacy and the State in Twentieth Century Africa*, Macmillan Press: London.
Soyinka, W. (1998), *Open Sore of a Continent*, Oxford University Press: Oxford.
Udogu, E. I. (1994), 'The Allurement of Ethnonationalism in Nigerian Politics: The Contemporary Debate', *Journal of Asian and African Studies*, Vol. 29, No. 3–4, pp. 159–171.
Udogu, E. I. (1995), 'The Military, Civil Society and the Issue of Democratic Governance: Toward Nigeria's Fourth Republic', *Journal of Developing Societies*, Vol. 11, fasc. 2, pp. 206–220.
Vaughan, O. (1994), 'Communalism, Legitimation, and Party Politics at the Grassroots: The Case of the Yoruba', *International Journal of Politics, Culture, and Society*, Vol. 7, pp. 419–440.
Vaughan, O. (1995), 'Assessing Grassroots Politics and Community Development in Nigeria', *African Affairs*, Vol. 94, No. 377, pp. 501–518.
Vaughan, O. (2000), *Nigerian Chiefs: Traditional Power in Modern Politics, 1890s–1990s*, University of Rochester Press: Rochester, NY.

6 Ethnic Politics and the Decay of the State in Kenya

F. WAFULA OKUMU

Introduction

Today, Kenya's socioeconomic structure, its politics, and even the state itself are warped by ethnicity to the extent that 'tribalism' or 'ethnicity' (two concepts that would be used interchangeably in this chapter) has become a common frame of reference and national ideology. As some ethnic groups claim their turn to control the state, ethnic mistrust and hatred is being bred and expressed through bloody incidences of ethnic clashes. The infusion of tribalism into politics has also contributed to stalemates in the democratic transition, constitutional reforms, and the anointment of Moi's successor. Mutuma Mathiu (1998) best illustrates this prevalence of ethnicity in Kenyan politics and its impact on the state in a hypothetical 'Second Coming' of Jesus Christ. Mathiu points out that on his return, Christ will be disappointed with Kenyans for not heeding his warning that 'any Kingdom divided against itself is laid to waste; and a house divided against itself falls.' According to Mathiu, Jesus would see not only a divided ruling party but also a divided opposition. He will then

> look to the four winds and see tribes, each with its son under its arm saying: Now appoint from among us a president to judge all the other tribes. Give us a king to judge others. He would look, with disgust, into the hearts of the duplicitous chaps who have thus rigged their tribesmen [and women] to proffer them as the next Saul. And perhaps He would repeat: I have come to cast fire upon the earth, and how I wish it were already kindled (Mutuma Mathiu in *Sunday Nation* (Nairobi), December 20, 1998).

This quote clearly illustrates the state of desperation that Kenyans are in as they witness a paralysis of their political system and the failure of the politicians to run the state properly. The fact that some are now seeking deliverance from Providence is a reflection of their deep frustration and despair, and damning indictment of the present crop of leaders. The central thesis of this chapter is that as Kenya marches into the new millennium and the end of Moi's rule, it is doing so with a decaying state and a nation that has been fragmented by ethnic politics. To underlie this thesis, I point out extensively how ethnic politics has become a major obstacle to the development of a modern nation-state and construction of Kenyan nationalism. I also analyze how the politicization of ethnicity has introduced political violence and undermined democracy in Kenya. Before positing my solutions, I will review some proposals that are being presented as possible solutions to the problems facing the Kenyan nation-state.

The decaying Kenyan state

The Kenyan state is decaying at an alarming rate. To paraphrase the English poet William B. Yeats, Kenya is falling apart as its center cannot hold. There are a number of reasons that explain why the state in Kenya is collapsing. One explanation is that the state is being fragmented by the excessive political and economic claims made on it by various ethnic groups and their leaders. The state in Kenya is seen as a prize that has to be won and used to enhance the material well-being of the various ethnic groups. As a result, there are now historical claims based on previous assumptions that each ethnic group deserves and must get its opportunity to control and exploit the state.

Raymond C. Taras and Rajat Ganguly (1998, p. 226) attribute the collapse of African states to 'ethnonationalism' and a retreat into ethnic identities. However, argue Taras and Rajat, this collapse is not a recent phenomenon. It was preceded by hasty colonial withdrawals and hasty African takeovers that created 'nascent independent states' in which the struggle for power between political leaders was ethnicized. By conditioning people to think 'in ethnic categories' and then inflating and politicizing their significance, leaders like Moi have diverted attention of the populace away from the more fundamental matters of power and resources (Taras and Ganguly, 1998, p. 242).

The second explanation for the accelerated decay of the Kenyan state is due to poor leadership that uses ethnicity as a means of sustaining itself in power. This has been amply demonstrated by the Moi administration. Indeed, ethnic considerations are behind Moi's maintenance of a large cabinet and a bloated bureaucracy. Unnecessary ministries have been created to reward ethnic groups for their loyalty or maintain a facade of a 'national outlook.' Also tribal considerations were behind the creation of numerous ethnic constituencies and administrative districts such as Teso, Elgon, Kuria, and Tharaka since Moi came to power. These ethnic manipulations have come with astronomical financial costs to the country.

The decay of the Kenyan state is clearly illustrated by a crumbling infrastructure and failed educational system. There is almost zero investment, both domestic and foreign; bank lending rates are high and people are over-taxed. Due to institutional corruption and bureaucratic inefficiency, hospitals have no medicine, schools have no supplies, farmers cannot market their products, and almost a third of the country's gross domestic product (GDP) has disappeared mysteriously. This culture of corruption and misuse of *mali ya uma* (public property) has permeated all levels of government and non-government institutions.

I. William Zartman (1995, p. 5) contends that when a state decays, it also becomes paralyzed and inoperative. Consequently, a decaying state, such as Kenya loses its societal cohesion, fails to make laws and preserve order, loses legitimacy and authority to act in the public good, and loses popular support and control over the population. Besides competence, delivery of services and good governance, other casualties of such a state are the socioeconomic system, national unity, development and democracy. In truth, such a scenario creates political instability, and in the proceeding analysis we will trace how ethnicity has contributed to this malaise.

Political ethnicity in Kenyan politics

Political ethnicity in Kenyan politics and society can be traced to the advent of colonialism when the British used some ethnic groups to conquer or rule others (Tignor, 1976; Ogot, 1996). Before the arrival of the British, most ethnic groups had coexisted in harmony. The Kenyan state never existed until the beginning of the 20th century when Kenya was established as a British settler colony and land of adventure. In their seminal works, Gideon Were, Gideon Muriuki and Justin Willis noted that ethnic groups were created for the expediency of the colonial rule (Were, 1967; Muriuki, 1974; and Willis, 1993). Throughout colonial rule, all non-Europeans were categorized and referred to according to specified ethnic groups and placed under 'tribal administrations' which were used indirectly to colonize Kenya (Mwaruvie, 1996). After being assigned to a 'tribe,' an African was treated according to the stereotypes invented for his or her 'tribe.' For instance, while Kenyans from western tribes were usually employed as house servants, members of central tribes generally labored on plantations and members of the pastoralist tribes were often preferred as guards of the master's property. The stereotype the British attached to the Kikuyus as 'untrustworthy' has remained to the present day and even found expression in politics. During colonialism, the British deliberately divided Africans, denied them the education needed to run a government effectively and to compete in a money economy after their departure.

After institutionalizing ethnicity, the British left Kenya hastily without preparing the Kenyans in the art of state management and democratic practice. Consequently, nation-building became a top priority of the Kenyatta government. It was a gigantic task for him. Before leaving, however, the British made an effort to deny Jomo Kenyatta and the Kenya African National Union (KANU) the opportunity to lead an independent Kenya by openly favoring the Kenya African Democratic Union (KADU), which was a party of minority groups that had come together to counter the Kikuyu-Luo dominated KANU. While KANU's manifesto sought a unified nation-state, KADU's promoted *majimboism* (ethnic federalism) as a system of government that would guarantee and protect the interests of the minor ethnic groups from being dominated by the largest ethnic groups.

The onus of building a new nation-state was entrusted to a cadre of neophytes who had no experience and training in running a state, let alone building a united nation-state system. The new state administrators and managers were placed in a serious disadvantage due to their inexperience and inadequate education. Few of these politicians and bureaucrats, even those who had European and American education, were skilled in policymaking and policy implementation (Ingham, 1990, pp. 6–7). In short, the British did not make adequate attempts to train Kenyans in the management of the state and the practice of democratic politics. It did not take long for this first generation of leaders, administrators, and managers to acquire a warped understanding of public service. On assuming new offices, they started feeling immense pressure to 'fulfil long-standing obligations to families and supporters by exercising patronage on their behalf' (Ingham, 1990, p. 7). This in turn led to unbridled nepotism and corruption. These two elements have come to characterize the Kenyan state since independence in 1963.

Kenyatta's priority was to fulfil the promise of delivering rapid development to the African population that had deliberately been exploited and neglected during the colonial rule. But there was a price tag attached to new development projects initiated in different areas of the country. In fact, development was to be dispensed on the basis of allegiance of the region's leaders to Kenyatta. Kenyatta deliberately interacted with the people through their 'leaders' who in turn came to see themselves as representatives of their tribal, rather than national, interests. It is ironic that Kenyatta, while trying to build a 'Kenyan nation', was also sowing seeds of national fragmentation and destruction of the state by introducing 'tribal leaders.'

After coming to power in December 1963, Kenyatta went on a powerhunt and in the process institutionalized 'tribalism.' The first effort in power consolidation came in January 1964 when he sought British military support to control an army battalion that tried to mutiny for higher pay and rank promotions. To prevent future military threats to his government, he reduced the dominance of the Kambas and Kalenjins, the two ethnic groups that made up the bulk of the army. He neutralized the number of Kamba officers by selectively recruiting Kikuyus to high positions in the military and police. He also created a special paramilitary force, General Service Unit (GSU), with a Kikuyu officer corps for the purpose of clamping down government opposition.

To consolidate his power further, Kenyatta assumed the leadership of all key institutions in the country, from the military to the party and university. He was not only the president of the country, but was also head of the ruling party. His wide-ranging powers included appointment of the cabinet (including the vice president), the judges, permanent secretaries, military commanders, provincial commissioners, heads of parastatals, and heads of other high offices. Kenyatta exercised patronage in filling these offices and made it clear to the appointees that they were serving at his discretion and pleasure. While most of the key positions, such as Attorney General and Chiefs of Internal Security, were reserved for Kikuyus, he 'distributed offices to members of other ethnic groups in such a way as to ensure that all parts of the country enjoyed some of the benison patronage' (Ingham, 1990, p. 96).

Kenyatta, the former student of the renowned anthropologist Bronislaw Malinowski, was astute in employing African traditions to accumulate power. For instance, he dismissed the concept of political opposition as alien to African traditions while stressing the one that holds the father in high esteem. In African tradition, fathers are highly respected, feared, and seldom challenged in their decisions and actions even when they are sometimes 'irrational'. By claiming to be the 'father of the nation' Kenyatta demanded reverence for his wisdom and generosity. Hence, it came as no surprise when Kenyatta harassed Oginga Odinga's Kenya People's Union (KPU) into extinction in 1969 (Wildner, 1992). Although Kenyatta acquired absolute power and total national allegiance, he was particularly concerned by the Luo's treatment of Odinga as their 'father.' He resented this open display of disloyalty and went to work by launching a systematic campaign aimed at bringing the Luos to their knees.

Kenyatta had instilled in the Luos a burning desire for the presidency when he made Oginga Odinga the vice-president. The Luos felt that they were entitled to the second most powerful position in the land by virtue of being the second most populous ethnic group in the country. Hence, Kenyatta's appointment of Odinga as his deputy came to be seen as a way of pacifying the Luos. But Kenyatta did not only strip power from the position but also tried to muzzle Odinga. However, as Odinga's criticism of government policies increased, Kenyatta labeled him a 'communist' and a 'tribalist,' among other things. Odinga was painted as a Luo leader working in concert with foreign interests, particularly Russian and Chinese, to take over power and establish a socialist government. When Odinga formed KPU, it was labeled a 'Luo party' despite its national manifesto, membership, and appeal. To prove to the Luos that he was in control of the country and had the power to teach them a lesson for their opposition to his rule, Kenyatta made a trip in October 1969 to Kisumu, the main city in Luoland. In a public rally he held there, he chastised the Luos for their challenge to his government. He pointedly accused Odinga for fomenting trouble, and threatened to crush all those who opposed his government. In the aftermath of riots that ensued following the speech, a number of people were killed, Odinga was placed under house arrest, and KPU was proscribed for 'national security interest.' To punish Luos further, Kenyatta suspended or abandoned all government-supported development projects in the region. Henceforth, 'national security interests' became synonymous with the president's security, interest and survival.

Kenyatta was further miffed by the Luo's continued treatment of Odinga as their leader, king-maker, and spokesman after the assassination of Tom Mboya, an ambitious, and promising statesman. Mboya, who was one of the staunchest KANU members, had started building a national base in anticipation of Kenyatta's departure from the scene due to poor health (Goldsworthy, 1982). As Mboya's meteoric star rose higher, some Kikuyu leaders attempted to block his rise to power by changing the constitution. In the end, Mboya's ambition to become the next president of Kenya was stopped by an assassin's bullet. This assassination stirred up Luo solidarity and erased any ethnic divisions that might have existed between the southern and northern Luos. Luo anger at the assassination of Mboya, as expressed in massive demonstrations and the stoning of the presidential limousine, came to illustrate the depth and solidification of ethnicity in post-independence Kenyan politics.

In reaction to their emotional outpouring of anger, Kenyatta branded all Luos, even those opposed to Odinga, together and treated them as ungrateful and wayward children. Ultimately, the Luos became thirstier for power and entrenched themselves deeper in the opposition. The treatment of Odinga and Luos was a powerful message sent to all other ethnic groups, particularly those that felt short-changed in sharing the fruits of independence. All the ethnic groups were constantly reminded of the plight that might befall them if they followed the path taken by the Luos. The responsibility of keeping ethnic members in line fell to the whole community who controlled each member's views on government. If a member of an ethnic group made remarks that the government felt were critical of its policies or actions, the leadership had to either dissociate the group from the individual or disown the individual. This was the case with Masinde Muliro, Jean-Marie Seroney, Martin Shikuku, George Anyona, and Chelagat Mutai, who paid dearly for their criticism of government policies.

After falling out with Oginga Odinga, a left-leaning vice president, Kenyatta started to rely heavily on a close-knit circle of Kikuyu friends and advisors. These associates were carefully chosen from his home district of Kiambu. In a short while, Kenyans started to grow suspicious and apprehensive of these associates whose arrogance and activities earned them a sobriquet—the 'Kiambu Mafia.' Their penchant for power became more pronounced in the mid-1970s when they engaged in a number of actions that amounted to a scorched-earth policy of dealing with the opposition and protecting their political and economic interests. As part of their plot, some of the politically active Kikuyus started taking an oath similar to that taken during the *Mau Mau* independence movement uprising. It was alleged that the Kikuyus were swearing to keep the presidency in the 'house of *Mumbi*,' the founding mother of the ethnic group.

Indeed, when it dawned on the Kikuyu elite that Kenyatta was mortal, they went to work to ensure that his successor would cater to their interests. They sought to change the constitutional clause that allowed the vice-president to automatically assume the presidency for 90 days should the president resign or die in office. When this effort was stifled, they developed a more sinister plan by creating a special paramilitary squad disguised as an anti-stock theft unit, or '*Ngorokos*,' as it was later called in reference to a cattle-rustling ethnic group. Their chilling conspiracy involved taking over the government when the gravely ill Kenyatta died and arresting vice-president Moi (a Kalenjin) and his supporters before he could assume power constitutionally (Karimi and Ochieng, 1980).

The intrigues, machinations, and assassination alleged to have been carried out by some Kikuyu political elites to maintain power by almost any means possible left a bitter taste in the mouth of many Kenyans. Hence, it was no wonder that when Moi formally assumed power on October 10, 1978, he had an overwhelming national support, particularly from non-Kikuyu ethnic groups. The assumption was that Moi would bring the 'Kikuyus down to the level of everyone else' in Kenya. It was hoped that the enormous powers the Kikuyus had in government and business would be reduced and transferred to the non-Kikuyus who had lost out during the Kenyatta regime.

However, to reassure the Kikuyus that he had no ill-feelings towards them and preferred them to be in his government rather than outside, like the Luos had been during the Kenyatta rule, Moi did two things. First, he promised to 'follow Kenyatta's footsteps,' implying that he would not upset the apple cart. To this end, he appointed Mwai Kibaki as vice-president and surrounded himself with Kikuyu advisors such as Charles Njonjo, the powerful Attorney-General and G. G. Kariuki (Throup and Hornsby, 1998, p. 29). With these associates, he made whirlwind tours of the Central Province and other predominantly Kikuyu parts of the country to boost his legitimacy among these people. However, this honeymoon was to be short-lived as Moi discovered that he could not continue relying on his Kikuyu handlers forever and decided to balance their influence by giving his inner circle a national outlook, wooing the Luos, and building his network of supporters and political operatives.

But his strategies did not work out as he had anticipated. The overtures he made to the Luos by appointing Odinga to head a parastatal were shattered when the latter denounced Kenyatta as 'a land grabber.' Moi alienated the Luos further when he barred Odinga from running for parliament in 1979. To bolster his fledgling presidency, Moi embarked on a populist, or more aptly put a *Bonapartist* agenda that was aimed at endearing him to all Kenyans. For example, in quick succession and on a whim, he issued decrees to supply milk to all school children, and all government departments to hire new employees equivalent to 10 percent of the existing workforce. He criss-crossed the country offering money to bystanders promising new projects, cheerleading the people in singing his new slogan of 'peace, love, and unity,' and warning or castigating imagined enemies and trouble makers. At the same time, Moi embarked on what became his trademark of accumulating power through 'divide-and-rule' tactics (Throup and Hornsby, 1998, pp. 48–50). Concerned, as it were, with the Kikuyus, Moi drove a wedge between them by arraigning Charles Njonjo, a southern Kikuyu, against Mwai Kibaki, a northern Kikuyu. Njonjo and his supporters undermined Kibaki's popularity by claiming that the latter was mismanaging the country's economy in his other portfolio as Finance Minister. Kibaki countered by rallying the Kikuyus behind him and selling himself as the best hope for the Kikuyu reclamation of power. After weakening his Kikuyu handlers, Moi went on a power consolidation drive. Starting in February 1982, he demoted Kibaki from the powerful Finance Ministry to Home Affairs, expelled Odinga from KANU, detained a number of suspected opponents under the draconian Preservation of Public Safety Act, and outlawed all political parties except KANU. The opportunity he needed to uproot all, real and perceived, enemies came with the August 1, 1982, coup attempt by a group of non-commissioned Air Force officers mainly of Luo origin. After the failed coup attempt, Moi purged 'traitors' in the system, court-marshaled and hanged Luo NCOs who had organized and attempted the coup. He also detained Odinga's son, Raila, and replaced high-ranking Kikuyu military officers with Kalenjins (Throup and Hornsby, 1998, p. 30).

Next to be purged was Charles Njonjo, against whom Moi launched an elimination campaign by spreading a rumor that he was conniving with a foreign power to overthrow the government. After whipping up anti-Njonjo sentiments, Moi moved swiftly by dropping him from the cabinet, forcing him to resign from parliament, suspending him from KANU, and appointing a judicial commission to investigate rumors made about him (Throup and Hornsby, 1998, pp. 34-37). After hounding Njonjo out of the power coterie, Moi cleansed the cabinet, parliament, and the civil service of 'other traitors,' perceived to be Njonjo cronies. However, it was understood by many Kenyans that the purpose of these purges was to reduce Kikuyu representation in government. As if on a rampage, Moi swept out almost all the Kikuyus from high-ranking government positions and replaced them with his own Kalenjins.

In what appeared to most Kenyans as a vendetta against Kikuyus, Moi targeted Kikuyu intellectuals and businesses for harassment and destruction. The intellectuals, who were branded agents of Kenya's envious foreign enemies, were suspected of being members of a radical underground movement called *Mwakenya*. To Moi, *Mwakenya* was not only a sign of their disloyalty to his government but another Kikuyu quest to grab the presidency from him. In a short time, he demoted Mwai Kibaki from the vice-presidency and replaced him with Joseph Karanja, another Kikuyu. However, after a shot stint, Karanja was dropped and replaced by a former mathematics professor, George Saitoti, who was also named Finance Minister. To complete the rout of Kikuyu power and influence, he banned 'tribal' organizations, such as the powerful Gikuyu Embu Meru Association (GEMA), recalled loans owed to government supported financial institutions by Kikuyu businessmen, and closed Kikuyu owned businesses, particularly financial lending institutions. After ten years in power, Moi had, indeed, 'cut the Kikuyus down to size.'

Just like Kenyatta saw the Luos, Moi has come to see his Kikuyu critics as 'hate-driven tribalists' under the influence of 'foreign Masters' (Warigi, 1999). In the heydays of Moi's tribal paranoia, tribalism was used as 'a code' for sinister intentions on the presidency. It was obvious then that a 'tribalist' was someone who 'came from a certain tribe, and probably served in some important position under the Kenyatta government, and was generally perceived to be disenchanted with the ...(Moi) regime (Warigi, 1999). Thus, the word 'tribalist' became not only an epithet for dismissing a Moi critic but also a code for a Kikuyu. Kikuyus have now become Moi's 'whipping tribe' whenever there is a political crisis. By fanning 'Kikuyuphobia,' Moi's regime has sustained itself in power despite its incompetent, corrupt and dismal performance.

Moi's survival strategy has been to ethnicize Kenyan politics. By playing the ethnic card he balkanized the state to his convenience. During his more than two decades in power, Moi has never passed up an opportunity to take cover under 'tribalism' whenever his mismanagement of the state was brought to light. To Moi any opposition to his policies and actions is tribally instigated. Consequently, nothing in Kenya seems to have escaped ethnicity. As Peter Anyang Nyong'o (1999) points out, Moi has also ethnicized poverty by deliberately neglecting some areas of the country deemed 'anti-Moi zones.' After depriving these areas of state development assistance, Moi has often ridden into them like a knight on a white horse, exhorted these ethnic groups to 'follow his footsteps,' conduct 'mammoth' fund-raising (*harambee*) for development projects that will bear his name, and imposed tribal leaders or spokesmen upon the collectivities (Warigi, 1999).

This 'king culture' has led to the popular practice of the ruling class assailing any challenge by waving the ethnic flag. Moi, like his predecessor, has promoted the norm by emphasizing during his presidency that 'for one to be politically big, even as big as sitting in the cabinet, doesn't count for a heck of a lot if you are not your tribe's spokesperson.' As a result, many Kenyans have made or destroyed their political careers by simply draping the tribal mantle on their shoulders. Some of these tribal leaders have become kpletomaniacs senselessly ripping the country apart. By dangling the presidency among different ethnic groups to win their support, Moi triggered a coronation race as most ethnic groups prostitute themselves before the president for this coveted prize.

To cling to power, Moi has designed and perfected a strategy of using ethnicity to further his objectives. This approach, similar to the colonial policy of dissecting and weakening strong ethnic groups, has been implemented in a number of ways. The most common practices are those of conducting 'mammoth harambees' in staunch or potential KANU constituencies, rewarding these 'zones' with cabinet appointments and new administrative districts that cater to specific ethnic groups, dangling the vice-presidency to different tribal leaders, and ethnic bashing or scapegoating. To reward his favored sycophants, he has let them loot the state in the name of their ethnic groups. Under Moi, corruption has been institutionalized to the point where it almost passes for official policy in both the public and private sectors of Kenyan national life. Government offices have become dens of corruption and state-owned corporations have either been turned into prizes to be awarded to political cronies and tribal leaders who lost elections or dumping grounds for political and government rejects who use them to doll out favors to members of their ethnic group. In truth, Moi's manipulative and poor leadership has contributed immensely to the politicization of ethnicity, severely undermined the democratic transition, and accelerated the decay of the Kenyan state.

The impact of ethnicity on party and electoral politics

After being prodded by the international financial donors and the pro-democracy forces in Kenya, Moi gave in to the clamors for the enlargement of the political space with a sinister warning that political parties would usher in ethnic politics and violence. His premonition was soon proven true when ethnic clashes broke out in the Rift Valley, Nyanza, and Western provinces. As the country prepared for its first multiparty elections since 1966, the strongest opposition party, the Forum for Restoration of

Democracy (FORD), disintegrated along ethnic lines into FORD-Kenya led by Oginga Odinga and supported by mainly Luos, and FORD-Asili led by Kenneth Matiba and supported by southern Kikuyus.

To guarantee KANU's dominance in Kenyan politics, Moi has manipulated his constitutional powers and state apparatuses to create ethnic political parties with grassroots support and patrons solidly reflective of their ethnic bases. Since the introduction of multiparty politics, leaders aspiring to the presidency have been forced to build and consolidate their ethnic bases before launching national campaigns. Consequently, Raila Odinga became a de facto Luo leader of the National Democratic Party (NDP); Nwai Kibaki, a Kikuyu, leader of the Democratic Party (DP); Michael Wamalwa Kijana, a Luhya (Bukusu), leader of FORD-Kenya; Charity Ngilu, a Kamba, leader of the Social Democratic Party (SDP). Other fringe political parties such as George Anyona's Kenya National Congress (KNC) and Shirikisho Party are also ethnically based. Even KANU, which claims to be a tent for all the minor ethnic groups, is widely viewed as an ethnically-based party due to its strong Kalenjin support.

As a reaction to Ngilu's failure to make a dent in national politics and her group's frustration with KANU for failing to deliver on its promises, some Kamba personalities have now formed a purely Kamba party to promote Kamba interests. Those behind this move argue that it is aimed at protecting the Kamba community from 'being used by other political parties to achieve hidden political agendas' (Shimoli and Odalo, 1999). The Kambas are disenchanted with Moi for only showing interest in the community during elections and thereafter abandoning it the moment the president's goal is achieved. The Kambas were miffed by Moi's new alliance with the Luo community, which became a recipient of the development projects and resources that were promised the Kamba ethnic group. The political marriage between the Luos and Moi's administration flowed from the fact that the former had started moderating its opposition to Moi's regime.

Although the Kambas are aware that they lack numerical clout to capture the presidency, they are betting on possible inclusion in any future coalition government. Indeed, according to a Kamba parliamentarian, if the new constitution allowed coalition governments then tribal parties would be the best means to protect tribal interests. He justified the Kamba's effort to form their own political party as a reflection of Kenyan political landscape that showed a tribal trend (Shimoli and Odalo, 1999). Following up on this artifice, the former Changamwe Member of Parliament (MP) formed the National Labour Party and received support from influential Kamba leaders to transform it into a full-fledged Ukambani party in the same class as the NDP (Luo) and FORD-Kenya (Luhya).

One clear characteristic of Kenyan electoral politics is its lack of ideologies that are likely to further national development and democracy. In part, it is because of this ideological paucity that ethnicity has flourished in Kenyan politics. In fact, the lack of political ideologies and commitment to political convictions has rendered the traditional role of political parties irrelevant. This is best symbolized by the habit of defections that take place before and after elections in Kenyan politics.

Kenyan opposition parties have become renowned not only for their consistent display of confusion and disorganization but also for their ethnic character and attempts to use tribalism to acquire power. In order to appeal for support in their quest for the presidency, political parties pander to tribal chauvinism. They claim that political ethnicity will guarantee tribal gains if they hold the highest position in the land. In the campaign leading to the December 1997 presidential and parliamentary elections, Mwai Kibaki, Wamalwa Kijana, Raila Odinga, Charity Ngilu and Daniel arap Moi (representing the party in government) acquired fanatical supporters from their respective ethnic groups in the competition to control national resources. The prevalent belief of these ethnic actors was that

> the prime duty of the Head of State was to feather his own nest and, in the process, feather that of his or her tribe. Thus, elections are meant to decide which tribe will "eat" next. The voters believe that the President is the patron of the tribe and is obliged to dispense favors to his or her own like a medieval chieftain (Mutahi, in the *Sunday Nation* (Nairobi), November 20, 1997).

The 1997 elections, like those of 1992, were dominated and decided by tribalism. However, the ethnic influence of voters has an economic angle as well. According to Kiraitu Murungi, in a publication entitled 'Ethnicity and Multi-Partyism in Kenya,' voters in the 1992 elections did not vote blindly on ethnic grounds. They voted for respective candidates

> on the basis of the traditional economic theory that *inoragia haria igwite* (when the elephant dies, it is the grass nearest that grows tallest). The Luos voted for a Luo presidential candidate because such a candidate was the best to access and allocate national economic resources to Luos. The Kikuyus voted for a Kikuyu presidential candidate for the same reason. The smaller tribes

thought they would be economically better off with President Moi who is also from a small tribe (Mutahi, in the *Sunday Nation* (Nairobi), November 20, 1997).

This further explains the corruption of politics through vote buying, hollow development promises and allocation of key government positions on tribal basis. After enduring years of abject poverty, the voters have come to see elections as means for putting food on the table. The state of desperation has subjected these poor voters to ethnic manipulation by those seeking power.

The question to grapple with is how did ethnicity hijack nationalism and become a predominant and destructive ideology in post-independence Kenya? Some have rationalized that ethnic influence on Kenyan politics can be explained by the fact that '[k]inship ties are still very strong in Kenya. The majority of Kenyans feel affiliated to the family, the clan and the tribe as is characteristic of peasant societies. Those three forms of social organization still remain the forces of socialization' (Mutahi, in the *Sunday Nation* (Nairobi), November 20, 1997). Colin Leys (1974) explained this political reality by pointing out that the peasantry as a class has not yet reached the limits of its development, and the symbiosis between it and the emerging urban-based classes is not yet fully developed either. It is this non-emergence of subjective class-consciousness that has allowed the persistence of clans or ethnic groups as units of social organization and modes of political expression. Expanding on this thesis Mutahi (in the *Sunday Nation* (Nairobi), November 20, 1997) points out that voters from a specific family, clan or tribe feel closer to

> one of their own because they share a common language, eating habits, rites of initiation and other cultural attributes. By belonging to a tribe, one gets a natural feeling of kinship towards other members of the ethnic group as they share a common ancestry or a place of origin and an historical heritage.

Another explanation is that ethnicity has been promoted by the political elite who see it as a means of enhancing their political capital. As pointed out earlier, there is a prevailing assumption in Kenya that for anyone to aspire to the highest office in the land, or to be closest to the president, one must first cultivate an ethnic base. The closer one is to the president, the higher the opportunities for capturing power, favors and privileges from the system. The pejorative slogan for this practice in Kiswahili is '*Kula ugali na Mzee,*' or 'eating cornmeal with the old man (the president).' The ramifications for all these are far-reaching, as we will attempt to elucidate in the following pages.

Ethnicity and presidential succession

As was noted earlier, Moi's rise to power was accelerated by the support he received from smaller ethnic groups who believed that they were marginalized by the predominately Kikuyu or Gikuyu regime of Mzee Jomo Kenyatta. They bought Moi's promises that he would represent their interests. Moi easily exploited the resentment the marginalized ethnic groups felt toward what they perceived to be Kikuyu arrogance (Githongo, 1998). Constitutionally, Moi can not run for a third term. Having been disappointed by the Moi administration, these groups are clamoring to put their sons and daughters in power so that their ethnic group could lay claims to the national fisc.

Although there is no established constitutional or legal order of how tribes should assume the presidency, it now seems that a precedent has been established for tribal rotation. Indeed, Githongo noted:

> The free-for-all scramble for the presidency has only set up a predatory cycle. If the Gikuyu 'ate' during the Kenyatta years and the Kalenjins have 'eaten' under Moi, others are afraid that whichever ethnic group comes to power will keep its snout permanently in the trough. In Africa, when one ethnic group 'eats' others are economically marginalized and impoverished. Look at Kenya. After alternate tribal 'feast' lasting more than 30 years, the country's economy has been brought to its knees (Githongo, in *The East African*, July 20–27, 1998).

Moi has also bred a culture of ethnic suspicion and rivalry by dangling the reins of power to different ethnic groups. Each ethnic group has already lined up its preferred political actor for the competition to succeed Moi. In fact, since 1992 former Agriculture Minister, Elijah Mwangale, has argued that

> after President Moi, it was the turn of Luhyas to eat...leaders of all shades have been saying the same thing. Leadership has come to be perceived as a banquet hall for the lucky few. In this situation, an

individual leader deposits his or her ethnic group at the entrance to the eating hall and proceeds to eat, in the guise of 'representing the interests of his people' (Matiangi, in the *Sunday Nation* (Nairobi), May 2, 1999).

On their part, the Kikuyus (the dominant ethnic group) have adopted a number of strategies to reclaim the presidency. They started this quest by forming an ethnically based political party in December 1991 when Mwai Kibaki opted to form the Democratic Party (DP) of Kenya instead of joining FORD. Although DP has drawn some votes from non-Kikuyu areas, its base and outlook is solidly Kikuyu. To enhance the opportunity for a Kikuyu president, Wangari Manthai (an internationally renowned environmentalist), made futile efforts to unite Kikuyu candidates behind one presidential candidate during the campaign for the December 1997 elections. In spite of the failure, attempts are still underway to unite for the purpose of capturing the presidency for the Kikuyus.

With the succession race turning into a messy political circus as a result of Moi's inability to groom and designate a successor, some of his lackeys started calling for a constitutional amendment to allow Moi to stay in power after the expiration of his mandated two terms. When Moi rebuffed these calls, an editorial in one of the daily newspapers cynically noted that this will give the country a brand new president who will give another entirely new clique, a totally new tribe, an opportunity to exploit the national wealth. The editorial also echoed the fact that the presidency has become an institution that allows ethnic groups to take turns in stealing from the state:

> Sharpen your teeth, Oh ye eaters, for a party will be thrown for you in 2002. Clear your throats, Oh he sycophants for there is a whole new vista of court poetry to be sung. Swell your ranks Oh ye proselytizers and tribalists, for there is a new standard to march to, a new bugle to answer to, a new master to wage war for (*Sunday Nation* (Nairobi), March 14, 1999).

This culture of perceiving the Head of State as the head of an 'eating tribe' can only be killed by changing the nature of the presidency. Murungi proposes a constitutional revision that will 'restrict anyone in political power from manipulating economic resources at his whim' (Mutahi, in *the Sunday Nation* (Nairobi), November 20, 1997). However, tribalism has also crept into, and undermined, the constitutional review process. The process turned messy and stalemated when tribalism was introduced into the nomination of members of the Constitutional Review Commission. Conscious of the fact that reforming the present Constitution will loosen its grip on power, KANU stalwarts are pulling all kinds of tricks from the 'tribal bag.' After agreeing in 1998 to the number of, and distribution formula for, members of the Commission, KANU later changed its position and sought to control the Commission by loading it with pro-KANU members. KANU hard-liners started muddling the nomination process when the women's political caucus presented its list that had no nominee who was politically aligned to the ruling party (*Weekly Review*, February 12, 1999). KANU challenged this list on the grounds that it had two Kikuyus; thus making it unrepresentative. When KANU also learnt that the National Council of Churches of Kenya (NCCK) had nominated a prominent constitutional lawyer, Wachira Maina, who also happens to be a Kikuyu, it launched a major and vicious campaign to 'preempt the selection of a Kikuyu nominee from the civil society' (*Weekly Review*, February 12, 1999).

By interpreting the succession of Moi in terms of tribes, politicians are merely exhibiting the typical mentality prevailing in Kenya that 'all politics are tribal.' Many Kenyans blindly follow politicians with presidential ambitions from their ethnic group regardless of the odds against their success. The main reason why many ethnic groups aspire to put one of their own in the highest office in the land is the widespread assumption that the holder of this office has the key to dispensing lucrative contracts, loans, jobs and other perks that are associated with political power.

Given the volatile political climate in the country, it seems KANU extremists are willing to use any means at their disposal, including ethnic violence, to derail efforts to reform the constitution and change the status quo. Certainly, it is in the party's interest to pursue this line of action. In the end, though, it is the Kenyan state that suffers from the politics of intolerance, mistrust and fear.

The impact of ethnicity on democratization

The democratization process in Kenya is being frustrated by ethnic political parties and suppressed fears and mistrust that ethnic groups have for each other (Githongo, 1998). Democracy has received a severe blow from the impact of political ethnicity on its leaders, the state and political groupings. The outcome is the polarization of the society which increased significantly following the introduction of multi-party democracy in 1991.

But democracy seldom flourish in situations in which ethnic groups fear and mistrust each other. Voting in Kenya, as in much of Africa, is often done along ethnic lines. Since the introduction of multi-party elections, it has been sadly observed that there are individuals and groups who will not vote for a candidate from another ethnic group so long as there is a candidate from their own—the issue of qualification or lack thereof is irrelevant. Further, in some cases, ethnic cultural discrepancies influence voting behavior. For example, in the 1992 elections, many Kikuyu voters rejected Oginga Odinga, despite his impeccable political record, because he was a member of the Luo ethnic group, which do not engage in circumcision rites (Amuka, 1996). To the Kikuyus, and Luhyas in particular, a man who is not circumcised is regarded as a 'boy' regardless of his age, academic achievements, and job qualification.

It is hard to disagree with Mugambi Kiai (1998) when he notes that among the many ills that ethnicity has wrought on Kenya is its threat to Kenya's democracy. As a tool of the political class, both in Government and in the Opposition, ethnicity has been used to seek favor from their local communities and in the process crucify proper 'plural' democracy. He notes further that ethnicity has been used as a political tool to counter or marginalize progressive ideas in post-independent Kenya. Moreover, the cloak of ethnicity has been used to incite people against each other in the ugly orgy of politically motivated violence in the struggle for power. And it is through ethnicity that a politically bankrupt elite has been able to retain power in Kenya despite their pillage of the economy. What is troubling to Kiai and others is that Kenyans have overlooked the fact that 'Kenya's rare great moments have come whenever ethnicity is ignored in their political lives.' One such moment was the struggle for independence that succeeded because the founding fathers dressed themselves in nationalistic cloaks. Indeed, it is a daunting, if not an impossible, task to build a democracy based on ethnic politics. As desperation sets in, most Kenyans have found themselves vulnerable to manipulation of their ethnic identities. Ethnic groups are either being confused and led to vote on ethnic lines or they are being instigated to resort to violence as a means of gaining or retaining control of the state, or at the minimum, increasing their participation levels in political and economic institutions. The result has been significantly increased levels in destructive ethnic mobilization. Most of the violence, of course, has not come exclusively from groups that feel politically marginalized but also from those fighting to retain the *status quo* and continue to maintain existing privileges.

Ethnic violence in Kenyan politics

One of the key elements in democratic politics is compromise. However, compromise does not seem to be commonly practiced in Kenyan politics. Most often, confrontation has become a widely preferred form of political interaction. The way Kenyan politics has been practiced under the leadership of President Moi defies the application of this basic rule of the game. Instead of peaceful resolution of differences and compromising on common sense basis, violence has become the first, rather than the final, resort to achieve political ends. Since the introduction of multi-party politics, there has been a growing tendency to instigate violence whenever those in power are challenged. Violence is becoming increasingly institutionalized as a conflict resolution method. Breakouts of ethnic violence in Kenya are becoming increasingly predictable. In the aftermath of the 1997 elections, orgies of violence were unleashed against the Kikuyus in the Rift Valley Province because Mwai Kibaki, the runner-up in that presidential race, had announced that he would challenge, in court, President Moi's victory.

The rationale for threatening Kibaki and the Kikuyus with violence was that such a petition was tantamount to disrespect for the 'sacrosanct' president. But what the president's supporters failed to realize, or realized but decided to ignore, was that Kibaki's petition was provided for in law (Ochieng', in the *Sunday Nation* (Nairobi), February 1, 1998).

Additionally, in both the 'Narok Declaration' and 'Nandi Hills Declaration,' warnings were issued to the effect that a war would be declared against the Kikuyu that would 'drive them out of [the] Rift Valley Province' (Ochieng', in the *Sunday Nation* (Nairobi), February 1, 1998). Nicholas Biwott, Moi's closest and longest serving confidant, choreographed these threats when he warned Kibaki against having an interest in capturing the presidency. To drive this point home, Kiptum Choge, a KANU parliamentarian, threatened that if 'some stupid magistrate arrives at a favorable ruling on Mwai Kibaki's petition against the election of President Moi, there would be automatic bloodshed throughout the country' (Warigi, in the *Sunday Nation* (Nairobi), February 1, 1998). Ochieng laments that such a warning

> is extremely unfortunate because this is no longer a threat to Mr. Kibaki alone. It is now a threat to the whole Judiciary. It is a warning to (Chief) Justice Zaccheaus Chesoni that the suit must be thrown out or Kenya will face civil war. It renders meaningless the

whole juridical process. To that extent, it is not a threat to the Judiciary alone. It is a threat to the whole country (Ochieng', in the *Sunday Nation* (Nairobi), February 1, 1998)

Gitau Warigi (in the *Sunday Nation* (Nairobi), February 1, 1998) opined that the idea of multipartyism seems to have

> failed to penetrate some people at the centre of power. One of the reasons politically-inspired clashes have become a fixture in Kenya is because these people have never learned to reconcile themselves to political pluralism. Political parties are in the business of capturing power. That is why they exist. For Mr. Kibaki to have designs on the presidency is proper, otherwise he has no business heading a political party.

Indeed, it is true that political violence in Kenya is attributable to a disturbing attitude of intolerance that, over the years, has grown with the politicization of ethnicity. The failure of President Moi to stop the spread of ethnic violence has led many to believe that he is behind its recurrence in post-one-party Kenya. This suspicion is given credence by the fact that no one has ever been convicted of promoting or perpetrating violence despite the existence of monumental evidence to prosecute the culprits. On the part of the government, it accuses the opposition of fomenting violence as one of its designs to topple the Moi administration.

Ethnic federalism and the future of Kenyan politics

There are a number of proposals that have been presented to address the looming catastrophe after Moi exits the political stage. The one that has gained a lot of attention and generated passionate debate is that of *majimboism* or ethnic federalism (Kimenyi, 1998). One of the most popular proponents of ethnic federalism in Africa, however, is Ali Mazrui (1998), who wonders why Africa has been reluctant in seriously considering it as a solution to its tumultuous ethnic upheaval. Mazrui argues that tribalism is deeply indented in Africa despite the acute psychological denial by Africans of its existence. In view of the fact that ethnic identity [and its politicization] is an African reality, he proposes the utilization of 'ethnic arithmetic' as a principle of representation. He cites Botswana, where ethnic representations are accommodated in the Senate and Ethiopia, where power has been decentralized to ethno-cultural groups, as places where this model appears to be working.

The *majimbo* proposal, as spearheaded by Coastal legislators and politicians, is being aggressively promoted as a panacea to ethnic politics and other ills bedeviling Kenya. Besides the coastal ethnic groups, the Kikuyus, Kalenjin, and Somalis are also seriously calling for ethnic states. The proposal made by the Coastal politicians calls for, among other things, ethnic states to control revenue sources, initiate all projects, run their own industries, and borrow money from external sources. These ideas have now been adopted as a party platform by the Shirikisho Party, which was founded on the eve of the December 1997 General Election, to fight for *majimbo* and the rights of the coastal peoples.

The proponents of *majimboism* have been ambiguous about the meaning of this concept. However, it is common knowledge that *majimboism* seeks to balkanize the country into ethnic kingdoms with ethnic districts catering to the interests of specific ethnic groups. Although the proponents have denied it, there is an underlying implication that under *majimboism* the ethnic states or regional governments will confer citizenship. Some have mused whether *majimboism* will entail splitting the country into tribal federations with autonomous tribal states with their own armies, foreign policies, currencies, infrastructures, presidents, bureaucracies, legislatures, and judiciaries (*Daily Nation*, July 8, 1998).

A full and frank discussion of this proposal has been severely undermined due to the lack of clear definition of federalism. But what is federalism? Operationally, the term federalism implies a system of government in which power is constitutionally divided between a central government and sub-national (state, regions, or provinces) or local governments. In a federal system, each of these levels of government receive their grants of power from the people and directly tax, regulate, or provide benefits to individuals. Powers granted to each level of government are not necessarily exclusive as some powers might be shared, while others may be denied and reserved to the people.

The proponents of *majimboism* have yet to provide specifics on the following questions: Should the new system be a unitary one with federal features or a federal system with unitary features? Do they want to form a federalism in which the central and sub-national governments exist almost autonomously or one in which there is sharing of power and responsibilities between the different levels of government? How will powers between governments be distributed? What powers will be delegated by the national government or sub-national governments? Will sub-national and local governments be created by the people or by the national government? Will sub-national governments be products of ethnic, cultural, linguistic, physiographic or economic factors? How will sub-national governments relate to each other? How will the issue of citizenship be determined in sub-national states? How will the rights and privileges of the citizens of one state be protected and guaranteed in the other? What will be the role of the national government in protecting citizens' rights? How will disputes between governments be resolved? How will policy or policies be harmonized if after an election the country ends up with governments in the hands of various political parties with completely different agendas? Who will be running the sub-national and local governments? Are they the same Kenyan 'politicians' who have increasingly distinguished themselves for their lack of political knowledge and skills in running the present government? Where will the money to run another tier of government come from? And finally, how will *majimboism* treat the cancer of corruption, rebuild the collapsed infrastructure, restore pride, harmony and honesty among Kenyans?

Mutava Musyimi (1998) argues that despite *majimboism's* claim that it will protect minorities, there is no guarantee that regionalism *per se* is an effective device for protecting minorities. He concludes that more often than not all that regionalism does is to open a new line of cleavage by fencing off new minorities where there initially were none. Moreover, there is a genuine concern that people of different ethnic groups will have no guarantees for security of their lives and property. This fear is based on the outbreak of violence in 1991, 1997, and 1998 that saw the Kalenjins, Saboats, Maasais, and Coastal groups cleanse their areas of Luos, Luhyas, Kikuyus and Kambas. The motives behind the proposals for federalism are also suspect and chilling when it is considered that they are being made by people who are afraid to lose their power and privileges in a democratic society and are known to nurse animosities against Kenyans of certain ethnic extraction.

It could be argued that the motive for calling for the establishment of a *majimbo* system of government is to expel persons of different ethnic and religious backgrounds from certain parts of the country to their 'ancestral lands.' The aim is to create tribal states or governments. *Majimboism* might not only be a death prescription for the nation of Kenya but also a resurrection of the colonial system of 'divide and rule' and a possible Trojan horse for institutionalizing tribalism.

Conclusion

As the Kenyan state 'decays' at an alarming rate and its experiment in democracy falters, there is a genuine fear that the country might slide into a Hobbesian state of nature. At the moment, mistrust, misunderstanding, and miscommunication are being fanned by ethnic chauvinists and bankrupt leadership that is sustaining itself in power by promoting tribal sentiments and dichotomies of 'us versus them.' The catastrophic consequence of this reality has been the abortion of the Kenyan nation-state and the retardation of its political system.

A measure of a political system's maturity is its capability, or capacity, to reconcile societal differences in a manner that enables all members and interests to flourish while keeping national beliefs in dominance. Such a system seeks compromise on divergent views while promoting its national interests. Kenya's path toward political maturity is being blocked by the prevalence of ethnicity in politics. Ethnicity has also impeded the process of national development and political ideologies that can direct the operation and management of the state. Kenya has yet to determine and put into practice her national political beliefs. Even as the country embarks on a road to rewrite its constitution, crucial questions of what Kenya's national beliefs are have yet to be addressed. One of the functions of the constitution is that of being a repository of national values. Let us take an example from the United States. In the Preamble of the U.S. constitution, American political values are enunciated as unity, welfare for all, justice, tranquility, and liberty. Additionally, Americans have also adopted constitutionalism, capitalism, democracy, freedom and equality as values that make up their political culture. For most of her history, classical liberalism has virtually been an unchallenged ideology.

The manipulation of ethnicity by an opportunistic political class has contributed significantly to the decline of the Kenyan state. Solutions to problems bedeviling Kenya do not lie in more doses of political ethnicity, such as *majimboism*. Kenyans need to carry out a thorough research and engage in a meaningful national debate to determine which political system and form of government that is best for serving the interests of all Kenyans regardless of their ethnicity, religion, race, gender, age, and region of origin. Monumental policy failures of the Moi administration should serve as lessons when designing or reconstructing a new Kenya. There is widespread fear that the collapse of the Kenyan state and the subsequent struggle for power that will ensue between various ethnic groups might lead to genocide, like the one that took place in Rwanda in 1994 or anarchy that is reining in Somalia.

To avert such apocalyptic scenarios, the following ideas should be reviewed. First, the reconstruction of a new Kenyan state must be preceded by riddance of the 'old breed' politicians who are morally corrupt and have promoted the politics of ethnicity; second, the political system, including the state must be completely democratized; third, both political and administrative boundaries must be redrawn to reflect fairness and equity; fourth, comprehensive changes must be made in the constitution to curb misuse and abuse of power and national resources; fifth, politicians and administrators must be re-educated and retrained in political and administrative skills; and sixth, Kenyans must embrace a new political culture that promotes the values of equality, justice, democracy and constitutionalism.

References

Amuka, P. (1996), 'The Romance of Nationhood: Kenya as Word and Desire', in Ogot, B. A. (ed.), *Ethnicity, Nationalism, and Democracy in Africa*, Institute of Research and Postgraduate Studies, Maseno University College: Maseno, Kenya.
Bayart, J.-F. (1989), *The State in Africa—The Politics of the Belly*, Longman Press: London.
Daily Nation (Nairobi), February 1, 1998.
Daily Nation (Nairobi), July 8, 1998.
Daily Nation (Nairobi), November 20, 1998.
De la Gorgendiere, L., King, K. and Vaughan, S. (1996), *Ethnicity in Africa—Roots, Meanings and Implications*, Centre of African Studies, University of Edinburgh: Edinburgh.
Economic Review, March 30-April 5, 1998.
Githongo, J. (1998), 'Kenyan Politics and Those Eating Chiefs', The *East African*, July 20–27.
Goldsworthy, D. (1982), *Tom Mboya: The Man Kenya Wanted to Forget*, Heinemann: Nairobi and New York.
Ingham, K. (1990), *Politics in Modern Africa: The Uneven Tribal Dimension*, Routledge: London and New York.
Karimi, J. and Ochieng, P. (1980), *The Kenyatta Succession*, Trans-Africa: Nairobi.
Kiai, M. (1998), 'The "King Culture" is Still Alive and Doing Well', *Sunday Nation*, September 13.
Kimenyi, M. S. (1998), 'Harmonizing Ethnic Claims in Africa: A Proposal for Ethnic-based Federalism', *Cato Journal*, Vol. 18, No. 1, pp. 43–63.
Leys, C. (1974), *Underdevelopment in Kenya: The Political Economy of Neocolonialism*, University of California Press: Berkeley, CA.
Mathiu, M. (1998), 'What Would Jesus Make of the Kenyans?', *Sunday Nation*, December 20.
Mazrui, A. (1998), 'The US Must Sell Federalism to Africa as Part of its Liberal Legacy',

Sunday Nation, February 22.
Muriuki, G. (1974), *A History of the Kikuyu, 1500–1800*, Oxford University Press: Nairobi.
Musyimi, M. (1998), 'How to Make Majimbo Work', *Daily Nation*, July 4.
Mutahi, W. (1997), 'Why Tribes Always Vote for Their Own', *Sunday Nation*, November 20.
Mwaruvie, J. M. (1996), 'Ethnic Imbalances in African States: A Challenge to Ideals of Nationalism and Democracy', in Ogot, B. A. (ed.), *Ethnicity, Nationalism, and Democracy in Africa*, Institute of Research and Post-Graduate Studies, Maseno University College: Maseno, Kenya.
Nyong'o, P. A. (1999), 'Makueni Shows Kenyans Where Real Power Is', *East African*, January 28-February 3.
Ochieng' P. (1998), 'Why Hatred and Bloodshed Will Hurt Warlords' Interests', *Sunday Nation* (Nairobi), February 1.
Ogot, B. A. (1996), 'Ethnicity, Nationalism, and Democracy—A Kind of Historiography', in Ogot, B. A. (ed.), *Ethnicity, Nationalism, and Democracy in Africa*, Institute of Research and Post-Graduate Studies, Maseno University College: Maseno, Kenya.
Simoli, E. Odalo, B. (1999), 'What Next for Kamba Politics?', *Sunday Nation*, January 24.
Taras, R. and Ganguly, R. (1998), *Understanding Ethnic Conflict—The International Dimension*, Longman Press: New York.
Throup, D. and Hornsby, C. (1998), *Multi-Party Politics in Kenya*, James Currey Publishers: Oxford.
Tignor, R. L. (1976), *The Colonial Transformation of Kenya, 1900 to 1939*, Princeton University Press: Princeton.
Tokin, E. (1996), 'Processes of Identity, Ethnicising and Morality', in De la Gorgendiere, L., King, K. and Vaughan, S. (eds.), *Ethnicity in Africa—Roots, Meanings and Implications*, Centre of African Studies, University of Edinburgh: Edinburgh.
Warigi, G. (1998), 'Instigators of Carnage Never Accepted Political Pluralism', *Sunday Nation*, February 1.
Weekly Review, February 12, 1999.
Were, G. S. (1967), *A History of the Abaluyia of Western Kenya, 1500–1930*, East African Publishing House: Nairobi.
Wildner, J. A. (1992), *The Rise of the Party-State in Kenya*, University of California: Berkeley, CA.
Willis, J. (1993), *Mombasa, the Swahili and the Making of the Mijikenda*, Clarendon Press: Oxford.
Zartman, I. W. (1995), 'Introduction: Posing the Problem of State Collapse', in Zartman, I. W. (ed.), *Collapsed States: The Disintegration and Restoration of Legitimate Authority*, Lynne Reiner: Boulder, CO.

7 The Ekutay: Ethnic Cabal and Politics in Sierra Leone

ALFRED B. ZACK-WILLIAMS

Introduction

Since March 1991, both civilian and military governments of Sierra Leone have experienced major-armed challenges by a group of rebels led by the Revolutionary United Front (RUF). In May 1997, the RUF was joined by rebellious elements within the national army, which ousted the newly elected civilian administration of Ahmed Tejan Kabba. The Armed Forces Revolutionary Council (AFRC), as the junta called itself, soon entered into a coalition with the RUF, and invited the latter's leader, Foday Sankoh to assume the leadership of the nation. The two fighting forces were integrated into what became known as the 'Peoples Army'. It needed coordinated and sustained efforts of the peacekeeping force of the Economic Community of West African States (ECOMOG), to remove the alliance of AFRC and RUF from the capital in 1998. However, in January 1999, despite the fortification of the capital by ECOMOG troops, the rebels were able to breach the city defenses, entered the capital, released thousands of prisoners and unleash widespread violence on the civilian population.

The initial *cause celebre* of the RUF was the overthrow of the dictatorial one-party system of the All Peoples' Congress (APC) which had ruled the country since 1968, initially under its charismatic leader and founder, former trade unionist, Siaka Probyn Stevens. Stevens ruled Sierra Leone with an iron fist until 1985 when to the chagrin of most Sierra Leoneans he announced his retirement and his aim to be succeeded by his kinsman and Force Commander, Brigadier-General Joseph Saidu Momoh. But Momoh was a phlegmatic individual with no base of support either within Congress, or civil society. The army was the basis of his support as he continued his role as conduit of the political temperature between a repressive regime and the army; in particular, he kept the lid on an otherwise volatile army.

In this chapter, attempts will be made to examine how ethnicity has been constructed in Sierra Leone by a faction of the ruling elite in order to maintain its hegemony, and how the successor regime proved its inability to utilize ethnicity in a corporatist manner in order to reproduce ethnic hegemony. I will also argue, that the policy of relying on ethnic cabal on the part of the successor regime, as well as the growing crisis of peripheral capitalism, which intensified the process of social exclusion and alienation gave rise to the emergence of a social movement, which challenged the state hegemony. I will also endeavor to analyze its origin, structure and why this actor in the civil society became so important at this juncture in the country's political history. I shall argue that this rise of the *Ekutay* in 1981 was a direct result of questions being raised concerning the 'ethnic group worth' of the hegemonic ethnic group, the *Limbas*, in an atmosphere of impending economic crisis, and the question of who should succeed the aging dictator. Similarly, the rise to prominence of the *Ekutay* after 1985 can be explained not only in terms of the change of personality and style of the leader, but also in the need for ethnic legitimacy and hegemonic continuity in a milieu of serious economic crisis. But above all the 'process of democratization' has tended to render relations more acute by undermining the mechanisms through which ethnic relations are regulated and fostering anxiety reactions (Ottaway, 1999, pp. 299–311). The call for multi-party democracy in the wake of Stevens' resignation helped to shake the ethnic balance within Congress, leading to the reassertion of ethnic identities thus threatening the fragile unity built by Stevens.

Ethnicity not tribalism

Until quite recently, the concept of ethnicity has been under-utilized within radical Africana. This is in spite of the rise of a 'new ethnicity' in discourse between Africa and the imperialist nations. For example, Aidan Campbell (1997, pp. 53–79) has argued that since the end of the Cold War, the West has been trying to nurture a 'new African elite' and this is based on the promotion of a favorable attitude towards ethnicity. Two main reasons could be discerned from this state of affairs: Firstly, the 'Manichaean relic' of colonial anthropology meant that many social scientists continued to theorize 'tribalism' in Africa as the main, if not the sole source of social action, whilst class action, and much later, ethnicity were seen as features of pluralistic liberal democracy. Note for instance, how the fratricidal strife in former Yugoslavia is reported as 'ethnic conflict' and that of Africa as tribalism or tribal killing. In this discourse tribalism is seen as the site of primordial loyalties and consciousness, and the inherent assumption is that tribalism is an African phenomenon *sui generis*. It is this assertion that led Archie Mafeje to unleash his diatribe against classical anthropology. Thus be warned: '...if tribalism is thought of as peculiarly African, then the ideology itself is particularly European in origin' (Mafeje, 1971, pp. 263–281). Paradoxically, whilst rejecting 'tribalism' as a tool for analyzing social action, Mafeje ended up by reconstituting tribalism as an ideological tool in the hands of the new elite, which in turn produce false consciousness for the ethnically-led. Thus he observed:

> This is not to deny the existence of tribal ideology and sentiment in Africa. The argument is that they have to be understood—and conceptualised—differently from modern conditions. There is a real difference between a man who, on behalf of his tribe, strives to maintain its traditional integrity and autonomy, and the man who invokes tribal ideology in order to maintain a power position, not in the tribal area, but in the modern capital city, and whose ultimate aim is to undermine and exploit the supposed tribesmen...if anything, it is a mark of false consciousness on the part of the supposed tribesmen, who subscribed to an ideology that is inconsistent with their material base and therefore unwittingly respond to the call for their own exploitation. On the part of the new African elite, it is a ploy or distortion they use to conceal their exploitative role (Mafeje, 1971, pp. 258–259).

Secondly, as a direct result of the 'Manichaean relic' and what they saw as the need to reconstitute African studies as a discipline alongside other area studies, many radical Africanists have moved to a position where class has become the dominant, if not the sole mover of history, and hence the only unit of social analysis. Other contradictions such as gender, ethnicity, intra-ethnicity, and regionalism are seen as secondary, and as such would disappear once the primary contradiction of class is resolved. However, a class-analytical approach need not forestall recognition of these other contradictions as Larry Diamond has observed:

> ...a class-analytical approach is not incompatible with an appreciation for the real culture and symbolic interests underlying

ethnicity, nor does it require any assumption of false-consciousness. Rather, it offers clues as to how and why certain mass interests get mobilized politically, to the exclusion of others (Diamond, 1987, p. 119).

In recent years, however, largely as a result of widespread social upheavals in major metropolitan cities, the collapse of communism in Eastern Europe and the end of the Cold War, questions of race and ethnicity have been forced back onto the academic agenda. The net result is that ethnicity and ethnic consciousness are now being recognized as universal phenomenon, hence the need to develop useful theories and concepts.

In this respect Donald Horowitz's (1985) *Ethnic Groups in Conflict* provides useful analytical tools in understanding the politics of ethnicity in a country like Sierra Leone. For Horowitz, ethnicity is an ascriptive category based on a myth of a common descent, shared history and distinctive cultural traits. Whilst pointing to the universal nature of ethnicity, his major concern was with ethnicity in Africa, Asia and Latin America. He utilized certain categories to illustrate different genres of ethnicity. For instance, he alluded to centralized ethnic system, where a few groups are so large, or so powerful as to threaten to dominate the center; dispersed ethnic system, where such domination of the center is not feasible; ranked system, where stratification is synonymous with ethnic membership; and 'unranked system' where parallel ethnic groups co-exist with each group, internally stratified. Some of these characteristics influence Sierra Leonean politics.

Ethnicity and the paternalistic state: 1947–1961

The process of decolonization in Sierra Leone was characterized by ethnic squabbling between the Creole elite on the one hand, led by H. C. Bankole-Bright and the then Protectorate elite led by Sir Milton Margai (Wyse, 1989). This is not to suggest unison of interest among the 'protectorate' elite, who in turn were divided between the traditional elite and the educated elite (Wyse, 1989, p. 106). According to Cartwright, this conflict helped to delay the process of self-government and decolonization (Cartwright, 1978). The Creoles who had been prominent in commerce and the colonial bureaucracy, demonstrated 'anxiety reaction' once the 1947 Constitutional proposals, which laid the basis for majority rule, were announced. They saw in these proposals the dashing of their hopes as successors to the departing colonial power. Indeed, the proposals which formed the basis of the 1951 constitution, to the extent that the model of selection for the Protectorate representatives was through the Protectorate Assembly, a body dominated by the chiefs, it also dashed the hopes of the Protectorate intelligentsia, as well as strengthening the position of the chiefs.

It is not surprising that the party that won the 1957 election, the Sierra Leone Peoples' Party (SLPP), came to depend on the chiefs for its support, and little attempt was made to build a grassroots party which would have by-passed the chiefs (Wyse, 1989). The latter were used to harass opponents, particularly in the south, the bastion of SLPP support. This over-dependence on the chiefs produced further problems for the ruling party. Firstly, the Creole elite pursued their interests via the United Progressive Party (UPP), though serious efforts were made to appeal to the spokesmen of discontent in the Protectorate, demanding control on the chiefs abuses and offering legal and moral support (Cartwright 1978). Secondly, a prolonged peace was broken with riots in the north in 1955 against perceived oppressive traditional leaders; and Freetown followed the next year with a general strike that ended in wide-spread violence. In 1958, a schism arose within the ruling SLPP, when Mr. Albert Margai (younger brother of the leader of the SLPP) broke away to form a new party, Peoples National Party (PNP). The ethnic vanguard of the PNP consisted of Mende and Creole educated elite.

The formation of the PNP was quickly followed by the emergence of a political party based on the educated elite of the diamond-rich, Kono District. The Kono Progressive Movement (KPM), led by Tamba Mbriwa drew its support from those 'tributors' (young men) in Kono who had not benefited from diamond mining (Hayward, 1972, pp. 1–28; Zack-Williams, 1995). The KPM attacked the mining policy of the Government of Milton Margai, a policy that enriched non-Konos as well as the chiefs in the diamond rich chiefdoms. In order to broaden its appeal, KPM joined forces with Edward Blyden's Sierra Leone Independence Movement (SLIM) to form the Sierra Leone Independence Progressive Movement (SLIPM).

By the time a constitutional conference was called in 1960, the Chief Minister, Mr. Milton Margai was able to summon a United Front of all political parties in the country, with the exception of SLIM, whose leader refused to co-operate with the Government in protest over its mining policy. In this way, Milton Margai was able to hold the ethnic coalition together, as long as he could count on the support of the chiefs in the diamond rich Kono District. The philosophy of continuing cooperation with the former colonial powers, the 'open door' economic policy and respect for traditional authority all helped to forge a national consensus. Despite this benevolent stance, he was criticized by the Creoles and Northerners for allocating a disproportionate share of cabinet positions to the Mende.

Economic and political authoritarianism, ethnicity and the post-colonial state in Sierra Leone

Post-colonial politics in Sierra Leone have been accompanied by prolonged economic decline, as successive civilian and military governments failed to arrest the nation's economic decline (Zack-Williams, 1990, pp. 22–33; Kandeh, 1998, pp. 91–111). For example, in 1995 GNP per capita stood at $180, a fall of 3.6% from the figure of a decade earlier; GDP, which grew just 1.6% between 1980 and 1990, fell by 4.2% between 1990 and 1995. What this suggests is that Sierra Leoneans were better off in 1980 than they were in 1995. Given this economic decline and its impact on government revenues, it is not surprising that life expectancy at birth was just 40 years (World Bank, 1997). Sierra Leone remains as one of the poorest nations in the world. Between 1985 and 1995, average annual inflation was 61%. In 1980 there was a net outflow of private capital to the tune of $7 million, but by 1995 the figure had risen to $28 million, and in that same year total external debt stood at $1,226 million or 158% of GNP.

It all started so well, in 1961 with the achievement of independence from Britain. Sierra Leone, described in its colonial apogee as 'the Athens of West Africa', carried much hope as the beacon of parliamentary democracy in the continent (Collier, 1970). It had inherited a relatively efficient civil service, an independent judiciary, and a relatively dynamic press. However, it was not long before this small nation of 4.5 million people followed its Anglophone neighbors by substituting praetorian guards for the tribunes. Indeed, the early warning signs were there, but these were clearly ignored by the governing classes upon whom independence had been foisted.

At independence, the nation's destiny was placed in the hands of the country's oldest political party, the Sierra Leone Peoples' Party led by the avuncular Sir Milton Margai. The latter, a conservative who acted as a conduit between the traditional chiefs whom he revered and the Western educated elite of whom he was always apprehensive. The 'old man' died in 1964 and was succeeded by his younger and more radical brother Sir Albert Margai He succeeded in splitting the party, which was always seen as a coalition of the ethnic elite of the south and north (Cartwright, 1970; Helm, 1978; Thompson, 1997). This action exacerbated ethnic tension. Sir Milton's Foreign Minister, John Karefa Smart, resigned in protest at being over-looked for the premiership and together with a number of other party stalwarts joined the opposition All Peoples' Congress formed in 1960 as a movement demanding elections before independence. Sir Albert's attempt to transform the political landscape by introducing a republican constitution and a one-party state made the regime unpopular with a skeptical public (Koroma, 1996).

Northerners were further alienated from the SLPP after Sir Albert dropped from his government mainly northerners who had questioned his appointment. These requital actions together with the mismanagement of the economy, in particular the crisis of the Sierra Leone Produce Marketing Board (SLPMB), which affected the prices farmers received for their produce, led to poor performance of the SLPP at the polls in the elections of 1967 (Sawi, 1972). The opposition APC capitalized on the Government's unpopularity, accusing Sir Albert of trying to impose republican status on a royal-loyal Sierra Leonean populace. Not surprising, the government was defeated at the polls, and before the country could lay claim as the first country in sub-Saharan Africa to vote out an unpopular regime, Brigadier Lansana, an 'ethno-client' of the Prime Minister (Kandeh, 1998) intervened by arresting both the Governor-General and the leader of the opposition, Mr. Siaka Stevens, who had been invited to form a new Government.

Brigadier Lansana himself was promptly removed from power within forty-eight hours by middle ranking officers who invited one of their numbers, Colonel Andrew Juxon-Smith, to head a military government, the National Reformation Council (NRC). This regime lasted a year before it was ousted by a group of non-commissioned officers calling themselves the Anti-corruption Revolutionary Movement (ACRM) who then invited Stevens from his self-imposed exile in neighboring Republic of Guinea to lead a civilian administration. Stevens wasted no time in forming a broadly based national government but it was not long before opposition members were sacked from the administration. The APC's base of support was largely in the Northern Province and Western region made up of Limbas (8.4%), Temne (29.8%), Creoles (2%) of the total population. Stevens, who was originally a minister in the SLPP government, but lost his seat as a result of election petition, resigned from the party largely because of the government's unwillingness to call election before independence in 1961, which presumably would have created an opportunity for Stevens' return to

Parliament. APC fostered the image of a radical party, and one determined to challenge not only the conservatism of the SLPP, particularly the latter's over-dependence on the traditional chiefs, but also its ethnic constellation of Southern domination. Contacts with Eastern Europe via trade unionists such as I. T. A. Wallace-Johnson and Stevens himself, helped Congress to foster an image of socialism. The party's symbol was the rising sun implanted on a bright red background. These Eastern contacts were used to distribute patronage to education hungry Sierra Leonean youth that wanted to pursue further education in these distant lands. Through these 'socialist scholarships', Congress was able to advance the façade of a radical political movement, but was also able to attract a large number of the youth of the country, particularly those from modest backgrounds who could not afford to attend schools in Europe or the United States.

In reality, politics under APC rule remained bifurcated as the north/west alliance continued to deny state power to the south/east alliance which formed the foundation of the SLPP. Indeed, Yusuf Bangura has argued that polities with 'two relatively equal and politicized ethnic groups constitut(ing) more than half of the population will inevitably be bifurcated. The most extreme of such bifurcation, he noted, is Rwanda and Burundi, which he called *two ethnic bi-polarity*, consisting of two [major] ethnic groups, Sierra Leone polity is defined as *multi-ethnic bi-polarity*' (Bangura, 1999, p. 29). While Sir Milton was able to hold together a grand coalition of Northern, Eastern and Southern elite against perceived threat from the politically impotent, but culturally hegemonic Creoles, Stevens despite his maternal link to the Southern Mende, was unable to carry the south in any free elections. In the eyes of the Southern people, Congress was too inextricably linked with northern domination. In his quest for state hegemony, Congress encountered several countervailing forces: the highly politicized Paramount chiefs; deep-seated opposition from the SLPP; opposition from the United Democratic Party formed in 1971 and led by John Karefa Smart, a former SLPP stalwart; and dissent from within Congress and the army. In one such alleged coup plot in which a number of individuals, including the Force Commander was killed by Stevens, a Corporal in the Republic of Sierra Leone Military Forces (RSLMF), was dismissed in the 1970s only for Foday Sankoh to emerge as leader of the rebel movement, the Revolutionary United Front. As part of his state hegemonic project, and more specifically in his attempt to control the diamond rich districts, Stevens set up a whole network of informal markets, the 'shadow state' (Reno, 1995; Zack-Williams, 1995). It is through this channel that patronage was distributed and denied. Those who were prepared to work with Congress were rewarded, and those who were critical of Congress were either removed from office or punished.

As with all state hegemonic projects, coercion was a major tool for political domination and control. It has been noted elsewhere that thuggery, political chicanery and political authoritarianism became the hallmark of Stevens' rule (Zack-Williams, 1999). By 1971 the national coalition had been transformed into a *de facto* one-party state. Stevens' dreaded deputy, S. I. Koroma, desensitized the population to thuggery and political chicanery in an effort to stay in power, and much of this violence was perpetrated against opposition forces in the Southern and Eastern Provinces, loci of much of the early rebel activities.

All Peoples' Congress (APC) Government, 1968–1985

APC rule of Sierra Leone can be divided into two distinct periods: 1968–1985 and 1985–1992. The consolidation of the one-party state; the decline of politics through generalized disenfranchisement; and the gradual collapse of the economy marked the first period. Elections were held in 1973, 1977, 1982 and 1986 all effectively within a one-party milieu, with opposition candidates being physically prevented from filing nomination papers or campaigning. In 1978, the one-party constitution was formally approved by Parliament as it was postulated as the 'antidote to ethnic politics and electoral violence' (Kandeh, 1998, p. 93), and a *sine qua non* for national integration and economic development. As Kandeh has pointed out, the elections of 1982 held under the new one-party constitution 'turned out to be more violent than previous elections' (Kandeh, 1998, p. 93). The process of the politics of decline and the decline of politics was accompanied by economic decline as shown in Table 7.1. The period was characterized by stagflation. As production fell, so did export earnings and government revenues, but the government's decision to continue printing money triggered off hyperinflation.

The causal factors for what was by now seen as a major crisis were both internal and external in dimension. By the late 1970s, foreign investments had dried up, except for the *rutile* and bauxite industries, and the country as we have seen above had become a net exporter of capital. The situation was exacerbated by the oil price increase after 1973, steady deterioration in the price of the country's major exports, as well as the fall in the unit value of the country's exports. Local infant industries were decimated through lack of access to foreign exchange, which was needed to purchase raw materials (Zack-Williams, 1985, pp. 43–58). In addition to these external factors, economic mismanagement, institutionalized corruption and lack of transparency led to policies that brought the nation to its knees. By the mid-1980s, it had become clear, even to the most casual observer of the Sierra Leone scene, that the country had entered a major crisis. Successive visits to the International Financial Institutions (IFI) for help tended to worsen the situation as the medicine (or conditionalities) almost killed the patient. While structural adjustment helped to down-size the bureaucracy by getting rid of ghost workers, it also impacted on vulnerable groups such as the urban/rural poor, children, women and the aged (Zack-Williams, 1995a). The constant atomization of state activities posed a threat to the legitimacy of the state. For many people (particularly the youth), the government did not affect their lives, and unemployment grew among school graduates fostering a sense of alienation.

Table 7.1   Average rate of growth in per capita income, 1970–1995 in Sierra Leone

1970–1975	1975–1980	1980–1985	1985–1995*
-0.9	-0.7	-5.6	-3.6

Note: *1985–1995 is average annual growth
Sources: UN National Accounts Statistics: Analysis of Main Aggregate, 1985; World Bank (1997), *World Development Report, 1997*, Oxford University Press: New York.

This alienation produced a restive urban and rural population, led by school children, students and some *declasse* members of society. The state responded through growing authoritarianism and the strengthening of the highly personalized rule of Stevens, as well as through corporatism. Stevens armed his personal army, the Internal Security Units, later called State Security Department (SSD), whom Sierra Leoneans promptly termed Siaka Stevens Dogs. The SSDs were armed to the teeth, whilst the national army of whom Stevens was very suspicious after several alleged attempted coups, was starved of ammunition. This policy of favoring the Cuban trained SSD at the expense of the army led to widespread concerns in the army. In order to hold down the lid on any potential rebellion, Stevens drew potential rivals—the Army Commander, the Inspector-General of the Police, leaders of organized labor and leaders of women's associations—into his cabinet. It was not long before concerns were being expressed about the under-representation of Mendes in Stevens' administration.

APC rule 1985–1992

In 1985, Stevens named Major-General Momoh, the Force commander as his chosen successor. This was a surprise to many observers who thought that his long serving Vice-President, S. I. Koroma would have succeeded him. Several reasons have been noted for Stevens' failure to appoint Koroma. Abdul K. Koroma has pointed to the poor health of the Vice-President following a road accident in 1977 to which Stevens constantly alluded; the election of Temne Tribal Headman in Freetown saw the Vice-President backing the losing candidate, whilst Stevens' choice, Chief Ahmed Multi-Kamara won the day. Abdul Koroma also argued that S. I. Koroma's 'open declaration of kinship with the Mandingo (minority ethnic group, see Table 7.2), and pledging a closer working relationship with them henceforth', was exploited by his detractors to undercut his standing among the Temnes nation-wide, who for many years had viewed him as their political figure (Koroma, 1996). It has also been argued that Stevens felt that his long-time lieutenant was too unpredictable to assume power, and it was widely believed that Stevens was concerned that Koroma might not only deviate from his policies, but might even put him on trial to account for his Stewardship (Zack-Williams, 1997a).

In the following analysis attempts will be made to demonstrate that the influence of *Ekutay* (a fraternal association) impacted on Stevens' choice of a successor. For example, it is widely believed that once Stevens informed Momoh of his decision, the latter went straight to consult with Chief Dura, a prominent member of this ethnic cabal who re-assured Momoh that the cunning Stevens was not setting a trap for him. Of the *Ekutay*, Kandeh has noted:

> The police chief, commander of the armed forces, and several prominent ministers were members of Momoh's ethnic cabal. Membership in this group became such a prized currency that even non-Limbas sought affiliation, if not membership (Kandeh, 1998, p. 110).

The peculiar character of Sierra Leonean politics can be seen against the backdrop of the country's demography. Table 7.2 points to the demographic predominance of the Mende and Temne ethnic groups who collectively account for just over 60% of the country's total population. No other ethnic group carries such numerical significance. The third largest ethnic group is the Limba which accounts for just under 8.5% of the population. The 'ethnic hegemony' which this group gained and maintained following the victory of the APC in 1967/68, could not have been sustained under a less skillful leader than Siaka Stevens, who was considered an 'ethnic Bonarparte' in the country's politics. Steven's exit from national politics, however, had a significantly negative impact on the confidence of the Limba elite, as his successor, Momoh proved to be a weak and phlegmatic leader.

Table 7.2   Demographic distribution and ethnic groups in Sierra Leone

Ethnic group	*Percent of total population*
Mende	30.9
Temne	29.8
Limba	8.4
Kono	4.8
Fula	4.0
Koranko	3.7
Kissi	3.5
Sherbro	3.4
Soso	3.1
Loko	3.0
Mandingo	2.3
Krio	2.0
Yalunka	0.7
Vai	0.3
Gola	0.2
Kro	0.2
Bassa	0.1

Source: Bangura, Yusuf, 'Strategic Policy Failure and State Fragmentation: Peace-keeping, Security and Democratization in Sierra Leone', Paper presented at the Bellagio Conference on Regional Peacekeeping, National Demilitarization and Development in Africa, organized by the Institute of Global Cultural Studies, Binghamton University and Rockefeller Foundation, Bellagio, Italy, June 7–11, 1999.

Momoh's candidature was quickly ratified by the Central Committee of Congress. And in a hurriedly convened congress, he was returned as leader of the party after being nominated by S. I. Koroma at the behest of Stevens. The country was split over the succession. The Temne and other non-Limba northerners felt aggrieved; those in the south were at best nonchalant, waiting to see who was going to be his deputy. Those who welcomed the new leader hoped that he would introduce military discipline in a corrupt and highly patrimonial bureaucracy. Sensing the unpopular nature of the Stevens' regime, the new President tried to distance himself from the former's policies, describing his government as a 'New Order' regime, based on 'constructive nationalism' (Kandeh, 1998, p. 110). He quickly reached an accommodation with the IMF and the World Bank for a standby credit as a *quid pro quo* for the usual conditionalities. In doing so, Momoh went the whole hog, thus unleashing social forces that he could not control.

Coincidentally, as the conditionalities began to have their social consequences on a vulnerable population, the demand for a return to multi-party democracy took momentum as both domestic social forces and donors pressed for an end to the monolithic state. This was strongly resisted by the party apparatchiks. E. T. Kamara, the bullish secretary-general of the APC warned those particularly from the southern and eastern provinces who were calling for political pluralism, that in a one-party state such demands were tantamount to treason, and as such, criticisms should stop forth with. At this point the activities of the *Ekutay* took momentum, as ethnic anxiety spread, and Momoh implored the citizenry in a broadcast to the 1990 annual convention of the association, to organize themselves into ethnic associations.

The manner of Mommoh's appointment and his personality posed major problems and threatened his leadership. As we have seen his appointment alienated the Temnes, the ethnic group from which rebel leader Foday Sankoh hailed; and though the Mende felt rehabilitated by the appointment of one of their number, Francis Minah, as Vice-President, yet several were suspicious of an 'ethnic up-start.' One such critic was Minah himself, a former SLPP stalwart who used the President's growing unpopularity to organize a putsch. Minah from Pujehun District, one of the first areas to be ravaged by the civil war, was tried and executed for being an accomplice to treason, a law which he himself had put on the statute book as Attorney-General under Stevens. Furthermore, Momoh needed to build up a political base within the party, which had been dominated by S. I. Koroma and his supporters. He was lacking in political skills and experience; after all, he had spent years as a 'Praetorian Guard', even as a member of Parliament to ensure that the lid was kept on disgruntled soldiers. He lacked the charisma and shrewdness of his patron. These structural weaknesses meant that he became more dependent on party-bureaucrats and the ethnic cabal, the *Ekutay*, locally known as the *Binkolo Mafia* (Kandeh, 1998, p. 94). These weaknesses soon became apparent, as structural adjustment took its toll, political and economic indiscipline mounted. Indeed, it was not long before the bad old days of Stevens' rule were now being celebrated as the golden era. The rising unpopularity of the phlegmatic new order President impelled him more systematically into the hands of the Binkolo Mafia, who were now responsible for major decisions including appointments in the parastatals and civil service.

The Ekutay: ethnic cabal and a search for ethnic worth

Despite the major role the *Ekutay* is alleged to have played in the decision-making process in Sierra Leone prior to the civil war, very little has been written about its origin, nature, membership and how it worked (Turay, 1990). The *Ekutay* was founded on Good Friday 1981 following an invitation from Stevens to important members of the Limba community to a meeting in Konadri Dee at Kafu Bullom Chiefdom. The invitees came from two important Limba voluntary associations: The Limba Tribal Union which was formed in 1945, and later changed to the Limba Friendly Society in 1960 after the formation of the APC; and the *Sibathae* formed in 1971. The *Sibathae* acted as a pressure group in order to mobilize support for the economic and social welfare of the kinsmen. At the end of the meeting, Stevens was elected as Chairman, C. A. Kamara-Taylor and Joseph Momoh were elected first and second vice chairmen respectively.

The aims of the *Ekutay* include the following: to promote the interests of the entire group in all sectors of Sierra Leone society; to promote the cultural, educational and economic advancement of the Limbas; foster unity and brotherhood among its kinsmen by materially supporting Limba farmers to enable them to be self-sufficient in food production; in recent years, in order to realize these goals, the association has shifted its activities toward more political functions, by seeking to protect and maintain Limba political figures in the country (Turay, 1990).

The structure of the Ekutay

The association has branches all over Sierra Leone, but its main national organs are the National Executive Council (NEC), consisting of the Chair, Vice Chair, Financial Secretary, General Secretary, Assistant General Secretary, Treasurer and Public Relations Officer. The NEC is responsible for liaising with the two other bodies, the Council of Chiefs and the Area Organizations as well as for organizing the annual conference, usually held at Binkolo Bombali District. At the annual conference, the Secretary General submits his report, and this is the locus of policy decisions, intra-ethnic conflicts resolution and cultural activities and networking. The plenary session is opened to all and Krio, the *lingua franca,* is the mode of communication whilst the conflict resolution and policy making sessions are restricted to members of the *gbagbani* secret society and here Limba is the language of communication.

The Council of Chiefs (COC) consists of nine Paramount Chiefs from the ethnic areas inhabited by Limbas. The role of the Chiefs is to mobilize support for the organization, in particular to ensure that candidates sympathetic to the Congress are returned in any elections. In this respect, Limba chiefs were only repeating the functions bestowed on chiefs in the south and east of the country by the SLPP. In fact, the chiefs remained the foci of political mobilization, as no attempt was made at involving the people in the political process. The COC is also responsible for mediating in conflicts between members, as well as organizing local initiation ceremonies.

The area organization is effectively responsible for regional and district branches. There is a Western Area Branch; two branches in Koinadugu District, situated in Kasonka Chiefdom and Warawara Bafodia Chiefdom; three branches in Bombali District situated in Sela Limba Kamakwie, Biriwa Limba Kamabia District, Kafe-Samiria-Mabonto and Kalansogoia-Bumbuna Tonkolili District. In 1990, as a sign of the growing importance of the association, the Secretariat was located at Charlotte Street, adjacent to the (APC) Party Headquarters (Turay, 1990).

The rise of the Ekutay and its prominence after 1984

The first point that we need to stress is that the utilization of ethnic cabal to mobilize support, allocate favors, and to safeguard power for elite entrenchment is not new in post-independence politics in Sierra Leone. Abner Cohen (1971, pp. 427–448), in a seminal paper, has analyzed how the Creoles utilized membership in free-masonry in the struggle to maintain dominance in the post-colonial bureaucracy and other professions. Cohen pointed to the proliferation both in the number of lodges established, as well as the number of people joining Masonic lodges, who were predominantly Creoles during the intensive struggle with the elite of the interior for control of the post-colonial bureaucracy. Free-masonry, like the Ekutay, is an exclusive institution whose *raison d'être* is the creation of brotherhood and to provide an opportunity for establishing informal links with powerful individuals. He contends that one often hears of gossip in Freetown society to the effect that all appointments and promotions in certain establishments are 'cooked in lodges.'

In a similar fashion, Sierra Leoneans complain that during the Momoh regime, the *Ekutay* became more powerful than both Parliament and the Cabinet, and that it was the source of most public appointments. Little wonder, then, that a member of the Association remarked:

> ...looking at the 'new order' regime of President Saidu Momoh and the composition of his Cabinet—President Joseph Saidu Momoh, Ben Kanu, E. T. Kamara, William S. Conteh, P. H. Kamara, Birch Conteh, Bambe Kamara, are all members of the association. The association has changed its role to a political power base, the retention of tribal privileges and the acquisition of social statuses...The *Ekutay* Friendly Association plays an advisory role towards the implementation of government policies and therefore it has become influential in Government circles (Turay, 1990, pp. 14–15).

The author drew attention to the large number of *Ekutay* members who in the late 1980s came to dominate the bureaucracy and the parastatals. These include the Armed Forces Commander, the Inspector General of Police, the head of the state-owned Sierra Leone Commercial Bank, the National Development Bank, the Chief Medical Officer, the Chair of the National Power Authority, the Chair of the National Authorization Office, as well as the Secretary General of the ruling party. Clearly, like the Creoles and

Masonic lodges, not all members of the Limba ethnic group are members of the *Ekutay*. Whilst only the relatively well off are able to join the organization, these tend to be patrons of those who are unable to join, but who hope to benefit via patronage. In the context of the Creoles, Cohen noted:

> Thus although only the relatively well to do are in lodges, these are in fact the patrons of those who are not members. Patronage involves both privileges and obligations and it is difficult for a man to remain in this position without keeping in close relationship with other patrons who occupy strategic positions in the society (Cohen, 1971, p. 437).

There are several reasons for the rise of the *Ekutay* after 1981. Firstly, as we have seen, at this time the economy had started showing increasing signs of over-heating stemming from inflationary pressures from the extravagant spending for the OAU Heads of state conference, and the subsequent deflationary effects of the IFI inspired structural adjustment policies. The *Ekutay* should be seen as an attempt by Stevens to extend his 'shadow state,' as well as an act of state corporatism under the exigencies of IFI conditionalities (Nyang'oro and Shaw, 1989). Stevens was concerned that his northern ethnic allies in particular, the Temnes, could not be easily counted upon for support, and the Creoles were becoming even more critical. Thus, the critical maxim circulated in Freetown in the wake of the OAU conference: 'OAU for you IOU for me.' It should also be noted that following the declaration of a one-party system of Government in 1978 in the wake of widespread student rebellion, Stevens had decided to call a 'candidate-choice election' for 1982 (Kandeh, 1998). The formation of the *Ekutay* was an attempt by Stevens to consolidate the base of his support, and to provide a carrot for those would be supporters, who might be tempted to join the already repressed opposition.

A second reason for the retort to the ethnic cabal strategy on the part of the Sierra Leonean political elite has to do with the nature of politics in Sierra Leone. As we have noted earlier, post-colonial politics in Sierra Leone has been characterized as highly bi-polar, whereby all freely held elections (1967 and 1996) in the country have tended to produce a similar result in terms of ethno-regional affiliation. The bi-polarity, it is argued, is a functional consequence of the ethnic structure of the country as noted in Table 7.2, with the two largest groups, the Mende (located in the east and south) and Temne (in the north) accounting for 60% of the population.

Apart from the Limba who account for 8.4% of the population, no other groups exceeds 4%, thus this type of *multi-ethnic bipolarity* tends to produce bifurcated electoral outcomes, around one of the two dominant ethnic groups, but with no single ethnic group being capable of dominating politics. In this regard Bangura observed:

> This pattern of ethnic distribution in which the two largest groups vastly outnumber other groups in their respective regions may explain why most groups in the South coalesce around the Mende; whereas those in the North revolve around the Temne, although the Limba, especially under Momoh's presidency (a Limba) have made efforts to change this dynamic (Bangura, 1999, p. 29).

He argued that in diffuse multi-polarity, politics is unlikely to be dominated by ethnicity, as politics is likely to be localized. Thus, he noted that this endemic split in the ranks of the national political elite has posed a major threat to democracy, as well as being an obstacle to sustainable peace in the country, as many leaders and elite supporters failed to defend the democratically elected Government of Ahmed Tejan Kabba which was ousted by the AFRC in May 1997. Bangura warned that if Sierra Leone should avoid the excesses of ethnic bi-polarism, then, the politics of winner takes all is to be abandoned in favor of an institutionalized national unity government, whereby individuals from opposition parties could be invited in any future governments. However, looking at the Senegalese experience of co-opting leaders, Richard Joseph has warned that we need to distinguish between 'power sharing' and 'resource sharing' since control of the major instruments of government tends to reside with the incumbent party (Joseph, 1998).

The third explanation could be found in the socio-political position of the Limba ethnic group within Sierra Leone. As we have seen, the Limbas constitute a highly fragmented group with up to twelve dialects and account for only 8.4% of the total Sierra Leone population. They constitute one of the least mobile groups in the country, with a relatively low incidence of Islamization and Christianity prior to independence in 1961 (Moseley, 1987). For example, in 1881 only 200 Limbas were counted in Freetown, and this figure rose to only 1,600 in 1911 during the period of Limba consciousness (Turay, 1990). Migration was still largely confined to the young, single males, who continuously returned to their villages regularly thus inviting an undeserved reputation as unreliable workers. In their new environments as late comers to wage labor and to Western education, they worked as palm wine *tappers*, distillers of illicit gin (*Omole*), and street potering (*Worok*). Additionally, there were involved in casual jobs such as in the docks and building sites, petty trade (mainly women and girls), as unskilled workers in the public Works and Sanitary Departments, and as domestic workers to wealthy families. Prior to 1950s, great strides were made by both religious groups to incorporate Limbas into their flocks. Nonetheless, the disadvantaged position of the Limbas continued and as late as 1979, two-thirds of Limba household heads had never attended school, a proportion rising to 90% for those over 50 years old (Moseley, 1987, p. 130). The number of Limba migrants in the capital, however, rose to 40,000, indicating a subjective sense of 'ethnic confidence' with the Government of the APC.

Siaka Stevens (1984) in his autobiography points to the contempt in which other ethnic groups in the country held the Limbas: being associated with boisterousness, dirty work, and 'bush.' Other ethnic groups always questioned, as such, the 'ethnic worth' of the Limbas. Thus the crisis of the early 1980s, must have triggered off a collective paranoia among the Limba elite, as they felt that their grip on power was being eroded, even before (as we have noted above) their youth had been invested with social capital. From this point of view, the *Ekutay* may be seen as 'collective anxiety reaction' in order to create breathing space for ethnic project completion, by improving the 'relative group worth' and re-enforcing collective self-esteem of the ethnic group. Sierra Leone with its relatively dispersed ethnic system presents a situation in which no single group could dominate the center. For any group to rule, it needs the co-operation of others adjacent or distant. As Horowwitz observed: 'dispersed ethnic system abets interethnic co-operation, while the structure of centralized ethnic system impedes it' (Horowitz, 1985, p. 39). For this reason, the *Ekutay* was not totally exclusive.

The *Ekutay* could be seen as an attempt by one group that has captured the state, but is reluctant to concede power. Earlier on, we have noted how the SLPP tried to cling to power by inviting Brigadier Lansana to foil a peaceful transition in 1967. In order to make the association more acceptable to other ethnic groups, at least the formal setting of the association is opened to non-members, and proceedings are conducted in Krio, the *lingua franca*. In a speech at the 1990 convention in Binkolo, President Momoh urged his countrymen to form their own cultural and friendly associations. The neighboring Kuranko elite took up the challenge by establishing the *Feronsola*.

Finally, the prominence of *Ekutay* members in major decision-making positions cannot be disconnected from the nature of the Momoh regime. We have seen that he inherited an economy in crisis, the corrective measures impelled by IMF conditionalities exposed vulnerable groups to poverty, thereby unleashing uncontrollable social forces. This was one reason why unlike Momoh, Stevens was not prepared to go all the way with IFI conditionalities. Furthermore, as we have seen, Momoh was not a seasoned politician. Though he had spent ten years in Stevens' cabinet, this was meant for him to keep the army loyal to the President.

The manner of his appointment to the Presidency meant that he had many enemies within the party, and therefore to survive, he had to placate several party apparatchiks. Since he did not have a strong political base within the party, Momoh's indecisiveness had to give in to the powerful young men who now constituted the *Ekutay*.

Ekutay and the civil war

Whilst several commentators have pointed to the external influence in the civil war in Sierra Leone (Richards, 1996), most point to the internal imperatives which led to the emergence of the RUF. For example, the issue of youth crisis is central to the analysis of some scholars (Abdullah, 1997, pp. 45–76). The collapse of the economy, the institutionalization of corruption and political authoritarianism provided fertile recruiting grounds for the RUF. Whilst it is true that no one ethnic group has been singled out for RUF odium of a 'lottery for life' (Richards and Fithen, 1999, p. 6), yet it is clear that there is an 'anti-ethnic' dimension to the war. Foday Sankoh, the leader, is a northern Temne, whose disgruntlement with the (Limba dominated) APC system stemmed from seven years of service in the RSLMF in which he was repeatedly passed over for promotion on spurious, clientelist grounds. When the movement was launched, Sankoh's aim was to remove the APC from power, and in no time an alliance was forged with the most alienated ethnic and social sectors in society—the chronically rootless young Sierra Leoneans. In order to foster unity, the movement decreed Krio as the language of communication.

The gradual 'sobelisation' (a concept analogous with looting and pillaging of property and diamonds) of the highly politicized army meant that the government could not rely upon its support to defeat the rebels (Zack-Williams, 1997a, 1999). After experimenting with external intervention fores such as the British Army Gurkhas, whose commanding officer was killed by the rebels, and the South African based Executive

Outcomes (EO), the government soon disbanded its army in the height of the civil war (Richards and Fithen, 1996) and became dependent on peacekeeping forces provided by the Economic Community of West African States Monitoring Group (ECOMOG) led by regional power Nigeria, and ethnic hunters-turned fighters such as the *Kamajors*, the *Kapras* and the *Tamaboros*. Whilst ECOMOG troops were able to both defend the capital and to push the AFRC/RUF coalition out of the capital, defense of the provincial towns after the departure of EO was left to the various ethnic hunters now renamed Civil Defense Forces (CDF). Each CDF defended its area of *indigenism*: the most renowned were the *Kamajors* who together with the EO were able to attack areas within the Gola Forest controlled by RUF, including their base camp in Zogoda, and defending Bo, the country's second biggest city from rebel incursions.

Conclusion

In this chapter, I have argued that ethnicity and ethnic cabals are not a new phenomena in Sierra Leone politics. As in other African polities, leaders manipulate ethnicity even though officially they claim a commitment to overcome it (Ottaway, 1999). Attention was drawn to how ethnic consciousness became a major factor in the period of competitive politics of de-colonization, in the struggle between the Creole and the Protectorate elite. Like the Masonic lodges utilized by the Creole elite to entrench their position within the bureaucracy, at a time of competitive political activities, so the Limba elite in the late-post-colonial period tried to set up the *Ekutay* to achieve similar goals. The call for democratic pluralism, as well as perceived ethnic challenges within the ruling party, created a sense of ethnic anxiety among this faction of the elite. As we have seen from Cohen's analysis, ethnic cabals tend to have greater meanings in periods of intense competition for control of the state. The ethnic structure alone could not account for the rise of the association. The deteriorating economic conditions after 1981, leading to anxiety reaction by the Limba elite also furthered the process. The position occupied by this ethnic group, within the Sierra Leonean social structure helped to compound 'anxiety reaction.' Momoh's precarious hold on state power meant that those who were entrenched within the party had a greater say in decision making because of greater dependence on APC apparatchiks. These factors surrounding the rise of the *Ekutay* were all determinants, which led to the rise of the RUF and the civil war in that country.

Whilst it could be argued that the RUF did not politicize ethnicity in its war against the system and the people, yet the rise of the AFRC consisting of the rump of the former Sierra Leone army was a direct response to the rise of the Kamajors which were seen by the Limba dominated junta as the new Praetorian Guards of the Tejan Kabba civilian administration (Zack-Williams, 1997, pp. 373–380). It was this faction of the 'peoples army' which gained universal notoriety when they kidnapped a group of United Nations peacekeepers, including five British military officers in August 1999.

References

Abdulllah, I. (1997), 'Bush Path to Destruction: The Origin and Character of the Revolutionary United Front (RUF/SL)', *The Journal of Modern African Studies*, Vol. 36, No. 2, pp. 203–235.

Bangura, Y. (1999), 'Strategic Policy Failure and State Fragmentation: Peacekeeping, Security and Democratization in Sierra Leone', A paper presented at the Bellagio Conference on Regional Peacekeeping, National Demilitarization and Development in Africa, Institute of Global Cultural Studies, Birmingham University, England.

Campbell, A. (1997), 'Ethical Ethnicity', *Journal of Modern African Studies*, Vol. 35, No. 1, pp. 53–79.

Cartwright, J. R. (1970), *Politics in Sierra Leone 1947–67*, University of Toronto Press: Toronto.

Cartwright, J. R. (1978), *Political Leadership in Sierra Leone*, Croom Helm Publishers: London.

Cohen, A. (1971), 'The Politics of Ritual Secrecy', *MAN*, No. 6, pp. 427–448.

Collier, G. B. (1970), *Sierra Leone: An Experiment in Democracy*, New York University Press: New York.

Diamond, L. (1987), 'Ethnicity and Ethnic Conflict', *Journal of Modern African Studies*, Vol. 25, No. 1, pp. 117–128.

Hayward, F. M. (1972), 'The Development of a Radical Political Organization in the Bush: A Case Study in Sierra Leone', *Canadian Journal of African Studies*, Vol. VI, No. 1, pp. 1–28.

Horowitz, D. L. (1985), *Ethnic Groups in Conflict*, University of California Press: Berkeley, CA.

Joseph, R. A. (ed.) (1998), *State, Conflict and Democracy in Africa*, Lynne Rienner Publishers: Boulder, CO.

Kandeh, J. D. (1998), 'Transition Without Rupture: Sierra Leone's Transfer Election of 1996', *African Studies Review*, Vol. 41, No. 2, pp. 91–111.

Kandeh, J. D. (1992), 'Politicization of Ethnic Identities in Sierra Leone', *African Studies Review*, Vol. 35, No. 1, pp. 81–99.

Koroma, A. K. (1996), *Sierra Leone: The Agony of A Nation*, Andromed Publications: Freetown, Sierra Leone.

Mafeje, A. (1971), 'The Ideology of Tribalism', *Journal of Modern African Studies*, Vol. 9, No. 2, pp. 263–281.
Moseley, K. P. (1987), 'The Safroko Limba Community in Freetown: An Interim Report', *Sierra Leone Studies at Birmingham, 1985*, Center for African Studies, University of Birmingham, England.
Nyango'oro, J. E. and Shaw, T. M. (eds.) (1989), *Corporatism in Africa: Comparative Analysis and Practice*, Westview Press: Boulder: CO.
Ottaway, M. (1998), 'Ethnic Politics in Africa: Change and Continuity', in Joseph, R. A. (ed.), *State, Conflict and Democracy in Africa*, Lynne Rienner: Boulder, CO.
Reno, W. (1995), *Corruption and State Politics in Sierra Leone*, Cambridge University Press: Cambridge.
Richards, P. (1996), *Fighting for the Rain Forest: War, Youth and Resources in Sierra Leone*, James Currey and Heinemann: Oxford.
Richards, P. (1999), 'Post-modern Warfare in Sierra Leone: Reasserting the Social in Global-Local Construction of Violence', Mimeo.
Sawi, F. M. B. (1972), *The SLPMB: 1949–67*, M.Sc. Thesis, University of Birmingham, England.
Stevens, S. (1984), *What Life Has Taught Me*, Kensal Press: Buckinghamshire, UK.
Thompson, B. (1997), *The Constitutional History and Law of Sierra Leone 1961–1995*, University Press of America: New York.
Turay, J. B. S. (1990), 'Ekutay Friendly Association and the Promotion of Limba Consciousness', *Manuscript*, Fourah Bay College, University of Sierra Leone.
Wyse, A. (1989), *The Krio of Sierra Leone: An Interpretive History*, C. Hurst and Company: London.
Zack-Williams, A. B. (1985), 'Comments on the Manufacturing Sector in Sierra Leone', *Africa Development*, Vol. 10, No. 4, pp. 43–58.
Zack-Williams, A. B. (1990), 'Sierra Leone: Crisis and Despair', *Review of African Political Economy*, No. 49, pp. 22–33.
Zack-Williams, A. B. (1995a), 'Crisis and Structural Adjustment in Sierra Leone: Implication for Women', in Emeagwali, G. T. (ed.), *Women Pay the Price: Structural Adjustment in Africa and the Caribbean*, Africa World Press: Trenton, NJ.
Zack-Williams, A. B. (1995b), *Tributors, Supporters and Merchant Capital in Sierra Leone: Mining and Underdevelopment in Sierra Leone*, Gower-Avebury Press: Aldershot, UK.
Zack-Williams, A. B. (1997a), 'Kamajors, "Sobel" and the Militariat: Civil Society and the Return of the Military in Sierra Leonean Politics', *Review of African Political Economy*, Vol. 24, No. 73, pp. 373–380.
Zack-Williams, A. B. (1997b), 'Labor, Structural Adjustment, and Democracy in Sierra Leone and Ghana', in Siddiqui, R. A. (ed.), *Sub-Saharan Africa in the 1990s: Challenges to Democracy and Development*, Praeger Publishers: Westport, CT.
Zack-Williams, A. B. (1999), 'Sierra Leone: The Political Economy of Civil War 1991–1998', *Third World Quarterly*, Vol. 20, No. 1, pp. 143–162.

8 The Limits and Possibilities of Conflict-Reduction Strategies in Africa's Polyethnic States*

JOHN BOYE EJOBOWAH

Introduction

One of the most pressing problems as the world enters the 21st century is how to minimize intrastate ethnic conflicts. Although there was the general expectation that the end of the Cold War might usher in a 'New World Order' of peace and stability, what emerged were ferocious domestic conflicts that promised more misery than the standard interstate confrontations of the post-World War II era. Even Europe was not spared what some had erroneously regarded to be a pre-modern sludge, as the 'ethnic cleansing' vocabulary was introduced into political discourse by Yugoslavia through its acts of mass expulsion and elimination of non-Serbian groups (Christie, 1998, p. 1).

In Africa, communal conflicts were the driving force behind the spectacle of state collapse in Burundi, Rwanda, Somalia, Zaire, and, to some extent, Liberia and Sierra Leone. They surely brought Nigeria to the brink of collapse in 1994. In South Africa, where the state has robust institutions, the Zulu factor posed a grave threat to the 1990–1993 democratic transformation (Johnston, 1998, p. 129). Timothy Sisk and Andrew Reynolds (1998, p. 1) have noted that between 1992 and 1994, more than twenty sub-Saharan countries experienced democratic transitions; however, several have suffered reversals. Angola, Sierra-Leone, Burundi, Niger, The Gambia, and Uganda were failed cases. Eritrea is at war with Ethiopia while Zimbabwe is limping under the authoritarian rule of Robert Gabriel Mugabe. Indeed, the situation is similar to what obtained in the early years of independence when secessionist movements emerged in eighteen out of fifty two states (Young, 1993, p. 29). The difference is that, in the past, the rival superpowers were as opposed to political recognition of ethnicity as was the dominant social science scholarship of the period. This encouraged states to adopt hegemonic controls that involved outright suppression of ethnic claims or co-optation of key elites of dissenting groups, if the former proved too costly or ineffective.

In contemporary times, the political environment that nurtured this approach to conflict reduction no longer exists: the Cold War is dead, and the forces of capitalism have vanquished socialism. Liberal democracy is marching through the world and African states have been forced (by internal and external pressures) to open up political spaces for self-expression. These developments required an approach to conflict reduction different from the state's hegemonic controls of the first three decades of independence. However, in most cases, democratization of the political landscape proceeded without accommodative arrangements freely negotiated by group elites. Where there were peace agreements, e.g., Abuja for Sierra Leone and Bicesse for Angola, negotiations were either limited to individuals who were actually waging wars or their outcome could not be implemented.[1] The failure to negotiate social compacts that specified terms of political union that would be reasonably just and democratic denied the second wave of independence of its foundational stability.

In the literature on African politics, we increasingly read about arguments that multiparty democracy opened spaces for political mobilization of differences that blew into violent conflicts. For example, Harvey Glickman (1995, pp. i–ii; 1997, p. 37) notes that 'ethnic and sectional conflicts, hidden and forcibly repressed by African regimes, wells up as politics becomes freer, and as competitive elections occur.' Thus, the solution for Africa is viewed in terms of conflict resolution, not democracy (Lemarchand, 1997, p. 95). The former appears to be separated from, and not regarded as a process in the design of, the latter. This essay does not share that view. Rather than blaming and turning away from democracy for not mitigating political instability in a number of African states, this work regards its institution as involving the negotiation of *ex ante* agreements on the accommodation of groups. Thus, this chapter will attempt to explore ethnic conflict reduction within the context of democracy. It will examine the limitations of selected strategies for conflict reduction and analyze the possibilities that exist for mollifying ethnic clashes within the framework of scholarly works. To achieve these objectives, the chapter will critically examine prescriptive arguments by some empirical theorists for the successful operation of democracy. The writers are Arthur Lewis, Eric Nordlinger, Arend Lijphart and Donald Horowitz. But what is democracy and why has it 'failed' in many multiethnic states?

Liberal democracy and its limitations

Democracy is a word that is commonly used today. It is often used to mean periodic election and removal or retention of government by the people, and is also used to mean multiparty competition for power. Democracy reflects all these dimensions. Indeed, following Robert Dahl (1971, pp. 2–3), I take it to mean a political system in which government is responsive to the preferences of its citizens, considered as political equals. Theoretically, a government of one man/woman could be responsive even if not elected by the governed, but this will not pass for democracy. For a system to be democratic, citizens must have the right to contest for government and to elect and cashier public officials. It is these constraints that make government responsive to the preferences of the citizens.

Until recently, democracy was practiced in purely formal liberal terms. The state was regarded as a neutral turf and its legislation dissociated from the substantive good of groups and their views about how life should be lived (Rawls, 1993, 1971). Individuals were regarded as the source of moral claims and, for this reason, were treated as bearers of equal rights. Consequently, the political arena was viewed as a market place where everyone had equal opportunity to compete in accordance with universal rules formally inscribed in constitutional texts. Thus, 'liberal democracy' conducted the business of politics with reference to constitutional rules that were believed to be impartial, dispassionate and governed everyone equally (Taylor, 1994, pp. 56–58). Its theory assumed ethnic homogeneity, as well evidenced in the works of John Locke, Jean Jacque Rousseau, John Stuart Mill, and John Rawls. One of its greatest promises was that, at the political market place, the supposedly impartial rules would ensure the emergence of a free, representative and responsive government. Empirically, this proved to be problematic in ethnically plural states as the supposedly impartial rules represented the interest of dominant ethnic groups. In most states, this resulted in political disorders as public rules conflicted with some ethnic and cultural norms.

The form of democracy that African countries inherited at independence from their former colonial rulers was supposed to have been representative of the model described above. In almost all the newly independent countries, however, the ethnic background of electors influenced their choice of political representatives. In some countries, ethnic communities trained the first generation of political leaders so that they would have their own share of elites that would inherit power from the departing colonial rulers. They taxed themselves to establish their own secondary schools and to send their most promising sons and daughters to prestigious European universities with the aim of having their members in power. Consequently, governments that emerged bore the identity of, and were responsive to, groups that brought them into office. Public law and policy were made to the advantage of the dominant groups and to the disadvantage of others. Thus, democracy displayed a double face: universal in its claims to justice but exclusionary in practice. The failure of liberal democracy to generate inclusive political regimes and the resultant enduring violent conflicts have prompted political scientists to conduct empirical inquiries with a view to deriving constitutional measures that would nurture democracy. Their studies suggest that ethnically plural states have to revise the Anglo-American model of democracy to make for political inclusion. They argue that the surest way of fostering injustice and unrest in such states is to replicate the proceduralist model that emphasizes majoritarian rule (Lijphart, 1995, p. 221; Horowitz, 1991, p. 164; Lewis, 1965, p. 71).

Beside the empirical investigations, there are philosophical inquiries into ways of revising liberal theory to take account of ethnic differences. This is also in response to conflicts generated in the Occident by the strains and tensions of liberal democracy and the recognition that there are over 5,000 ethnic groups that have to coexist in the 184 independent states of the world (Kymlicka, 1995, p. 1). The philosophical revision of liberal principles will not receive attention here; instead, the focus is on empirical arguments that prescribe democratic arrangements for conflict-reduction.

Strategies for conflict reduction

It was in 1965 that Sir Arthur Lewis, the Nobel Prize winning economist, first made a scholarly analysis and recommendation of power sharing as a democratic solution to the politics of exclusion and violence in West Africa. After a careful study of politics in the region, Lewis came up with the view that ethnic pluralism was not the cause of democratic failures; rather, the political institutions and philosophies inherited from Europe were the source. He thought that liberal democracy could be made to work if three measures were adopted to reform it.

The measures are: a federal constitution that permits different ethnic regions to look after their own affairs and prevent richer areas from contributing too heavily to subsidize the rest of the country; proportional representation of groups in the legislature; a coalition government in which parties are represented in proportion to their electoral performance if they meet a certain percentage threshold, say 20 percent, of the total vote (Lewis, 1965, pp. 51–55, 66, 73–74 and 79–83). These measures boil down to 'consociationalism.'

'Consociation' is about formal accommodative institutions negotiated by group elites. Its principles were derived from the features of political arrangements invented and put in place by political elites in Austria, Belgium, Netherlands, Switzerland, Lebanon and Malaysia at various periods in the 20th century, to bring intense conflict under control. Eric Nordlinger, who produced a monograph on consociational theory in 1972, used the general characteristics of the arrangements in these countries to formulate six conflict reduction measures for deeply divided societies. The measures are: 'stable governing coalition between . . . the major conflict organisations'; the 'principle of proportionality' whereby offices are distributed according to the relative size of 'segments'; mutual veto, which requires government decisions to be agreed upon by all 'conflict organisations'; 'depoliticization' whereby conflicting groups agree not to involve government in policy areas that might touch on segment's values; 'compromise,' which entails mutual adjustment of interests; and, 'concession' by a stronger to a weaker group (Nordlinger, 1972, pp. 21–29).

Nordlinger excluded federalism for a number of reasons; the most important was that the drawing of internal boundaries would create new minorities with ties to another group that has been separated. Worse still, federalism with its grant of internal self-determination might promote secession and civil wars (Nordlinger, 1972, pp. 31–32). For these reasons, he regarded it as contributing to conflict exacerbation. He also regarded the then conventional strategies like nation-building and spatial isolation of conflict-groups as ineffectual and counter productive.

Arend Lijphart, one of the earliest and perhaps most famous consociational writers, has presented four defining characteristics of the model that overlap with the ones listed above. Like Nordlinger, he derived them from techniques used by the already mentioned European countries. The defining features are: the consensus principle by which executive power is shared by all parties in a grand coalition; mutual veto in decision making; proportionality principle in the distribution of offices and allocation of resources; and segmental autonomy expressed through federal arrangement (Lijphart, 1984, pp. 23–24, 1977, pp. 25–44). In recent times, Lijphart has prioritized the features by listing the sharing of executive power as the first and group autonomy as the second most important attributes. He refers to these two as the 'primary characteristics' of consociational democracy. Proportionality and mutual veto are listed as third and fourth respectively, and are referred to as 'secondary characteristics' (Lijphart, 1999, pp. 3–4).

Donald Horowitz, one of the world's foremost experts on conflict reduction, shares the consociationalists' argument that multiethnic co-operation is what deeply divided societies need, but disagrees with the means to it. He thinks the measures are incapable of achieving the purpose for which they are prescribed (Horowitz, 1998, pp. 6–10; 1985, pp. 571–575). Consequently, he prescribes a different set of strategy, which consists of electoral laws and territorial institutions that induce politicians and their followers to co-operate across group lines. The territorial institution is federalism that fragment groups in political sub-units while the electoral institution is alternative voting or plurality *plus* distribution, which are majoritarian systems. With the fragmentation of groups in federal units, the electoral system will reward politicians and parties with power, if they take account of the interest of voters from groups other than theirs (Horowitz, 1998, pp. 9–18; 1991, chapter 5).[2] He regards the arrangement as having internal incentives to harness selfish calculations for interethnic co-operation. Therefore, there will be no need for minority rights as they would be superfluous.

When the prescriptions of Nordlinger, Lijphart, and Horowitz are unpacked, we have the following emerging as the main strategies for conflict reduction. First are consociational arrangements that carefully share power among group elites. The main elements are:

- a grand coalition government by which all parties share executive power;
- group autonomy through federal arrangements.
- an electoral system that makes for proportional representation of groups; and

- mutual veto.

All the writers mentioned above prescribe these components of consociationalism, the exception is Horowitz who views them to be inadequate.

Second main strategy is electoral system. The inventories of measures for conflict reduction have as their common goal the politics of interethnic moderation and conciliation, the difference is the means, and it is here that the electoral system receives a lot of emphasis. Consociationlists recommend Proportional Representation (PR) system as a way of avoiding minority exclusion. On the other hand, Horowitz prescribes the plurality *plus* distribution or alternative voting methods that are majoritarian, but could produce politics of moderation in divided societies. They work by requiring parties to reach across to groups to obtain electoral support. Thus, politicians have to reach out and accommodate not because they are altruistic, but because their self-interests require that they do so. As bridges are built, so group interests get intertwined overtime to yield conciliatory institutions (Hortowitz, 1991, p. 150; 1998, p. 10). This incentive approach, according to Horowitz, must apply to all elected officials for it to be effective.

Third main strategy is the construction of federal sub-units to devolve power to groups that would otherwise not have shared in it. While the arrangement has the advantage of granting internal self-government to groups, Horowitz views it as a structural component of an electoral incentive package for which he considers legislative constituencies also important. It is when the sub-units and constituencies are self-governing that ethnic based parties can be induced to reach out to units other than theirs as they compete for control of the central government. To this end, the boundaries need not enclose homogenous groups, for the incentive to accommodate could thaw frozen majorities and minorities (Horowitz, 1991, pp. 99–100 and 216–213).

Possibilities of conflict reduction: an overview

Regardless of the differences between the consociationalists and Horowitz, it would be necessary to examine the conditions required for each of the two sets of strategies to work, given the variation among African states in the number and forms of group configuration, their pattern of interaction, and demand types. I begin with the consociational prescriptions.

The consociational package

The package presented by Lijphart, Nordlinger and Lewis appears to be a coherent one whose modules fit nicely together. At what could be regarded as the pillar of the package is spatial separation of groups in a federal arrangement that keeps each within its own bounds. This foundational module calls in another module: the electoral system of PR that allows ample scope for group representation in the national legislature. This in turn calls in a coalition government of parties representing various groups. Then, veto powers. So, it works as a complete system, and might not be efficacious if one or two modules are adopted.

What would be required for the system to work successfully? A precondition that arises is the existence of recognizable and determinate groups that would be granted regional/state status within a federal arrangement. These actors, organized in political parties, would negotiate a coalition government at the center. A grand coalition, which Lijphart considers to be the crown jewel of the arrangement, is difficult to form and sustain if group elites are either factionalized or engaged in internal competition, as is often the situation. It is more difficult to bring into being if there are indeterminate or countless ethnic and sectional groups, as is the case in countries like Uganda, Zaire, and Nigeria. Lijphart made the point when he noted that: 'Actually, a society with relatively few segments, say three or four, constitutes a more favorable base for consociational democracy than one with a relatively many segments, and a much more favorable base than a fractionalized society' (Lijphart, 1977, p. 56). So where there are countless politically active groups, some are sure to be left out; and where all are thought to have been sufficiently included, the indeterminacy of some would result in the emergence of new and excluded segments that preclude the coalition from being grand.

Take the case of Zaire that has about 250 ethnic groups, which some scholars have grouped into 23 on grounds of similarity in language, culture and geographic contiguity (Kimenyi, 1997, p. 24). A coalition of parties representing 23 groups might see the emergence of new politically conscious groups from within, protesting exclusion from the arrangement. Or, the autonomy and legitimacy of leaders of any of the 23 groups could be undermined by the emergence of rival subgroup leaders opposed to compromises. The latter phenomenon is known as outflanking. Thus, elites of a relevant ethnic community making compromises are likely to be frustrated by rival elites emerging from the flanks to repudiate them on ground that they do not represent the various subgroups within, or to denounce them as traitors. In a multiethnic society in which the various collectivities are politically active, grand coalition is difficult if not impossible because of conflicting interests. It is not surprising that no single state in Africa has ever had it. In fact, consociation has not worked anywhere except in Switzerland and Belgium where its characteristics were extracted from (Zartman, 1998, p. 328). South Africa's transitional constitution that is claimed to have followed very closely to Lijphart's reasoning did not work as a grand coalition. Three years into the working of the government of national unity, the National Party exited, preferring to work from outside the government as a vibrant opposition.

Secondly, consociational system presumes a society whose conflict groups accept some basis for unity other than the immediate gains to be derived from coalition agreement. Lijphart (1977, p. 82) made an oblique reference to this when he spoke of overarching loyalties moderating the intensity of cleavages. Where loyalties that transcend ethnicity do not exist or are very weak, as is the case in most deeply divided societies, a multiethnic coalition, assuming it were possible for one to come into being, would require concessions as argued by Nordlinger. Mutually conflicting claims and interests would have to be adjusted and softened, but with the expectation that greater benefits would be derived from the resultant arrangement. Eventually, when a party feels that its expected benefits are not coming early enough or do not outweigh what it has traded, it would consider itself a loser for having given up too much. Recrimination rents the air and the coalition breaks down if there are no means for rectifying their weak position. There are numerous examples of such collapses and two would be cited here. In Nigeria, a second republic governing coalition formed by the Hausa-Fulani controlled National Party of Nigeria (NPN) and the Ibo dominated National Peoples Party (NPP) fell apart when the latter realized that its share of contracts and other forms of patronage were not coming as expected. In Malaysia, a coalition of Malay, Chinese and Indian parties during independence was unsettled because of a later realization by the Malay party that its expectation of economic advancement for Malays, in return for which Chinese had been given citizenship status, did not materialize.

Third, and related to what has just been noted, consociationalism requires that ethnic elites be committed to power sharing without reservation. The commitment is rooted in the notion that leaders of a particular group cannot govern in exclusion or impose hegemonic controls without risking severe conflict. It is a commitment that is driven by self-interest: the interest to govern. If elites of one group want to rule the entire country, they have to reach across ethnic fault-lines, take moderate position on issues, and accommodate others. A multiethnic coalition becomes impossible the moment rival group-elites believe they can govern alone. For example, in Uganda the 1962-1964 coalition between the Milton Obote led Uganda Peoples Congress (UPC) and the Kabakka Yekka (KY) was formed because the UPC could not govern alone. When Obote appointed the Kabaka of Buganda as president, he was praised as a moderate who could reach across deep divides. However, soon after his party got enough defectors from KY legislators to command majority in the national assembly, it felt confident that it could govern by itself. Thereafter the coalition suffered death.

Fourth, and arising from the third, is that consociationalism requires societies that are disposed to norms of compromise. Those that have history of intense ethnic hatred, conflict and genocide may not harbor it. Mutual distrust and thirst for revenge would make it unappetizing. Take the case of Burundi where Hutu insurrection in 1965, 1972 and 1988 led to catastrophic Tutsi reprisals. The 1965 abortive Hutu coup brought forth retribution that saw the elimination of their elites in the military during the rest of the decade, while the genocide that followed the 1972 insurrection was with the purpose of destroying their present and future civilian elites, including primary school children (Lemarchand, 1993, 164). The violent mode of procedure that has typified the county's political life is uninviting to politics of mutual bargaining, compromise and accommodation. Although an inclusive constitutional arrangement was adopted in 1993, Tutsi soldiers sacked the broad-based democratic government that emerged from it, and President Melchoir Ndadaye (the first Hutu president in Burundi) was executed (Human Rights Watch, 1998, pp. 15-17; Evans, 1977, pp. 26-27). This in turn elicited several rounds of interethnic killings and a huge outflow of Hutus to Rwanda. The next cycle of violence that pitched Tutsi militias against Hutu gangs following the genocide in Rwanda, would validate Lemarchand's (1993) argument that, where 'the recourse to violence has become institutionalized into an almost routine-like mode of behavior, compromise and accommodation (become) all the more difficult' (Lemarchand, 1993, p. 168).

Federal arrangement

The federalist device either in the form presented by consociationalists or Horowitz is one that deals with ethnic pluralism by institutionalizing it constitutionally (Elazar, 1994, p. 25). As a form of government in which political power is divided between constitutionally defined domains, it is the quintessence of limited government operating under the rule of law (Macpherson, 1994, p. 10). Thus, it safeguards freedom by recognizing that people have divided ties and loyalties and by providing the appropriate space for their expression. However, its adoption would require some background conditions.

Firstly, ethnic cleavages have to be territorially discrete (in the consociationalists approach). Unless they are geographically clustered, groups can hardly be separated in federal units. In countries like Rwanda and Burundi where Tutsis and Hutus are mixed, without fault-lines separating one from the other, federalism will not create space for group autonomy and might have no effect in conflict reduction. On the other hand, where there are clusters of groups and internal political boundaries do not take account of ethnic configurations (as in Horowitz's approach), differences cannot be territorially defined and represented. In which case federalism might be meaningless. It is equally unappetizing where ethnic minorities are scattered or hemmed within territorially discrete majorities. In this case the creation of federal units might have a cascading effect, as unprotected minorities would emerge to ask for autonomy. The failures of Nigerian federalism in resolving ethnic claims may best illustrate how difficult the arrangement could be in a society where there are minority groups within majority groups or where the boundaries are unclear. William Zartman (1998, p. 328) has shown that despite its offensive during the Ogaden War of 1977–1978, the Somali could not declare victory because of their inability to find a line where they could claim to have liberated all Somalis from Ethiopian rule.

The second requirement is that groups have to be internally coherent and should be able to sustain a state/province economically. If they are not coherent, federalism will generate new groups with new claims to autonomy as already discussed above. If they are not economically viable, resources will have to flow from entities occupied by groups that are well endowed. The institutional channel for the transfer of resources will be the central government that has the role of securing the well-being of the entire country. In some cases, significant transfer of resources may provoke political uprising or secession by the well endowed. In other cases, it may gradually increase the power of the center to the point that the federating states/provinces lose their autonomy. In both cases, they unavoidably lead to federation breakdown as the Nigerian experience has shown. Mindful of this, negotiators of the interim South African constitution of 1993 rejected suggestions for ethnic federalism (Rothchild, 1997, p. 56). Each of the nine provinces that were established under the constitution had its own legislative and executive bodies but dependent on the center for about 88% of its administrative funds. Without ethnic provinces there was no fear that a redistributive policy would heighten differences and precipitate sectional uprising. It is no accident that the South African arrangement is not federal, despite the features it displays (Lijphart, 1995, pp. 223–224), and Eric Nordlinger actually excluded federalism from his list of conflict-reduction measures.

Electoral incentives

The electoral instruments (of Horowitz) have a lot of promise because they could induce politicians to engage in interethnic cooperation. But, they require heterogeneous constituencies and political parties formed along ethnic lines without which candidates do not need to appeal across ethnic lines. For example, states/provinces have to contain a number of groups, and candidates contesting for governorship/premiership offices may have to appeal to voters from groups other than theirs in order to win. In the same way, legislative constituencies for both the national and state assemblies have to contain clusters of ethnic groups for this model to operate. Countries having numerous groups are more likely to meet this demographic condition.

Besides, it is difficult to establish a relationship between multiethnic support in the election of legislators and accommodative behaviour at the national level. For example, take a scenario in which each of the units of a federation has a specified number of federal legislative constituencies, each containing three, four or five ethnic groups. In this scenario, the need for candidates to take account of the interest of groups outside their constituencies will not arise. Undoubtedly, they will make cross-ethnic appeals and take moderate position in order to win, but this is in relation to the few groups within their respective constituencies. The pursuance of inter-group accommodation and moderation politics at the local level does not translate into accommodative behaviour at the national level.[3] Political toleration among minority groups in one state or constituency does not translate into toleration of majority groups at the national level. Therefore, in a country where ethnic groups are few, it is unnecessary to deliberately activate group divisions in order to have heterogeneous federal constituencies that would make for multiethnic support in the election of legislators. The critical targets for conflict reduction are the parties that have to produce the prime minister and cabinet (in a parliamentary system) or the president with a cabinet (in a presidential system). It is they that have to be induced to reach out to groups in other units in order to reduce possible conflicts and a sense of marginalization.

Conclusion: looking ahead

On the whole, the empirical writers aim at providing a theory of democracy that would reconcile multiple identities in Africa's polyethnic states, but their prescriptions raise a number of difficulties, as discussed above. The difficulties do not imply that the prescriptions are useless; rather, they suggest that some would apply in some settings and not in others.

Take the case of Arthur Lewis' model of consociationalism defined by a federal arrangement, proportional representation of groups in the legislature, and representation of parties in the cabinet in proportion to electoral performance. These measures (with exception to the first) constituted the core of the Transitional Constitution that brought racial and ethnic reconciliation to post-apartheid South Africa. The constitutional adoption of a cabinet inclusive of parties that met a certain threshold of electoral votes was said to be the brainchild of Joe Slovo, the late communist party negotiator. In fact, South Africans dubbed the principle for the inclusive cabinet the 'Slovo Formula,' but it was Arthur Lewis who first enunciated it over 30 years ago. Nigeria was to borrow the principle in 1995 when its constitutional negotiators produced a draft constitution that provided for competing parties representation in cabinet in proportion to their performance at the polls. Although the provision was not included in the 1999 constitution, President Olusegun Obasanjo went on to constitute a cabinet whose members were drawn informally from all the three registered political parties. The effect has been the amelioration of adversarial politics that characterized previous democracies in Nigeria. The example of these two countries illustrate the possibilities that the Lewis model could have for other ethnically diverse countries like Uganda, Zaire and Kenya where there are a few large and several small ethnic groups, and exclusion tends to be pronounced.

Furthermore, take the case of Lijphart model that is defined by ethnic federalism, Proportional Representation (PR) system of election, grand coalition, and mutual veto. While some of these are fraught with difficulties, it is undeniable that the PR method makes for adequate representation of groups in elective decision-making institutions. South Africa has used it successfully. Nigeria has had no need for it because the boundaries of its legislative constituencies follow groups very closely, and thus make for adequate representation of diverse identities in the country. The major problem with the PR method is that in a parliamentary system it freezes the minority status of ethnic minorities' parties by permanently excluding them from the executive branch of government (Horowitz, 1998, pp. 6–8). But there are ways of mitigating this exclusion as we have noted earlier.

It is also undeniable that ethnic federalism, with all its possible problems, is an essential institution for reducing conflict and ensuring the triumph of democracy in societies where ethnic groups are recognizable and occupy a discrete territorial space. Empirical evidence shows that the political malaise that afflicted Uganda and the protracted civil war that struck Sudan were inexorable outcomes of the centralizing tendencies in these countries' regimes. In Ethiopia, years of political instability have given way to the realization by its current leadership that a new federal arrangement fits with the 'realities of the country's ethnic character.' Consequently, laws were enacted declaring the 'rights of nations to administer (their) own affairs within their defined [geoethnic] territory' (Rothchild, 1997, p. 56). The possibilities that federalism offers were acknowledged by an international conference on 'federalism and ethnicity' organized by the Swiss Peace Foundation on the occasion of the 50th anniversary of the UN and attended by more than 80 experts in political science and international law. The conference issued the 'Charter of Basel' in which it recommended a federal arrangement as the most appropriate framework for political participation and confidence building in multiethnic states, notwithstanding some of the difficulties pointed out by Nordlinger (Bachler, 1997, see also Ekeh, 1997).

Finally, Horowitz's approach defined by the combination of electoral formula and federal arrangements that induce group elites to cooperate across group lines is not without promise in states with multiple ethnicity. It is more promising if legislative constituencies and state/provincial boundaries run around groups to provide clear ethnic fault-lines or strata that group elites have to reach across to take reconciliatory position on issues and make political marriages to produce parties whose elites cut across ethnicity. The Nigerian Fourth Republic has achieved some measure of success in using the electoral mechanism and ethnicity to generate political parties composed of a complex array of group elites from all sections of the country. The Alliance for Democracy (AD) began as a national pro-democracy party but sank into a sectional one, but is attempting to regain its image by broadening its elite membership. The outcome of the broad ethnic elite membership is political moderation and mutual accommodation. Juan Linz (1978, pp. 67–68) was right when he argued in the late 1970s that an electoral law that rewards efforts at cooperation diminishes political crisis and raises the prospects for stability. In the Nigerian case, moderation was furthered by President Obasanjo's sagacious inclusion of all the parties in his cabinet. Other deeply divided African states could emulate the Nigeria situation within the broader context of Horowitz's prescriptions.[4]

Acknowledgments

*I wish to thank David Black and E. Ike Udogu for their helpful criticisms and suggestions for improvement.

Notes

1. The Abuja agreement was focused on the interest of some combatants and overlooked the interest of groups. Even then, D. Roosevelt Johnson, who was the *de facto* leader of the Krahn ethnic group, was excluded from the council of state. The Bicesse Accord was unsuccessful because it could not be enforced. Jonas Savimbi reneged on it and resumed fighting following his poor performance in the first round of the 1992 election.
2. These prescriptions are a revision of the ones he made in his 1985 book *Ethnic Groups in Conflict*. There, he recommended the following strategies: the creation

of lower level political units with a view to proliferating points of power and taking the heat off the centre; an electoral system that places high premium on multiethnic support in the election of state officials; the adoption of policies that encourage alignments based on interest other than ethnicity; and affirmative action programs to reduce disparities between groups (Horowitz, pp. 597–599).

3. Unless we are assuming Edmund Burke's argument that Parliament is a deliberative assembly where the general interest ought to guide members, in which case the prescription for multiethnic electoral support becomes superfluous.

4. It is therefore immaterial whether the system of government is presidential or parliamentary. What is important is the strategy that makes for inclusive government and complex intertwining of group interests. In this respect, the debate between Juan Linz and Donald Horowitz in the Fall (1990) issue of *Journal of Democracy* over the merits of the two types of government was unnecessary.

References

Bachler, G. (1997) (ed.), *Federalism Against Ethnicity*, Verlag Rugger Publishers: Zurich.
Bentham, J. (1988), *Principles of Morals and Legislation*, Prometheus Press: Buffalo.
Christie, K. (1998) (ed.), *Ethnic Conflict, Tribal Politics*, Curzan Press: Richmond, Surrey.
Dahl, R. (1971), *Polyarchy: Participation and Opposition*, Yale University Press: New Haven, CT and London.
Ekeh, P. (1997) (ed.), *Wilberforce Conference on Nigerian Federalism*, State University of New York: Buffalo.
Elazar, D. (1994), *Federalism and the Way to Peace*, Institute of Intergovernmental Relations: Kingston.
Evans, G. (1997), *Responding To Crises in the African Great Lakes*, Oxford University Press: New York.
Glickman, H. (1995) (ed.), *Ethnic Conflict and Democratization in Africa*, New Brunswick, NJ: African Studies Association.
Glickman, H. (1998), 'Ethnicity, Elections, and Constitutional Democracy in Africa', in Reynold, A. and Sisk, T. D. (eds.), *Elections and Conflict Management in Africa*, United States Institute of Peace Press: Washington, D.C.
Horowitz, D. (1985), *Ethnic Groups in Conflict*, University of California Press: Berkeley.
Horowitz, D. (1991), *A Democratic South Africa?*, University of California Press: Berkeley.
Horowitz, D. (1998), 'Constitutional Design: An Oxymoron?', Corrected version of a paper presented at the Annual Meeting of the American Political Science Association, Boston, September 3–6.
Human Rights Watch (1998), *Proxy Targets: Civilians in the War in Burundi*, Human Rights Watch: New York.
Johnston, A. (1998), 'Ethnic Conflict in Post Cold War Africa: Four Case Studies', in Christie, K. (ed.), *Ethnic Conflict, Tribal Politics*, Curzon Press: Richmond, Surrey.
Keller, E. (1998), 'Transnational Ethnic Conflict in Africa', in Rothchild, D. and Lake, D. (ed.), *The International Spread of Ethnic Conflict*, Princeton University Press: Princeton.
Kimenyi, Mwangi S. (1997), *Ethnic Diversity, Liberty and the State: The African Dilemma*,

Edward Elgar: Cheltenham.
Lemarachand, R. (1993), 'Burundi in Comparative Perspective: Dimensions of Ethnic Strife', in McGarry, J. and O'Leary, B. (eds.), *The Politics of Ethnic Conflict Regulation*, Routledge: London.
Lemarchand, R. (1997), 'Ethnic Conflict Resolution in Contemporary Africa: Four Models in Search of Solutions', in Bachler, G. (ed.), *Federalism Against Ethnicity?*, Verlag Rugger: Zurich.
Lewis, A. (1965), *Politics in West Africa*, Oxford University Press: London.
Lijphart, A. (1977), *Democracy in Plural Societies: A Comparative Explanation*, Yale University Press: New Haven.
Lijphart, A. (1984), *Democracies: Patterns of Majoritarian and Consensus Government in Twenty-One Countries*, Yale University Press: New Haven.
Lijphart, A. (1991), 'The Alternative Vote: A Realistic Alternative for South Africa?', *Politikon*, Vol. 18, No. 2, pp. 91–101.
Lijphart, A. (1995), 'Prospects for Power-Sharing in the New South Africa', in Reynolds, A. (ed.), *Elections '94 South Africa*, St. Martins Press: New York.
Lijphart, A. (1999), 'Power-Sharing and Group Autonomy in the 1990s and the 21st Century', paper read at the conference on Constitutional Design 2000, University of Notre Dame, South Bend, Indiana, December 9–11.
Linz, J. (1976), 'Crisis, Breakdown, and Reequilibration', in Linz, J. J. and Stepan, A. (eds.), *The Breakdown of Authoritarian Regimes*, The Johns Hopkins University Press: Baltimore, MD.
Macpherson, J. (1994), 'The Future of Federalism', in Randall, S. and Gibbins, R. (eds.), *Federalism and the New World Order*, University of Calgary Press: Calgary.
McGarry, J. and O'Leary, B. (1993), 'Introduction: The Macro-Political Regulation of Ethnic Conflict', in McGarry, J. and O'Leary, B. (eds.), *The Politics of Ethnic Conflict Regulation*, Routledge: London.
Nordlinger, E. (1972), *Conflict Regulation in Divided Societies*, Occasional Paper, Centre for International Affairs, Harvard University, Cambridge.
Reynolds, A. and Sisk, T. (1998), 'Elections and Electoral Systems: Implications for Conflict Management', in Reynolds, A. and Sisk, T. D. (eds.), *Elections and Conflict Management in Africa*, United States Institute of Peace Press: Washingtom, D.C.
Rothchild, D. (1997), *Managing Ethnic Conflict in Africa*, Brookings Institution Press: Washington.
Rothchild, D. and Lake, D. (1998), 'Containing Fear: The Management of Transnational Ethnic Conflict', in Rothchild, D. and Lake, D. (eds.), *The International Spread of Ethnic Conflict*, Princeton University Press: Princeton, NJ.
Sartori G. (1976), *Parties and Party Systems*, Cambridge University Press: Cambridge.
Walzer, M. (1994), *Thick and Thin*, University of Notre Dame Press: Notre Dame.

Young, C. (1992), 'The National and Colonial Question and Marxism: A View from the South', in Motyl, A. L. (ed.), *Thinking Theoretically about Soviet Nationalities: History and Comparison in the Study of the USSR*, Columbia University Press: New York.

Zartman, I. W. (1998), 'Putting Humpty-Dumpty Together Again', in Rothchild, D. and Lake, D. (eds.), *The International Spread of Ethnic Conflict*, Princeton University Press: Princeton.

9 Western Discourse and the Socio-Political Pathology of Ethnicity in Contemporary Africa

PEYI SOYINKA-AIREWELE

Introduction

Western attitudes, myths and images significantly influence the contemporary historical drama in African countries, particularly in the construction of ethnicity as a stigma and socio-political malady in *the African context*. The visual, theoretical and empirical treatment of ethnicity, race and social divisions by the international media, Western intellectual and foreign policy establishment and the role of racial attitudes in such a treatment has had a critical impact on much of the modern African political and intellectual class.

The following pages employ a cross-disciplinary approach in seeking to capture and convey the salient nuances of ethnicity in Western discourse and their implications for African socio-political development. This chapter focuses on four central issues: The power of representation as a tool of domination; the negative rendering of African ethnicity in Western media and the impact of such discourse on the continent's political and intellectual elite; the crisis of ethnic related state violence engendered partly by the insidious framing of African ethnicity; and the search for progressive alternatives within the complex socio-economic and political matrices of contemporary Africa.

The incessant struggle for socio-political reforms in the African continent indicates that this is a propitious time for a frontal confrontation with the realities of ethnicity, race and other social cleavages. Indeed, a cursory overview of the literature reveals an overwhelming concern with the problem of 'divisiveness' or 'polarization' and its consequences for development in Africa. Such concerns are not entirely misplaced. Irredentist wars, internal conflicts and state disintegration inspired by ethno-political tensions have gradually defined the continent, and in contrast to the early post-colonial postulations, sub-state identities are increasingly regarded as obdurate variables, particularly impervious to the entreaties, arguments and policies of government and academic theorists.

A considerable number of African and Western scholars view ethnicity simply as a social construct, arguing that in African societies, for instance, the force of ethnicity lies in the way in which latent primordial characteristics are given a contemporary construction through socialization and mobilization. Kieh, writing on the conflict nexus in Africa, observed that 'the perennial locus of these conflicts is that a small compradorial class has monopolized power, and excluded the majority of the population. But, in their endeavor to advance their agendas, various factional leaders, often masquerading as the champions of suppressed ethnic groups, tend to divert these conflicts from the central issues that occasioned them' (Kieh, 1996, pp. 106–107).

Monga (1996) and other commentators have also accurately dismissed the universal invocation of ethnicity or tribalism as the source of Africa's woes and as the justification for authoritarianism in modern African states. Monga's incisive criticism of much of Western scholarship on this matter are overdue contributions to the understanding of political and social change in Africa. He argues that ill-founded assumptions about political culture and the 'ideological mystification of "tribalism,"' have been used by African governments to sidestep and eliminate debate on their political brutality and economic failures.

However, he rejects any political or social arrangement based on an acknowledgment of social or ethnic divisions on the grounds that it is indicative of the political double standard with which African societies are treated in scholarly discourse. Certainly, the racial and ethnic cleavages in the United States for instance, have not resulted in a call for consociationalism. Yet in this aspect of Monga's contention, a disinclination to accept the paradigm of ethnicity outside of its association with the negative can be clearly perceived.

It is this philosophical tension that must be confronted, explored and resolved by African societies as they seek to undergo transformations towards internally determined goals.

Representation and power

Grinker and Steiner (1997) have reminded us that it is the so-called 'master' authors of anthropology who have constructed the sites from which students of African studies view the histories, societies, and cultures of Africa. Yet, while such representation, as Hozic (2000, p. 13) notes, can obviously be an 'unfettered replica of the *other*, alternately, it can be a projection of the subject's own desires, a self-centered conversation with oneself for which the *other* is only a convenient excuse. . . [or indeed]. . . a reflection of that Lacunian *other* to which both the imagining subject and the imagined object are subsumed, possibly a structure such as capitalism, patriarchy or imperialism.' In the context of the physical and material subjugation of Africa, and the search for an endorsement of Western activities within the region, it is not surprising that the continent has been 'invented, constructed and defined' negatively in many works produced in Western Europe and elsewhere.

Writing on 20th century native 'Indians' in North America, Dorris alluded to the power of representation as a tool of cultural domination when he noted that the *ad initiam* refusal of Europeans to call Native Americans societies by their own names is symptomatic of the wider issues of cultural domination. 'The imputation of a solitary ethnicity to several hundred heterogeneous societies and nations was accomplished for one purpose only: it suited the convenience, psychology and bureaucracy of Euro-American management' (Dorris, 1979, p. 75). It is instructive that colonial administrators in Africa have been accused of adopting the reverse policy: the 'invention of tribalism.' Obviously, the historical reality of this imposed discursive and administrative framework, does not, in itself, support the popular conclusion that self-differentiating, politicized ethnicities in Africa were therefore, the result of European machinations. But, as Dorris (1979) further observed, every effort has been made to enclose the non-western world into a European schema, and then to label, discredit and misrepresent or obscure at will. Johannes Fabian highlights the translation of inscription and representation into exercised power:

> Colonial expeditions were not just a form of invasion; nor was their purpose inspection. They were determined efforts at inscription. By putting regions on a map and native words on a list, explorers laid the first and deepest foundations for colonial power. By giving proof of the 'scientific' nature of their enterprise they exercised power in a subtle form—as the power to name, to describe, to

classify (cited in Grinker and Steiner, 1997, p. xviii).

Beyond the physical expeditions, contemporary Western construction of African ethnicity derives its power from the nature of the gaze itself, which, stripped of obvious political, economic, or military gain, still transforms the un-desired post-colony, into a 'no-one's wasteland', of 'strategically unimportant lands featuring hostile peoples and hostile terrain with no or little possibility for lasting order or positive change' (Hozic, 2000, pp. 21, 16).

Such inscriptions have had profound ramifications on the continuing political and social saga of these post-colonies, and on their efforts to construct national policies within the framework of Western domination and perceptions.

Indeed, W. E. B. Dubois in his eloquent depiction of this dilemma noted: 'It is a peculiar sensation, this double consciousness, this sense of always looking at one's self through the eyes of others, of measuring one's soul by the tape of a world that looks on in amused contempt and pity' (cited in Dorris, 1979, p. 49). 'Amused contempt and pity' is apparent even in the patronizing efforts by an increasingly politically correct academic globe to accede to the demand for a restructuring of the distorted intellectual and media frames through which Africa has for so long been indiscriminately represented. Southall's response is illustrative of this disturbing attitude, seemingly based more on the need to placate than to acknowledge and rectify the distortion of imaging and representation as a projection of Western cultural domination. In his words, 'Since the birth of African nationalism, tribalism has always been a sore subject and for very good reasons. Some nationalists have *even gone so far* as to claim that tribal divisions were the deliberate creation of a Machiavellian colonial policy of divide and rule... Anthropology claims to be a universal discipline ...it is naturally *embarrassed* by the colonialist taint, which besmirches it in so much of the tiers monde' (Southall, 1997, pp. 43 and 49; emphasis added). More damning in this seemingly innocuous essay on the 'Illusion of Tribe,' is Southall's carefully worded appeal:

> If Western, and especially American anthropologists are to avoid the charge that they are prostituting the discipline to assuage their personality problems, they will have to take much more seriously the complementarity of the contribution required from the new breed of anthropologists *whose fathers or grandfathers were members of non-literate societies* ... Western anthropologists will

have to stop calling primitive and tribal the contemporary communities from which their colleagues of the new breed come. *This may be a case of which human feelings have to prevail over strict logic*...If asked what terms then can we use?...I should have to answer simply for the strategic moment, for the present critical and vital generation, that for the present the word primitive should be dropped from the vocabulary of social anthropology, *however much it wounds our romantic souls*, that the term 'tribe' should be applied only to the small scale societies of the past which retain their political autonomy, and that the new associations derived from them in the contemporary context should be referred to as ethnic groups as other members of the category are' (Southall, 1997, pp. 43 and 49; emphasis added).

If other members of the category are indeed referred to as ethnic groups, why must an appeal be issued to the 'romantic souls' of Western scholars to extend a similar rule to African societies? Southall's argument appears to be that the representation of African ethnicity should be modified 'simply for the strategic moment' and only as an outcome of Western sympathy for the feelings 'of the present critical generation' of Africans. Thus the projection of Western self-image continues—from an insensitive superior culture to a strategically accommodating but dominant observer of others, with the privilege of interpreting and inscribing.

Postulating a connection between the characterization and representation of African ethnicity in writing and media and the domestic responses to ethnicity does not imply that such imaging is the cause of ethnic conflicts. Such a facile proposition would fall in the ranks of suggestions that ethnic conflicts are a part of the savage, tribal African nature or that ethnic identity is alien to the African (in contrast to the rest of the world) and is a sole product of colonial machinations. The interaction between global imaging and what is described here as the socio-political pathology of ethnicity suggests that the internalization of the Western elaboration of 'African tribalism' and the socio-political responses to that conceptualization has served to exacerbate the traumas of multi-ethnic statehood in much of Africa. Such an interaction occurs within the framework of competition over power and resources and the complex web of development issues that shape the lives of Africans.

The inscription of difference and the stigmatization of ethnicity in Africa

Ali Mazrui (1978) warned that two problems await the analyst—the first is recognizing and rebelling against the arrogance of others and the second is recognizing and rebelling against one's own dependence and imitativeness. Thus, while Udogu states that it is safe to contend that many individuals might not consider it insulting to be referred to as ethnonationalist because the concept generally implies the love for one's ethnic group (e.g. Mandingo, Jewish, Serbian, Yoruba, Zulu, Russian, etc.) (Udogu, 1994, p. 159), scholars of African politics must remember that even the privilege of 'ethnonational' imaging was not extended to African ethnicity till very recently and only sporadically at the present.

As Appiah noted, the framing of Africa as tribal, savage and primitive is an inscription of difference, that is deeply implicated in the endurance of Western racism and hinders the capacity of the region to disrupt the cycle of social and political crisis that bedevil it (Appiah, 1992; Myers, Klak and Koehl, 1996). The Comaroffs' review of the form and content of European discourses on Africa reveals that together the continent was established as the dark stage of savagery, cannibalism and backwardness into which the white men wrote themselves. The representation of African ethnicity thus emerged out of a relationship of 'opposition and inequality' in which by a historical imperative Europe stood to Africa as 'civilization to nature,' 'savior to victim,' 'actor to subject' (Comaroff and Comaroff, 1997, p. 691).

Without dwelling at length on ethnicity and its various definitions, it is safe to state that ethnicity accounts for group identity that may transcend descent, linguistic, cultural or territorial boundaries. The debate is still waged over the origins of this phenomenon (Soyinka-Airewele, 1999; Mafeje, 1971; Ranger, 1985, 1997; Vail, 1997), but there is some consensus that ethnicity involves a form of common consciousness and social organization, which may be derived from primordial or utilitarian characterizations, refined over time and according to specific historical contexts. Such a collective consciousness may be harnessed to provide a framework for debate or action by elements within or outside the group. The pride in ethnonationalism to which Udogu referred takes its cue from this representation of ethnicity.

'Tribe' on the other hand, evolved rapidly into a pejorative concept as has been noted in this volume. Any wonder, then, that Grinker and Steiner note that whatever definitions we apply to the concept, the use of the term tribe invokes a serious problem in its implication of a distinction between Africa and Europe (Grinker and Steiner, 1997, p. 6). Myers and others have produced one of the most instructive of recent research on how the media cover conflicts in Africa, and help to enforce the 'tribal' stereotype in Africa. They note that US news media elected to cast their coverage of the civil war in Rwanda and Bosnia in two different frameworks to the public, despite the striking similarities between both wars. Each conflict has been marked by appalling atrocities, comparable estimates of war-related deaths and has remained obstinate despite Western intervention. Both conflicts have emerged in relatively small, rural and agricultural oriented and densely populated states.

The theater, political history and the progression of conflicts also indicate remarkable commonality—with legacies of Western imperialism in cultivating and exploiting strife, the role of ethnic identity in fomenting the struggles, as well as the terrain and strategies of warfare (Myers, Klak and Koehl, 1996). Yet, against this background, there has been a startling discrepancy in the international press coverage of these wars—a fact noted by Myers and other critical observers (Bates, Mudimbe and O'Barr, 1993; Moore, 1993).[1]

The inscription of difference is exhibited in many striking dimensions; for instance, computer-assisted discourse analysis applied to a study of reporting on Rwanda and Bosnia in a four year period reveals extreme discrepancies in the amount of coverage (a total of 560 referring to Rwanda and 14,114 referring to Bosnia) But of more relevance here is the analysis of language of civil war, ethnicity and tribalism. It became clear that the media coverage was value loaded and culturally biased as there is a near-total absence of tribal terminology in Bosnian stories, while it comprises the explanatory core of Rwandan articles. Myers and colleagues find that, of the one percent 'tribal references' in Bosnia articles, all but one of these articles is not even referring at all to Bosnian tribalism but rather to tribes in Rwanda and other parts of Africa. 'Typical of such references might be a sentence beginning with phrases such as 'ethnic warfare in Bosnia or for that matter tribal war in Rwanda...' (Myers, Klak and Koehl, 1996, p. 33).

The characterization of the Rwandan conflict as tribal warfare opened the floodgates of biased journalistic depictions. 'Rwanda's war was simply centuries-old tribal savagery,' an orgy of blood and terror 'unbounded by any rationality other than some sort of ritualistic, primitive logic.' Ten articles in a two-week period in 1994 described events in Rwanda as an 'orgy' of violence and revenge (Myers, Klak and Koehl, 1996, p. 33).

Yet in the Bosnian case, despite extensive documentation of repeated gang rape and mutilation of Muslim women, only one of the more than 14,000 articles during the four years of Myer's study uses the term 'orgy.' The selective cultural association is revealing as orgy is defined in Webster's dictionary 'as a secret ceremonial rite...usually characterized by ecstatic singing and dancing, drunken revelry or an excessive indulgence in an activity' (Myers, Klak and Koehl, 1996, p. 33).

The selective framing of the Rwandan conflict was not limited to the international media. A newly released 'scholarly' text on global issues, noted that 'in the former Yugoslavia, some 200,000 people were killed in what was called *"ethnic cleansing"*, and in Rwanda, approximately 800,000 were *massacred* in what appeared to be *"tribal violence"*' (Snarr, 1998, p. 57; emphasis added). The imagery conveyed in the contrasting phrases, 'killed' and 'ethnic' (for Yugoslavia) as against 'massacred' and 'tribal violence' (for Rwanda) within a single sentence, is eloquent testimony of the insidious nature of such representation of the African 'other'.

Self imaging versus reality in Western ethno-evolutionary mythology

Ethnicity has always been and does remain a global phenomenon. For now, at least, the assumption that modernization will lead to the suppression or disappearance of ethnic consciousness in Western societies and elsewhere is a myth.

Walker Connor (1994), for instance, has persistently drawn attention to the strength of ethnic loyalties, not merely in developing countries but in modern industrialized formations. Perhaps in response to such challenges the literature reflects a distinction between so-called 'plural societies' and 'divided societies.' It has become fashionable to describe 'advanced' Western societies as pluralistic, where plural refers to the existence of multiple, cross-cutting cleavages, based on partial, diverse interests (see Kuper, 1969; Dahl, 1971; Rueschmeyer and Stephens, 1993).

In these 'pluralistically divided societies,' it has been argued that where cleavages exist, the different groups are 'civil' towards each other, *acknowledge the equality of other individuals and groups* and share a national ethos of primary allegiance to the state and define themselves by such primary loyalties. Paradoxically, such literature began to emerge at a time when racial divisions and social inequalities were the cause of gross suffering, internal strife and decidedly 'uncivil behavior,' not only in Africa but also in many parts of Europe and North America.

In contrast to such 'advanced' societies characterized by such a vibrant civil society and 'non-cumulative conflicts' (Dahl, 1971), most African societies are defined in Western literature as 'divided societies,' with fixed and total identities, preclusive of a democratic political culture. They are therefore deemed to have a propensity for, or are disposed to, extremist tribal politics and conflicts. Tribalism, of course, is generally endowed with sufficient sense of primordiality, savagery and backwardness, especially in its form or genre in African societies.

Yet, as Hall notes, the Quebecan, the Basque, Catalan, Irish Separatist or Scottish demands for greater economic and political autonomy are not noted as backward, tribal, selfish or greedy even when they are clearly driven by the power calculus and economic considerations (just like similar groups in Africa). In Northern Ireland, religion is commonly presented as the root of Ulster's crises, but the conflict is much deeper than one of rival theologies (Hall, 1979, p. 141). Religion is simply the 'badge of ethnic identity' that divides the communities so deeply. Thus, Catholicism has been an integral part of Irish nationalism and identity, while Protestanism springs from the heritage of the descendants of the colonizers of Ulster (Hall, 1979, p. 141). Ethnic tensions and conflicts similarly bedevil Europe and North America.

Connor's juxtaposition of Mussolini's Manifesto of the Racist Scientist published throughout every village in Italy in 1938 with a more recent commentary on the relative vitality of local identities compared to Italianess is instructive. The former read in part:

> If Italians differ from Frenchmen, Germans, Turks, Greek, etc., this is not just because they posses a different language and different history, but because that racial development is different...a pure 'Italian race' is already in existence. This pronouncement [rests] on the very pure blood ties that unite present day Italians (Connor, 1994, pp. 217–218).

This is a prime illustration of the politicization of ethnicity by politicians, but the failure of Musssolini's attempt to eradicate the identities of the peoples of Italy is also evident in the following commentary:

> Most Italians will tell you sooner or later, that there is no such place as Italy. Oh yes, no doubt, as a geographical expression or a legal diplomatic entity, capable of entering into treaties and voting at the United Nations and suchlike unimportant things. But as a

nation—coherent, homogeneous, more or less like minded collection of people with a shared sense of pride and patriotism—as that, they will say, Italy remains an invention of you foreigners. We Italians are not really Italians at all—or anyway, often. We are Florentines, Venetians, Neopolitans, Bolognese. But Italians? Oh dear no! (cited in Connors, 1979, p. 218).

Unfortunately, the effective invention and projection of a 'modern post-ethnic' self image by the West has hindered the post-colonial efforts to come to terms with multi-ethnicity in African countries.

Stigmatization and the predicament of ethno-politics in contemporary Africa

Against the background of the foregoing analyses, it would be overly optimistic to expect that admitting a love for 'tribalism' would be a feature of post-colonial thought in Africa. Indeed, pre-independence nationalists and the first generation of African politicians and academics were primed to struggle against the landscape of ethnicity, the notion of primordial tribalism, and to seek to refashion their sense of themselves, through their politics and socio-cultural arena. The programs and policies for social transformation that arose from the stigmatization of African ethnicity might be a pragmatic attempt to address ethnic related tensions in the goal of state building. However, they also reflect an on-going struggle by African elite to resolve the contradictions of identity and 'enlightenment' evoked within them.

As Mudimbe (1988, 1994) argued, behavior patterns in Africa have been constructed and disseminated through the subjective lenses or 'fantasies' of the West. The impact of such representations and responses in the continuing saga of African politics is evident in the ethnic discourse of African political and intellectual elites, in the state policies that attempt to confront pluralism and the responses of international agencies to issues in Africa.

Impact on African political establishments

Official documents, statements and writings of almost all postcolonial African leaders, no matter their ideological position, reveal much consensus on ethnicity. In the words of President Mathieu Kérékou of the Republic of

Benin, it 'debased, divided and slighted the people' (Ismagilova, 1978, p. 50). As African leaders adroitly exploited ethnicity, while criticizing the West for its racially motivated negative imagery of Africa, there was also widespread acceptance that, semantics aside, ethnicity was atavistic. Leaders as diverse as the late President Ahmadou Ahidjo of Cameroon, Siaka Stevens of Sierra Leone, Mobutu Sese Seko of Zaire, all 'declared' a determination to eradicate 'tribal self awareness.'

In fairness to the African nationalists and intellectual cadres, political ethnicity created tensions and obstacles to the process of nation-building. Thus resort to ethnic 'propaganda of any kind' was criminalized and made punishable by imprisonment in some countries, including Mali. The government of Albin Nyamoya in Burundi went as far as declaring that ethnic names should not be used any longer so that they would not lead to differences between the inhabitants of one province or another (Ismagilova, 1978, p. 138). The tragic epilogue in Rwanda-Burundi demonstrates the ineffectiveness of such a frontal assault.

Does the framing of African culture and identity actually have any bearing on local attitudes to ethnicity and the crisis of post-colonial politics? Might it be argued that the severe reactions against ethnicity were logically motivated by the very tragic and real consequences of divisiveness, and the internally motivated goals of anti-imperialism, modern state development, peace and stability as well as perhaps the consolidation and preservation of incumbent regimes?

The answer might be all of the above. Obviously, in seeking to justify colonialism as a civilizing expedition, Western discourse aroused a groundswell of political, popular and intellectual opinion that permitted the construction of repressive policies ostensibly aimed at stemming neo-colonial influences in African affairs. Beyond that, the continued racially inspired imaging of Africa consolidated the 'them' versus 'us' pattern that underlay the rhetoric of power and dominance of African political elite for decades after independence.

But the Western gaze was more than a mere object of manipulation by African leaders for political purpose. It severely impacted on the 'double consciousness' of the elite themselves (caught between their 'Africanness and Europeanness'). Thus, it generated 'unobserved' contradictions in political philosophy, policies and actions. Nkrumah provides an excellent illustration of this. Much of his opposition to ethnicity was inspired as much by the consciousness and pressures of a watching hypercritical Western world as by the actual and potential problems of ethnicity. In a statement on unity in Ghana, he denounced the 'tribal opposition in

Ashanti, the Northern region, and the Ga people, among others. But his words reveal the importance of the international context:

> Ghana was the cynosure of all eyes, friendly and unfriendly. The world's press was represented in our capital, and what they missed, the opposition filled in for them with their own explanations. No occasion, no event, was too small to exploit in order to discredit both Ghana and the government before the world and reduce the high prestige which our struggle and attainment of freedom had won for Ghana. ...the disinclination to take salutary measures was also being misunderstood abroad, where it was being regarded as a trial of strength between us, the lawfully constituted government, and the subversive non-governmental elements. We watched the antics of the foreign press with misgiving. It seemed as though our overseas critics were intent upon destroying us before we ever got started (Nkrumah, 1979, p. 73).

Nkrumah went on to implicate the international media and intellectual coverage in his ultimate defection from 'classical' liberal democracy to a more authoritarian style of government. While the direct influence of the West in his change of political direction is disputable, the impact of Western imaging on his attitudes to ethnicity clearly is not. In spite of his 'radical' intellectual analysis, like other African leaders, Nkrumah was prey to the moral high ground the West ascribed to its relation to Africa. Thus many of his policy measures were announced with reference to the West. For instance, the preface to the Avoidance of Discrimination Bill, which effectively suppressed ethnic related activities, reads, 'In times of national emergency, the Western democracies have been compelled to limit their citizens' freedom...' (Nkrumah, 1979, p. 74).

The intellectual community

From the nationalist era preceding decolonization, a distinct incoherence was also apparent among many African intellectuals, relayed as a simultaneous rejection of racist framing of African culture and the subliminal acceptance of the conceptualization undergirding such frames. Anise, for instance, argues that ethnicity, or *'tribalism as it is properly known in African politics'* is the single most readily identifiable social-structural characteristic of contemporary African states (Anise, 1979, p. 314. emphasis added).

In largely defensive postures, African scholars have tried to explain away or justify the presence of such 'negative' social institutions: either through their glorification in politically correct anthropological lexicon, as unique/exotic African traits (i.e., however, 'barbarous, you must not speak or think ill of another culture'); or by passing the buck ('a colonial invention for divide and rule purpose'); or pyscho-alienation (the people are not actually 'tribal' neither do they actually feel this way—the elite simply manipulate them in the modern power stakes').

As Thandika Mkandawire astutely notes, the African academic has been disarmed in many ways: the state looms large in the financial support and survival of almost all African universities and the latter, modeled after their Western counterparts, were born in chains, including the chains of the dominant perspectives of the new political elite. Mkandawire cites Nkrumah:

> We do not intend to sit idly by and see these institutions which are supported by millions of dollars produced out of the sweat and toil of common people continue to be centers of anti-government activities. We want the university college to cease being an alien institution and to take on the character of a Ghanaian university, loyally serving the interest of the nation and the well-being of our people. If reforms do not come from within, we intend to impose them from outside, and no resort to the cry of academic freedom (for academic freedom does not mean irresponsibility) is going to restrain us from seeing that our university is a healthy university devoted to Ghanaian interest (Nkrumah, cited in Mkandawire, 1997, p. 20).

For the African intellectual, it would appear that the starting point in the study and negotiation of multi-ethnic politics must be the abandonment of rigid positions and counterproductive assumptions regarding ethnicity. That such inflexible assumptions about 'African tribalism' still prevail on the continent is evident in Mathata Tsedu's remarks in the article titled, 'Nigerian Grouping of Tribal Enclaves.' A South African, Tsedu was shocked by the fact that the political discourse during the Nigerian electioneering process was dominated by what was disparagingly called 'tribal politics.' He further exclaimed: 'when people like Wole Soyinka and other learned people give support to such tribal based organizations at the political level, the fate of Africa as a continent becomes truly precarious' (Tsedu, in the *Nigerian Vanguard*, March 4, 1999).

Tsedu's frustration at the political process is understandable especially as the question was posed: What are the lessons for my own country? But, this commentary may be disturbing on several accounts: the internalization of the stereotypical 'African tribalist' imagery of the West, the assumption that ethno-politics (tribal politics) is innately backward and inimical to development, and the blanket condemnation of politicians and activists who call for a political landscape that takes due cognizance of ethnic realities.

Like so many external and, indeed, 'native' observers, Tsedu does a 'disservice' to the so-called tribal masses and their positions in the contemporary political arena by the patent 'inability' to deconstruct the language and illusions of identity and power in the continent today.

Building the multi-ethnic state

The continuing creation and communication of external myths, realities and images of ethnicity has provided an arena in which a modern yet dependent Africa recreates and enacts ethnopolitics. The issue, though, is whether ethnopolitics is injurious to African politics.

Ofeimun's critique of the presumption that 'block-voting by an [ethnic] community is antithetical to democracy, constitutes tribalism, and is tantamount to 'treason' or a step away from secessionism'(Ofeimun, 1998, p. 47), raises issues that must be confronted in mediating Africa's political future. Moreover, Ofeimun queries: 'in what way is democracy offended when a whole people decide that they will not accept perceived domination ... by those they have not chosen? Why is it such a bad thing for people to seek common solutions for recognized needs? And for that matter, why should anyone support a democracy which insists that an ethnic group which feels that it has a grievance should not nurse it through a common stand in a supposedly free and fair election? (Ofeimun, 1998, p. 47).

It becomes clear that such questions arouse even more critical issues focused on the role of the state in the whole calculus of political ethnicity. The relevance of the state in Africa has been more frequently probed through the interpretive lens of political economy and globalization studies. Yet ethnic politics present equally disquieting issues. The first generation of African leaders were prepared to usher in an era of 'state building' that would be the logical outcome of the evolutionary perspective of political and social development and would be heralded by the forceful excision of ethno-nationalism (Vail, 1997, p. 52).

This traditional conceptualization of the role and strategic importance of the state is under siege, particularly for its contribution to a milieu of state terrorism within which ethnic identities have been revitalized (see Agbese, 1996). The emerging debate questions the role of the state as manager, arbiter and guarantor of the rights and participation of individuals as well as groups. It would appear that one of the many tasks facing African governments is that of finding new structures of representation, appropriate and vibrant, that are cognizant of the ethnic calculus.

Obadare, for instance, argued against the contemptuous condemnation of so-called 'intellectual tribalist' who seek a fundamental redefinition of the idea of state and nationhood. Representative of the critics addressed by Obadare, in the Nigerian situation, is U. Shodipe who recently wrote 'calumny in a season of goodwill' in which he states that everywhere 'there is an infectious liberal dawning ... a rousing clarity of national re-awakening', but into this garden of 'idyllic national unity' he identifies *the serpent of 'tribalism' and division* as a major cause for lamentation. Thus he berates those who are incapable of civilized accommodation' (Obadare, 1998, p. 50). Clearly, the stigmatization of ethnicity has become a part of the dominant discourse of Africans and Westerners especially in the area of political economy.

The power of the international media in the process of inscription continues to be a major factor in the creation of African political history. Acts of observation and construction of difference are no less controlling simply because they lack the apparatus of physical conquest and expropriation. (see Hozic, 2000). Stigmatizing discourse tends to obstruct the search for innovative and appropriate means of integrating disparate groups into politics and society and for mitigating the consequences of ethnopolitics in Africa.

Strategies and programs

The internalization of Western images of African ethnicity has plagued policy and politics in Africa, acerbated ethnic conflicts, and provided fertile grounds for political transmutations, ethnic manipulations and human rights abuses in African countries. The initial steps to political stability must therefore commence with a reconstruction of notions of ethnicity, acceptance of its presence, and construction of policies void of the discomfort that currently pervades discussion of ethnicity in the continent.

The broad spectrum of political and administrative strategies for the accommodation and management of ethnicity may be relevant: devolution of power to constituent (geo-ethnic) political groups, power sharing, respect for human rights and the rule of law, federalism (where necessary), among others (Osaghae, 1998, p. 16). Indeed, Mbaku (1996) has consistently argued that constitutional reform is an essential step in constructing effective and viable political arrangements for African societies. In even more recent research, he suggests that attention to institutional reforms will not only promote individual participation in democracy and development, but also yield dividends in peace and stability (Mbaku, 1998).

However, because of the existence of conflicting interest within and between groups, it is vital that the search for answers goes beyond functional power sharing. Agbese and Kieh (1993), suggest that addressing issues of social justice is imperative in this search for answers. This position is appropriate in the present socio-political climate in Africa.

Beyond that, and toward that goal, it would appear that the acceptance of multiculturalism, as a given, is an essential step. But the absence of such institutionalized and integrative acceptance of the ethnic-self is apparent even in African educational institutions (in stark contrast to their Western counterparts). In Africa, few programs, agencies or forums exist in which diversity can be addressed, celebrated or debated with a view to creating a basis for understanding its intricacies. It is disheartening, for instance, to acknowledge that very few, if any, African universities have a commitment to addressing the thorny, but real, issues of ethnicity probably because of its sensitivity. The intensely politicized tensions and violent conflicts between the oil producing communities in Southern Nigeria, has received media coverage, but not enough attention from the large academic community based therein to alter significantly the government policy in the area. The dynamic leadership that the intellectual community in Africa has often provided in the struggle against political authoritarianism can be transferred to that of resolving inter-ethnic tensions and underdevelopment. This could be achieved through increased curricular focus on multiculturalism, training in conflict management and resolution.

Conclusion

It is simplistic to blame the socio-political problems of Africa on the presence of ethnicity, even as we admit that the state response to ethnic loyalties and the manipulation of ethnic identity by political entrepreneurs do pose a grave threat to stability.

Ethnicity in Africa continues to be popularly perceived by some observers as a morally reprehensible African trait that needs to be excised in the continent. Yet ethnicity is not uniquely African, and neither are the acts of terrorism, warfare and conflict that emerge from the manipulation of racial or ethnic loyalties. Ironically, while at its apex in the post-colonial, post-Cold War age, Western framing of the African order is now deemed by many to depict 'reality', sapped of base desires and therefore, a mirror image of the object. In the present climate of 'mediated images "distant violence"', Hozic again asks, 'Why is the world watching?', and answers; 'consumed as an image but rejected as a territory, ethnic war zone emerges as a new kind of colony—*un-wanted, un-desired, un-called for*—and, thus, as a playground for a new type of capitalism' (Hozic, 2000, pp. 7, 4).

Clearly, ethno-nationalism remains a critical factor in African development and stability or lack thereof. But initiatives to resolve the innate philosophical tensions, this double consciousness, are more crucial than the mere deprecation of 'tribalism.'

In sum, a multi-dimensional approach through which ethnicity can be elaborated or made to work for development, democracy, community growth, and political stability is imperative. In such an approach, the *celebration* of multi-ethnicity in the social and educational systems is a crucial starting point. It is possible that on such a foundation the apparatus for conflict resolution, distributive justice and national cohesion can be constructed.

Note

1. While I focus here on the discrepancy between media coverage of Bosnia and Rwanda, other works confirm a distinct global hierachization, emerging from Western ethnocentrism, that also locates the Balkan in a similar 'tribal' frame of representation, relative to the 'more civilized West.' The reflections of an American foreign correspondent on his initial attitude to the Balkans conflict are instructive: 'This is the Balkans, it's ethnic rivalry, tribal warfare, the people are uncivilized, they've been doing it for centuries. It was a comforting explanation because it defined the violence as an anti-modern and anti-Western phenomenon—an exception. These people are different from the rest of us, I said to myself, they are like animals in a strange zoo' (Maass, 1996). Other scholars have deplored the treatment of the Balkan conflict as one of 'ethnic hatreds' (see, Gagnon, 1994).

References

Adam, H. (1995), 'The Politics of Ethnic Identity: Comparing South Africa', *Ethnic and Racial Studies*, Vol. 18, No. 3, pp. 457-475.

Adekanye, J. B. (1995), 'Structural Adjustment, Democratization and Rising Ethnic Tensions in Africa', *Development and Change*, Vol. 26, pp. 355-374.

Agbese, P. O. (1996), 'The Military as an Obstacle to the Democratic Enterprise: Toward an Agenda for Permanent Military Disengagement from Politics in Nigeria', *Journal of Asian and African Studies*, Vol. 31, No. 1-2, pp. 82-98.

Agbese, P. O. and Kieh, G. K. (1993), From Politics Back to the Barracks in Nigeria: A Theoretical Exploration', *Journal of Peace Research*, Vol. 30, No. 4, pp. 409-426.

Anise, L. (1979), 'Ethnicity and National Integration in West Africa: Some Theoretical Considerations', in Hall, R. L. (ed.), *Ethnic Autonomy—Comparative Dynamics*, Pergamon Press: New York.

Apaduria, A. (1996), *Modernity at Large*, University of Minnesota Press: Minneapolis.

Appia, K. (1992), *In My Father's House: Africa in the Philosophy of Culture*, Oxford University Press: New York.

Assefa, H. (1996), 'Ethnic Conflict in the Horn of Africa: Myth and Reality', in Rupesinghe, K. and Tishkov, V. A. (eds.), *Ethnicity and Power in the Contemporary World*, United Nations University Press: Tokyo.

Bates, R., Mudimbe, V. and O'Barr, J. (eds.) (1993), *Africa and the Disciplines*, University of Chicago Press: Chicago.

Campbell, A. (1997), 'Ethical Ethnicity: A Critique', *The Journal of Modern African Studies*, Vol. 35, No. 1, pp. 53-79.

Clifford, J. (1988), *The Predicament of Culture: Twentieth-Century Ethnography, Literature and Art*, Harvard University Press: Cambridge, MA.

Comaroff, J. and Comaroff, J. (1997), 'Africa Observed: Discourses of the Imperial Imagination', in Grinker, R. R. and Steiner, C. B. (eds.), *Perspectives on Africa: A Reader in Culture, History and Representation*, Blackwell Publishers: Oxford.

Connor, W. (1994), *Ethnonationalism: The Quest for Understanding*, Princeton University Press: Princeton, NJ.

Cook, W. W. (1979), 'Swim: Cultural Separatism in Contemporary Black Literature', in Hall, R. (ed.), *Ethnic Autonomy—Comparative Dynamics*, Pergamon Press: New York.

Dahl, R. A. (1971), *Polyarchy: Participation and Opposition*, Yale University Press, New Haven, CN.

Diamond, L., Linz, J., and Lipset, S. (eds.) (1995), *Politics in Developing Countries: Comparing Experiences with Democracy*, Lynne Rienner Publishers Boulder, CO.

Dorris, M. (1979), 'Twentieth-Century Indians: The Return of the Natives', in Hall, R. (ed.), *Ethnic Autonomy—Comparative Dynamics*, Pergamon Press: New York.

Eyoh, D. (1995), 'From the Belly to the Ballot: Ethnicity and Politics in Africa', *Queen's Quarterly*, Vol. 102, No. 1, pp. 39-51.

Gagnon, V. P. (1994), 'Ethnic Nationalism and International Conflict: The Case of Serbia', *International Security*, Vol. 19, No. 3, pp. 130-166.

Grinker, R. R. and Steiner, C. B. (eds.) (1997), 'Introduction: Africa in Perspective', in Grinker, R. R. and Steiner, C. B. (eds.), *Perspectives on Africa: A Reader in Culture, History and Representation*, Blackwell Publishers: Oxford.

Hall, R. L. (1979), 'Conceptual Overviews of Ethnicity and Ethnic Dynamics', in Hall, R. L. (ed.), *Ethnic Autonomy—Comparative Dynamics*, Pergamon Press: New York.
Hawk, B. (ed.) (1992), *Africa's Media Image*, Praeger Publishers: New York.
Horowitz, D. L. (1985), *Ethnic Groups in Conflicts*, University of California Press: Berkeley.
Horowitz, D. L. (1991), *A Democratic South Africa? Constitutional Engineering in a Divided Society*, University of California Press: Berkeley.
Horowitz, D. L. (1993), 'Democracy in Divided Societies', *Journal of Democracy*, Vol. 4, No. 4, pp. 18–38.
Hozic, A. A. (2000), 'Making of the Unwanted Colonies: (Un)imagining Desire', in Dean, J. (ed.), *Politics Theory: A Cultural Turn*, Cornell University Press: New York (forthcoming).
Huber, E., Rueschmeyer and Stephens, J. (1993), 'The Impact of Economic Development on Democracy', *Journal of Economic Perspectives*, Vol. 7, No. 3, pp. 71–85.
Huntington, S. P. (1968), *Political Order in Changing Societies*, Yale University Press: New Haven, CN.
Ihonvbere, J. O. (1994), 'The 'Irrelevant State', Ethnicity and the Quest for Nationhood in Africa', *Ethnic and Racial Studies*, Vol. 17, No. 1, pp. 42–60.
Ihonvbere, J. O. and Shaw, T. (eds.) (1998), *Illusions of Power: Nigeria in Transition*, Africa World Press: Trenton, NJ.
Ismagilova, R. N. (1978), *Ethnic Problems of the Tropical Africa. Can They be Solved?*, Progress Publishers: Moscow.
Kieh, G. K. Jr. (1996), 'Democratization and Peace in Africa', *Journal of Asian and African Studies*, Vol. 31, No. 1–2, pp. 99–111.
Lijphart, A. (1985), *Power Sharing in South Africa*, University of California Press: Berkeley.
Maass, P. (1996), *Love Thy Neighbor: A Story of War*, Alfred Knopf: New York.
Mafeje, A. (1971), 'The Ideology of Tribalism', *Journal of Modern African Studies*, Vol. 9, No. 2, pp. 253–262.
Mare, G. (1992), *Ethnicity and Politics in South Africa*, Zed Books: London.
Mazrui, A. (1972), *Cultural Engineering and Nation-Building in East Africa*, Northwestern University Press: Evanston.
Mazrui, A. (1978), *Political Values and the Educated Class in Africa*, University of California Press: Berkeley.
Mbaku, J. M. (1996), 'Effective Constitutional Discourse as an Important First Step to Democracy in Africa', *Journal of Asian and African Studies*, Vol. 31, No. 1–2, pp. 39–51.
Mbaku, J. M. (1998), 'Constitutions and Constitutional Discourse in Africa: Developing Institutional Structures for Peaceful Coexistence', *Civilisations*, Vol. 45, No. 1–2, pp. 229–269.
Mkandawire, T. (1997), 'The Social Sciences in Africa: Breaking Local Barriers and Negotiating International Presence', *African Studies Review*, Vol. 40, No. 2, pp. 15–36.
Monga, C. (1996), *The Anthropology of Anger: Civil Society and Democracy in Africa*, Lynne Rienner Publishers: Boulder, CO.
Moore, S. F. (1993), 'Changing Perspectives on a Changing Africa: The Work of Anthropology', in Bates, R., Mudimbe, V. and O'Barr, J. (eds.), *Africa and the Disciplines*, University of Chicago Press: Chicago.

Mudimbe, V. Y. (1994), *The Idea of Africa*, Indiana University Press: Bloomington.
Myers, G., Klak, T. and Koehl, T. (1996), 'The Inscription of Difference: News Coverage of the Conflicts in Rwanda and Bosnia', *Political Geography*, Vol. 15, No. 1, pp. 21–46.
Nkrumah, K. (1970), *Africa Must Unite*, International Publishers: New York.
Nnoli, O. (1980), *Ethnic Politics in Nigeria*, Fourth Dimension Press: Enugu, Nigeria.
Nyong'o, P. A. (ed.) (1993), *Arms and Daggers in the Heart of Africa: Studies on Internal Conflicts*, Academy of Science Publishers: Nairobi, Kenya.
Obadare, E. (1998), 'Memo to Uthman Shodipe', *The News* (Lagos, Nigeria), Vol. 11, No. 24, p. 50.
Ofeimun, O. (1998), 'Against the Threatening One Party State', *The News* (Lagos, Nigeria), Vol. 11, No. 24, p. 47.
Osaghae, E. E. (1998), 'Managing Multiple Minority Problems in a Divided Society: The Nigerian Experience', *Journal of Modern African Studies*, Vol. 36, No. 1, pp. 1–24.
Przeworski, A. and Limongi, F. (1997), 'Modernization: Theories and Facts', *World Politics*, Vol. 49, pp. 155–183.
Ranger, T. (1985), *The Invention of Tribalism in Zimbabwe*, Mambo Press, Harare, Zimbabwe.
Ranger, T. (1997), 'The Invention of Tradition in Colonial Africa', in Grinker, R. R. and Steiner, C. B. (eds.), *Perspectives on Africa: A Reader in Culture, History and Representation*, Blackwell Publishers: Oxford.
Schmitter, P. C. and Karl, T. L. (1991), 'What Democracy is...and is Not', *Journal of Democracy*, Vol. 2, No. 3, pp. 75–88.
Snarr, N. D. (1998), 'Human Rights', in Snarr, M. T. and Snarr, N. D. (eds.), *Introducing Global Issues*, Lynne Rienner Publishers: Boulder, CO.
Southall, A. W. (1997), 'The Illusion of Tribe', in Grinker, R. R. and Steiner, C. B. (eds.), *Perspectives on Africa: A Reader in Culture, History and Representation*, Blackwell Publishers: Oxford.
Soyinka-Airewele, P. (1999), '*The Nature or Nurture Debate and the Future of Ethnopolitics in Africa*', Working Paper, Alliance for Community Transformation (ACT).
Tsedu, M. (March 4, 1999), 'Nigerian Grouping of Tribal Enclaves', *The [Nigerian] Vanguard*, http://www.afbis.com/vanguard/vp304399.html.
Udogu, E. I (1994), 'The Allurement of Ethnonationalism in Nigerian Politics: The Contemporary Debate', *Journal of Asian and African Studies*, Vol. 29, No. 3–4, pp. 159–171.
Yankah, K. (1995), 'Displaced Academics and the Quest for a New World Academic Order', *Africa Today*, Vol. 47, No. 3, pp. 7–25.

Selected Bibliography

Books

Adam, Herbert and Guillomee, H. (eds.) (1979), *Ethnic Power Mobilized: Can South Africa Change?*, Yale University Press: New Haven.
Ake, Claude (1967), *The Theory of Political Integration*, The Dorsey Press: Homewood, IL.
Alba, Richard (1990), *Ethnic Identity: The Transformation of White America*, Yale University Press: New York and London.
Apaduria, A. (1996), *Modernity at Large*, University of Minneapolis Press: Minneapolis.
Apia, K. (1992), *In My Father's House: Africa in the Philosophy of Culture*, Oxford University Press: New York.
Armstrong, J. (1982), *Nations Before Nationalism*, University of North Carolina Press: Chapel Hill, NC.
Asiwaju, A. I. (ed.) (1985), *Partitioned Africans: Ethnic Relations across Africa's International Boundaries, 1884–1984*, C. Hurst and Company: London.
Bachler, G. (ed.) (1997), *Federalism Against Ethnicity*, Verlag Rugger Publishers: Zurich.
Banks, Marcus (1966), *Ethnicity: Anthropological Construction*, Routledge: London.
Banton, Michael (1967), *Race Relations*, Tavistock Publishers: London.
Banton, Michael (1993), *Racial and Ethnic Competition*, Ashgate Publishing Company: Brookfield, VT.
Banton, Michael (1998), *Ethnic and Racial Consciousness*, Longman Publishing Group: White Plains.
Barth, F. (1969), *Ethnic Groups and Boundaries*, Little Brown: Boston, MA.
Bates, R., Mudimbe, V. and O'Barr, J. (eds.) (1993), *Africa and the Disciplines*, University of Chicago Press: Chicago.
Bayart, J.-F. (1989), *The State in Africa—The Politics of the Belly*, Longman Press: London.
Bentham, J. (1988), *Principles of Morals and Legislation*, Prometheus Press: Buffalo.
Boutros-Ghali, Boutros (1992), *An Agenda for Peace: Preventive Diplomacy, Peacemaking and Peace-keeping*, United Nations Publications: New York.
Brass, Paul (ed.) (1985), *Ethnic Groups and the State*, Croom Helm Publishers: London.
Brass, Paul (1991), *Ethnicity and Nationalism: Theory and Comparison*, Sage Publications: New Delhi.
Brown, Michael E. (ed.) (1993), *Ethnic Conflict and International Security*, Princeton University Press: Princeton, NJ.
Brown, Michael E. (ed.) (1996), *The International Dimension of Internal Conflict*, MIT Press: Cambridge, MA.
Cartwright, John R. (1970), *Politics in Sierra Leone, 1947–67*, University of Toronto Press: Toronto.
Cartwright, John R. (1978), *Political Leadership in Sierra Leone*, Croom Helm Publishers: London.

Christie, K (ed.), (1988), *Ethnic Conflict, Tribal Politics*, Curzan Press: Richmond, Surrey.
Cohen, Abner (ed.) (1974), *Urban Ethnicity*, Tavistock Publishers: London.
Cohen, Anthony P. (1985), *The Symbolic Construction of Community*, Tavistock Publishers: London.
Cohen, Ronald and Middleton, John (1970), *From Tribe to Nation in Africa*, Chandler Publishers: Scranton.
Coleman, James S. and Sklar, Richard L. (1994), *Nationalism and Development in Africa: Selected Essays*, University of California Press: Berkeley.
Collier, G. B. (1970), *Sierra Leone: An Experiment in Democracy*, New York University Press: New York.
Connor, Walker (1993), *Ethnonationalism: The Quest for Understanding*, Princeton University Press: Princeton, NJ.
Couloumbis, Theodore A. and Wolfe, James H. (1990), *Introduction to International Relations: Power and Justice*, Prentice-Hall: Englewood, Cliffs.
Dahl, Robert A. (1971), *Polyarchy: Participation and Opposition*, Yale University Press: New Haven.
Davidson, Basil (1970), *The African Genius: An Introduction to Social and Cultural History*, Little Brown: Boston, MA.
Davidson, Basil (1974), *Africa in History: Themes and Outlines*, Macmillan Publishing Company: New York.
Davidson, Basil (1992), *Africa in History*, Free Press: New York.
De Silva, K. M. and May, R. J. (ed.) (1991), *Internationalization of Ethnic Conflict*, Pinter Publishers: London.
Diamond, Larry (1988), *Class, Ethnicity and Democracy in Nigeria: The Failure of the First Republic*, Macmillan Press: London.
Diamond, Larry, Linz, J. and Lipset, S. (eds.) (1995), *Politics in Developing Countries: Comparing Experiences with Democracy*, Lynne Rienner Publishers: Boulder, CO.
Donald, J. and Rattansi, Ali (eds.) (1992), *Race, Culture and Difference*, Sage Publishers: London.
Ekeh, Peter (ed.) (1997), *Wilberforce Conference on Nigerian Federalism*, State University of New York: Buffalo.
Elazar, D (1974), *Federalism and the Way to Peace*, Institute of Intergovernmental Relations: Kingston.
Emeagwali, Gloria T. (1995), *Women Pay the Price: Structural Adjustment in Africa and the Caribbean*, Africa World Press: Trenton, NJ.
Emerson, Rupert (1960), *From Empire to Nation: The Rise to Self-Assertion of Asian and African Peoples*, Beacon Press: Boston.
Enloe, Cynthia (1973), *Ethnic Conflict and Political Development*, Little Brown: Boston.
Enloe, Cynthia (1980), *Ethnic Soldiers*, University of Georgia Press: Athens.
Esman, Milton J. (1994), *Ethnic Politics*, Cornell University Press: Ithaca, NY.
Esman, Milton J. (ed.) (1995), *International Organizations and Ethnic Conflict*, Cornell University Press: Ithaca, NY.
Esman, Miltor, J. and Telhami, Shibley (eds.) (1995), *International Organizations and Ethnic Conflict*, Cornell University Press: Ithaca, NY.
Evans, G. (1997), *Responding to Crisis in the African Great Lakes*, New Oxford University Press: New York.

Selected Bibliography 189

Falola, Toyin and Ihonvbere, Julius (1985), *The Rise and Fall of Nigeria's Second Republic*, Zed Press: London.
Fanon, Frantz (1963), *The Wretched of the Earth*, Grove Press: New York.
Francis, Emerich (1976), *Inter-Ethnic Relations, An Essay in Sociological Theory*, Elsevier Scientific Publishing Company: New York.
Frankel, M. M. (1964), *Tribe and Class in Monrovia*, Oxford University Press: London.
Furley, O. W. (ed.) (1995), *Conflict in Africa*, St. Martin's Press: New York.
Geertz, Clifford (ed.) (1963), *Old Societies and New States*, Free Press: Oxford and New York.
Geertz, Clifford (1973), *The Interpretation of Cultures*, Basic Books: New York.
Geertz, Clifford (1981), *Negara: The Theatre State in Nineteenth Century*, Princeton University Press: Princeton, NJ.
Gellner, Ernest (1983), *Nations and Nationalism*, Blackwell Publishers: Oxford.
Glazer, Nathan and Moynihan, Daniel P. (eds.) (1975), *Ethnicity: Theory and Experience*, Harvard University Press: Cambridge, MA.
Goldsworthy, D. (1982), *Tom Mboya: The Man Kenya Wanted to Forget*, Heinemann Press: Nairobi and New York.
Gottlieb, Gidon (1993), *Nation Against State: A New Approach to Ethnic Conflicts and the Decline of Sovereignty*, Council on Foreign Relations Press: New York.
Gulliver, P. H. (ed.) (1968), *Tradition and Transition in East Africa*, University of California Press: Berkeley.
Gurr, Ted (1993), *Minorities at Risk: A Global View of Ethnopolitical Conflict*, United States Institute of Peace Press: Washington, DC.
Gurr, Ted and Harff, Barbara (1994), *Ethnic Conflict in World Politics*, Westview Press: Boulder, CO.
Gutkind, P (ed.) (1970), *The Passing of Tribal Man in Africa*, E. J. Brill Publishers: Leiden.
Hall, Raymond L. (ed.) (1979), *Ethnic Autonomy—Comparative Dynamics: The Americas, Europe and the Developing World*, Pergamon Press: New York.
Hawk, B. (ed.) (1992), *Africa's Media Image*, Praeger Publishers: New York.
Hayward, F. M. (ed.) (1987), *Elections in Independent Africa*, Westview Press: Boulder, CO.
Heraclides, Alexis (1991), *The Self-determination of Minorities in International Politics*, Frank Cass Publishers: London.
Horowitz, Donald (1985), *Ethnic Groups in Conflict*, University of California Press: Berkeley and Los Angeles.
Horowitz, Donald (1991), *A Democratic South Africa: Constitutional Engineering in a Divided Society*, University of California Press: Berkeley and Los Angeles.
Huntington, Samuel P. (1968), *Political Order in Changing Societies*, Yale University Press: New Haven.
Hutchinson, John and Smith, Anthony D. (eds.) (1996), *Ethnicity*, Oxford University Press: Oxford and New York.
Hutnick, Nimmi (1991), *Ethnic Minority Identity: A Social Psychological Perspective*, Clarendon Press: Oxford.
Hyden, G and Bratton, M. (eds.) (1992), *Governance and Politics in Africa*, Lynne Rienner: Boulder, CO.
Ihonvbere, Julius (1994), *Nigeria: The Politics of Adjustment & Democracy*, Transaction Publishers: New York.

Ihonvbere, Julius and Shaw, Timothy (1988), *Illusions of Power: Nigeria in Transition*, Africa World Press: Lawrenceville, NJ.
Ingham, K. (1990), *Politics in Modern Africa: The Uneven Tribal Dimension*, Routledge Publishers: London and New York.
Ismagilova, R. N. (1978), *Ethnic Problems of the Tropical Africa: Can they be Solved?*, Progress Publishers: Moscow.
Joseph, Richard (1987), *Democracy and Prebendal Politics in Nigeria*, Cambridge University Press: Cambridge.
Joseph, Richard (ed.) (1998), *Conflict and Democracy in Africa*, Lynne Rienner Publishers: Boulder, CO.
Karimi, J. And Ochieng, P. (1980), *The Kenyatta Succession*, Trans-Africa Publishers: Nairobi.
Kegley, Charles W. and Wittkopf Eugene (1997), *World Politics: Trends and Transformation*, St. Martin's Press: New York.
Kellas, James G. (1991), *The Politics of Nationalism and Ethnicity*, Macmillan Press: London.
Keyes, Charles (ed.) (1981), *Ethnic Change*, University of Washington Press: Seattle.
Kofele-Kale, N. (1981), *Tribesmen and Patriot: Political Culture in a Polyethnic State*, University Press of America: Washington, DC.
Kohli, A (ed.) (1986), *The State and Development in the Third World*, Princeton University Press: Princeton, NJ.
Koroma, A. K. (1996), *Sierra Leone: The Agony of a Nation*, Andromed Publications: Freetown, Sierra Leone.
Laitin, D. (1986), *Hegemony and Culture: Politics and Religious Change Among the Yoruba*, University of Chicago Press: Chicago, IL.
Laski, H. J. (1935), *The State as a Concept in Theory and Practice*, The Viking Press: London.
LeVine, V. T. (1971), *The Cameroon Federal Republic*, Cornell University Press: Ithaca, NY.
Lewis, Arthur (1965), *Politics in West Africa*, Oxford University Press: London.
Leys, C. (1974), *Underdevelopment in Kenya: The Political Economy of Neocolonialism*, University of California Press: Berkeley.
Light, Ivan (1972), *Ethnic Enterprise in America*, University of California Press: Berkeley.
Lijphart, Arendt (1977), *Democracy in Plural Societies: A Comparative Exploration*, Yale University Press: New Haven.
Lijphart, Arendt (1984), *Democracies: Patterns of Majoritarian and Consensus Government in the Twenty-one Countries*, Yale University Press: New Haven.
Linz, J. J. and Stepan, A. (eds.) (1976), *The Breakdown of Authoritarian Regimes*, The John Hopkins University Press: Baltimore, MD.
Lubasz, H. (1974), *The Development of the Modern State*, Macmillan Press: New York.
Mare, G. (1992), *Ethnicity and Politics in South Africa*, Zed Books: London.
Mazrui, Ali (1978), *Political Values and the Educated Class in Africa*, University of California Press: Berkeley.
Mazrui, Ali (1987), *The Africans: A Triple Heritage*, Little, Brown and Company: New York.
Mazrui, Ali (1990), *Cultural Forces in World Politics*, Heinemann Educational Books: Portsmouth, NH.

Mbaku, John M. (ed.) (1999), *Preparing Africa for the Twenty-First Century: Strategies for Peaceful Co-existence and Sustainable Development*, Ashgate Publishers: Aldershot, UK.
McGary, J. and O'Leary, B. (eds.) (1993), *The Politics of Ethnic Regulations*, Routldge Publishers: London.
McNeill, William H. (1986), *Polyethnicity and National Unity in World History*, University of Toronto Press: Toronto.
Monga, C. (1996), *The Anthropology of Anger: Civil Society and Democracy in Africa*, Lynne Rienner: Boulder, CO.
Montville, Joseph, V. (ed.) (1990), *Conflict and Peacemaking in Multiethnic Societies*, Lexington Books: Lexington, MA.
Moynihan, Daniel P. (1993), *Pandaemonium: Ethnicity in International Politics*, Oxford University Press: Oxford.
Mudimbe, V. Y. (1994), *The Idea of Africa*, Indiana University Press: Bloomington.
Muriuki, G (1974), *A History of the Kikuyu, 1500–1800*, Oxford University Press: Nairobi.
Nash, Manning (1989), *The Cauldrum of Ethnicity in the Modern World*, University of Chicago Press: Chicago and London.
Newbury, Catherine (1988), *The Cohesion of Oppression: Clientship and Ethnicity in Rwanda, 1860–1960*, Columbia University Press: New York.
Nkrumah, Kwame (1970), *Africa Must Unite*, International Publishers: New York.
Nnoli, Okwudiba (1978), *Ethnic Politics in Nigeria*, Fourth Dimension Press: Enugu, Nigeria.
Nnoli, Okwudiba (1995), *Ethnicity and Development in Nigeria*, Ashgate Publishing Company: Brookfield.
Nordlinger, Eric A. (1972), *Conflict Regulation in Divided Societies*, Harvard University Press: Cambridge, MA.
Nordlinger, Eric A. (1981), *On the Autonomy of the Democratic State*, Harvard University Press: Cambridge, MA.
Nyang'o, P. A. (ed.) (1993), *Arms and Daggers in the Heart of Africa: Studies on Internal Conflicts*, Academy of Science Publishers: Nairobi.
Nyang'oro, Julius E. and Shaw, Timothy M. (eds.) (1989), *Corporatism in Africa: Comparative Analysis and Practice*, Westview Press: Boulder, CO.
Ogot, B. A (ed.) (1996), *Ethnicity, Nationalism, and Democracy in Africa*, Institute of Research and Postgraduate Studies, Maseno University College: Maseno, Kenya.
Olorunsola, Victor A (ed.) (1972), *Politics of Cultural Subnationalism*, Doubleday and Company, Inc.: New York.
Patterson, Orlando (1977), *Ethnic Chauvinism: The Reactionary Impulse*, Stein and Day Publishers: New York.
Peel, P. D. Y. (1983), *Ijeshas and Nigerians: The Incorporation of a Yoruba Kingdom, 1890s–1970s*, Cambridge University Press: Cambridge.
Pemberton, J. and Afolayan, F. (1996), *Yoruba Sacred Kingship: A Power Like the Gods*, Smithsonian Institution Press: Washington, DC.
Post, K. And Vickers, M. (1973), *Structures and Conflict in Nigeria, 1960–1966*, Heinemann Press: London.
Rabushka, Alvin and Shepsle Kenneth A. (1972), *Politics in Plural Societies: A Theory of Democratic Instability*, Charles E. Merrill Publishing Company: Columbus, OH.
Randall, S. and Gibbins, R. (eds.) (1994), *Federalism and the New World Order*, University

of Calgary Press: Calgary.
Ranger, T. (1985), *The Invention of Tribalism in Zimbabwe*, Mambo Press: Harare, Zimbabwe.
Ranger, T. and Vaughan, Olufemi (eds.) (1993), *Legitimacy and the State in Twentieth Century Africa*, Macmillan Press: London.
Reno, W (1995), *Corruption and State Politics in Sierra Leone*, Cambridge University Press: Cambridge.
Reynolds, A. (ed.) (1994), *Elections '94 South Africa*, St. Martin's Press: New York.
Reynolds, A. and Sisk, T. D. (eds.) (1998), *Elections and Conflict Management in Africa*, United States Institute of Peace Press: Washington, DC.
Rex, John (1986), *Race and Ethnicity*, Open University Press: Milton, Keynes.
Rex, John and Mason, David (eds.) (1986), *Theories of Race and Ethnic Relations*, Cambridge University Press: Cambridge.
Ringer, Benjamin R. and Lawless, Elinor R. (1989), *Race-Ethnicity and Society*, Routledge Publishers: New York.
Rotberg, Robert and Mazrui, Ali (eds.) (1970), *Protest and Power in Black Africa*, Oxford University Press: New York.
Rothchild, Donald (1997), *Managing Ethnic Conflict in Africa*, Brookings Institution Press: Washington, DC.
Rothchild, Donald and Lake, D. (eds.) (1998), *The International Spread of Ethnic Conflict*, Princeton University Press: Princeton, NJ.
Rothchild, Donald and Olorunsola, Victor (eds.) (1983), *State versus Ethnic Claims: African Policy Dilemmas*, Westview Press: Boulder, CO.
Rothschild, Joseph (1981), *Ethnopolitics: A Conceptual Framework*, Columbia University Press: New York.
Rupesinghe, K. (ed.) (1989), *Conflict Resolution in Uganda*, Ohio University Press: Athens, OH.
Rupesinghe, K. (ed.) (1992), *Early Warning: Conflict and Resolution*, St. Martin's Press: New York.
Rupesinghe, K. and Tishkov, V. A. (eds.), *Ethnicity and Power in the Contemporary World*, United Nations University Press: Tokyo.
Said, Abdul and Simmons, Luis (eds.) (1977), *Ethnicity in an International Context*, Transaction Books: New Brunswick, NJ.
Schermerhorn, R. A. (1978), *Comparative Ethnic Relations*, University of Chicago Press: Chicago, IL.
Schwarz, F. A. O. (1965), *Nigeria: The Tribe, the Nation or the Race*, MIT Press: Cambridge.
Siddiqui, Rukhsana A. (ed.) (1997), *Sub-Saharan Africa in the 1990s: Challenges to Democracy and Development*, Praeger Publishers: Wesport, CT.
Sisk, Timothy D. (1996), *Power Sharing and International Mediation in Ethnic Conflict*, U. S. Institute of Peace Press: Washington, DC.
Smith, Anthony D. (1981), *The Ethnic Revival in the Modern World*, Cambridge University Press: Cambridge.
Smith, Anthony D. (1986), *The Ethnic Origin of Nations*, Blackwell Publishers: Oxford.
Smith, Anthony D. (1995), *Nations and Nationalism in a Global Era*, Polity Press: Cambridge.
Sollors, Werner (eds.) (1989), *The Invention of Ethnicity*, Oxford University Press: New

York.
Soyinka, Peyi (1988), *Ethnic Minorities in European Union: A Study of the Basques and Irish Republican Separatists*, Obafemi Awolowo University M.A. Thesis: Ile-Ife, Nigeria.
Soyinka, Wole (1998), *Open Sore of a Continent*, Oxford University Press: Oxford.
Sowell, T. (1981), *Ethnic America*, Basic Books: New York.
Stack, J. F. (ed.) (1986), *The Primordial Challenge: Ethnicity in the Contemporary World*, Greenwood Press: New York.
Taras, R. and Ganguly, R. (1998), *Understanding Ethnic Conflict—The International Dimension*, Longman Press: New York.
Thompson, B. (1997), *The Constitutional History and Law of Sierra Leone, 1961–1995*, University Press of America: New York.
Throup, D. and Hornsby, C. (1998), *Multi-Party Politics in Kenya*, James Currey Publishers: Oxford.
Tigmor, R. L. (1976), *The Colonial Transformation of Kenya, 1900–1939*, Princeton University Press: Princeton, NJ.
Tilly, C. (ed.) (1975), *The Formation of National States in Western Europe*, Princeton University Press: Princeton, NJ.
Udogu, E. Ike (1997), *Nigeria and the Politics of Survival as a Nation-State*, The Edwin Mellen Press: Lewiston, NY.
Udogu, E. Ike (ed.) (1997), *Democracy and Democratization in Africa: Toward the 21st Century*, E. J. Brill Publishers: Leiden, New York, Köln.
Van Der Berghe Pierre (1979), *The Ethnic Phenomenon*, Elsevier Scientific Publishing Company: New York.
Vaughan, Olufemi (2000), *Chiefs: Traditional Power in Modern Politics 1890s–1990s*, University of Rochester Press: Rochester, New York.
Wallmann, Sandra (ed.) (1979), *Ethnicity and Work*, Macmillan Press: London.
Waters, M. C. (1990), *Ethnic Options: Choosing Ethnic Identities in America*, University of California Press: Berkeley.
Watkins, F. M. (1934), *The State as a Concept in Political Science*, Harper and Brothers: New York.
Were, G. S. (1967), *A History of the Abaluyia of Western Kenya, 1500–1930*, East African Publishing House: Nairobi.
Wildner, J. A. (1992), *The Rise of the Party-State in Kenya*, University of California Press: Berkeley.
Willis, J. (1993), *Mombasa, the Swahili and the Making of the Mijikenda*, Clarendon Press: Oxford.
Wyse, A. (1989), *The Krio of Sierra Leone: An Interpretive History*, C. Hurst and Company: London.
Yeros, Paris (ed.) (1999), *Ethnicity and Nationalism in Africa: Constructivist Reflections and Contemporary Politics*, Macmillan Press: London.
Young, Crawford (1976), *The Politics of Cultural Pluralism*, University of Wisconsin Press: Madison.
Young, Crawford (ed.) (1993), *The Rising Tide of Cultural Pluralism: The Nation-State at Bay*, University of Wisconsin Press: Madison.
Young, Crawford (1998), *Ethnic Diversity and Public Policy: A Comparative Inquiry*, St. Martin's Press: New York.

Zack-Williams, Alfred B. (1995), *Tributors, Supporters and Merchant Capital in Sierra Leone Mining and Underdevelopment in Sierra Leone*, Gower-Avebury Press: Aldershot, UK.
Zartmann, I. William (ed.) (1991), *Conflict Resolution in Africa*, Brookings Institution: Washington: DC.
Zartmann, I. William (ed.) (1995), *Collapsed States: The Disintegration and Restoration of Legitimate Authority*, Lynne Rienner: Boulder, CO.

Journal articles

Adam, H. (1995), The Politics Of Ethnic Identity: Comparing South Africa', *Ethnic And Racial Studies*, Vol. 18, No. 3, pp. 457–475.
Adekanye, J. B. (1995), Structural Adjustment, Democratization and Rising Ethnic Tensions in Africa', *Development And Change*, Vol. 26, pp. 355–374.
Agbese, Pita O. (1996), Ethnic Conflicts and Hometown Associations', *Africa Today*, Vol. 43, No. 2, pp. 139–156.
Agbese, Pita O. (1996), The Military as an Obstacle to the Democratization Enterprise: Toward an Agenda for Permanent Military Disengagement from Politics in Nigeria', *Journal of Asian and African Studies*, Vol. 31, No. 1–2, pp. 82–98.
Agbese, Pita O. and Kieh, George K (1993), From Politics Back to the Barracks in Nigeria: A Theoretical Exploration', *Journal of Peace Research*, Vol. 30, No. 4, pp. 409–426.
Bariagaber, Assefaw (1998), The Politics of Cultural Pluralism in Ethiopia and Eritrea: Trajectories or Ethnicity and Constitutional Experiments', *Ethnic and Racial Studies*, Vol. 21, No. 6, pp. 1056–1073.
Bates, Robert (1974), 'Ethnic Competition and Modernization in Contemporary Africa', *Comparative Political Studies*, Vol. 6, No. 4, pp. 457–484.
Bonacich, Edna (1972), 'A Theory of Ethnic Antagonism: The Split Labor Market', *American Sociological Review*, Vol. 37, pp. 547–559.
Burges, Elaine (1978), 'The Resurgence of Ethnicity', *Ethnic and Racial Studies*, Vol. 1, No. 3, pp. 265–285.
Cambell, A. (1997), 'Ethical Ethnicity: A Critique', *The Journal of Modern African Studies*, Vol. 35, No. 1, pp. 53–79.
Connor, Walker (1973), 'The Politics of Ethnonationalism', *Journal of International Affairs*, Vol. 27, No. 1, pp. 1–23.
Connor, Walker (1978), 'A Nation is a Nation, is a State, is an Ethnic Group, is a ...', *Ethnic and Racial Studies*, Vol. 1, No. 4, pp. 378–400.
Cross, Malcolm (1978), 'Colonialism and Ethnicity: A Theory and Comparative Case Study', *Ethnic and Racial Studies*, Vol. 1, No. 1, p. 37–59.
Diamond, L. (1987), 'Ethnicity and Ethnic Conflict', *Journal of Modern African Studies*, Vol. 25, No. 1, pp. 117–128.
Eller, J. and Coughlin, R. (1993), 'The Poverty of Primordialism: The Demystification of Ethnic Attachments', *Ethnic and Racial Studies*, Vol. 6, No. 2, pp. 183–202.
Enloe, Cynthia (1978), 'Ethnicity, Bureaucracy and State-building in Africa and Latin America', *Ethnic and Racial Studies*, Vol. 1, No. 2, pp. 336–351.
Esman, Milton J. (1995), 'Ethnic Actors in International Politics', *Nationalism and Ethnic*

Politics, Vol. 1, No. 1, pp. 111–125.
Eyoh, Dickson (1995), 'From the Belly to the Ballot: Ethnicity and Politics in Africa', Queen's Quarterly, Vol. 102, No. 1, pp. 39–51.
Gans, H. (1994), 'Symbolic Ethnicity and Symbolic Religiosity: Towards a Comparison of Ethnic and Religious Accumulation', Ethnic and Racial Studies, Vol. 17, No. 4, pp. 577–592.
Gross, Michael L. (1996), 'Restructuring Ethnic Paradigms: From Pre-Modern to Post-Modern Perspectives', Canadian Review of Studies in Nationalism, Vol. 23, Nos. 1–2, pp. 51–65.
Gurr, Ted (1993), 'Why Minorities Rebel: A Global Analysis of Communal Mobilization and Conflict Since 1945', International Political Science Review, Vol. 14, No. 2, pp. 161–201.
Gurr, Ted (1994), 'Peoples Against States: Ethnopolitical Conflict and the Changing World System', International Studies Quarterly, Vol. 38, No. 3, pp. 347–377.
Handelman, Don (1977), 'The Organization of Ethnicity', Ethnic Groups, Vol. 1, pp. 187–200.
Hayward, F. M. (1972), 'The Development of a Radical Political Organization in the Bush: A Case Study of Sierra Leone', Canadian Journal of African Studies, Vol. 6, No. 1, pp. 1–28.
Hechter, M., Friedman, D. and Appelbaun, M. (1982), 'A Theory of Ethnic Collective Action', International Migration Review, Vol. 16, pp. 112–134.
Holmquist, F. and Ford M. (1994), 'Kenya: State and Civil Society the First Year after the Election', Africa Today, Vol. 41, No. 4, pp. 5–25.
Horowitz, D. (1971), 'Three Dimensions of Ethnic Politics', World Politics, Vol. 23, No. 2, pp. 244–251.
Horowitz, D. (1993), 'Democracy in Divided Societies', Journal of Democracy, Vol. 4, No. 4, pp. 18–38.
Hyden, G. and William, D. C. (1994), 'A Community Model of African Politics: Illustrations from Nigeria and Tanzania', Comparative Studies in Society and History, Vol. 36, No. 1, pp. 68–96.
Ihonvbere, Julius O. (1994), 'The "Irrelevant" State, Ethnicity, and the Quest for Nationhood in Africa', Ethnic and Racial Studies, Vol. 17, No. 1, pp. 42–60.
Ihonvbere, Julius O. (1996), 'Are Things Falling Apart? The Military and the Crisis of Democratization in Nigeria', Journal of Modern African Studies, Vol. 34, No. 2, pp. 193–225.
Ikime, O. (1968), 'Reconsidering Colonial Rule: The Nigerian Example', Journal of Historical Society of Nigeria, Vol. 4, pp. 421–438.
Kalu, Kelechi A. (1996), 'Political Economy in Nigeria: The Military, Ethnic Politics and Development', International Journal of Politics, Culture and Society, Vol. 10, pp. 229–247.
Kandeh, J. D. (1992), 'Politicization of Ethnic Identities in Sierra Leone', African Studies Review, Vol. 35, No. 1, pp. 81–99.
Kandeh, J. D. (1998), 'Transition Without Rupture: Sierra Leone's Transfer Election of 1996 ', African Studies Review, Vol. 41, No. 2, pp. 91–111.
Kieh, George K., Jr. (1996), 'Democratization and Peace in Africa', Journal of Asian and African Studies, Vol. 31, Nos. 1–2, pp. 99–111.
Kimenyi, M. S. (1998), 'Harmonizing Ethnic Claims in Africa: A Proposal for Ethnic-Based

Federalism', *Cato Journal*, Vol. 35, No. 2, pp. 43–63.
Konings, P. and Nyamnjoh, F. B. (1997), 'Anglophone Problem in Cameroon', *Journal of Modern African Studies*, Vol. 35, No. 2, pp. 207–229.
Lake, David A. and Rothchild, D. (1996), 'Containing Fear: The Origin and Management of Ethnic Conflict', *International Security*, Vol. 21, No. 2, p. 41–75.
Lal, B. B. (1983), 'Perspectives on Ethnicity: Old Wine in New Bottles', *Ethnic and Racial Studies*, Vol. 6, No. 2, pp. 154–173.
Lemarchand, R. (1968), 'Revolutionary Phenomena in Stratified States', *Civilisations*, Vol. 18, pp. 16–51.
Lemarchand, R. (1994), 'Managing Transition Anarchies: Rwanda, Burundi, and South Africa in Comparative Perspective', *Journal of Modern African Studies*, Vol. 32, No. 4, pp. 581–604.
Lenthner, H. (1984), 'The Concept of the State: A Response to Stephen Krasner', *Comparative Politics*, Vol. 16, pp. 367–377.
Lustick, I. (1979), 'Stability in Deeply Divided Societies', *World Politics*, Vol. 31, pp. 325–344.
Mafeje, A. (1971), 'The Ideology of Tribalism', *Journal of Modern African Studies*, Vol. 9, No. 2, pp. 253–262.
Maynes, Charles W. (1993), 'Containing Ethnic Conflict', *Foreign Affairs*, Vol. 90, pp. 3–31.
Mbaku, John M. (1996), 'Effective Constitutional Discourse as an Important First Step to Democracy in Africa', *Journal of Asian and African Studies*, Vol. 31, Nos. 1–2, pp. 39–51.
Mbaku, John M. (1998), 'Constitutional Discourse and the Development of Structures for Sustainable Development in Africa', *Journal for Studies in Economics and Econometrics*, Vol. 22, No. 1, pp. 1–36.
Mbaku, John M. (1999), 'Property Rights and the Exploitation of Africa's Environmental Resources: Preparing for the New Century', *Global Focus*, Vol. 11, No. 4, pp. 77–92.
Mbaku, John M. (2000), 'Minority Rights in Plural Societies', *Seminar* (Delhi), No. 490 (June), pp. 51–59.
McKay, J. (1982), 'An Exploratory Synthesis of Primordial and Mobilizationist Approaches to Ethnic Phenomenon', *Ethnic and Racial Studies*, Vol. 5, No. 4, pp. 394–420.
Mkandawire, T. (1997), 'The Social Science in Africa: Breaking Local Barriers and Negotiating International Presence', *African Studies Review*, Vol. 40, No 2, pp. 15–36.
Myers, G., Klak, T. and Koehl, T. (1996), 'The Inscription of Difference: News Coverage of the Conflicts in Rwanda and Bosnia', *Political Geography*, Vol. 15, No. 1, pp. 21–46.
Nagel, J. (1995), 'Resource Competition Theories', *American Behavioral Scientist*, Vol. 38, No. 3, pp. 442–457.
Newman, S. (1991), 'Does Modernization Breed Ethnic Political Conflict?', *World Politics*, Vol. 43, No. 3, pp. 451–478.
Nowroje, B. and Manby B. (1993), 'Divide and Rule', *Africa Report*, Vol. 38, No. 5, pp. 32–35.
Ojo, Olatunde J. B. (1981), 'The Impact of Personality and Ethnicity on Nigerian Elections of 1979', *Africa Today*, Vol. 28, No. 1, pp. 47–58.

Okamura, J. Y. (1981), 'Situational Ethnicity', *Ethnic and Racial Studies*, Vol. 4, No. 4, pp. 452–463.
Olzak, S. (1983), 'Contemporary Ethnic Mobilization', *Annual Review of Sociology*, Vol. 9, pp. 355–374.
Osaghae, E. E. (1991), 'Ethnic Minorities and Federalism in Africa', *African Affairs*, Vol. 90, No. 359, pp. 237–258.
Osaghae, E. E. (1995), 'The Ogoni Uprising: Oil Politics, Minority Agitation and the Future of the Nigerian State', *African Affairs*, Vol. 94, No. 376, pp. 325–344.
Posen, Barry R. (1993), 'The Security Dilemma and Ethnic Conflict', *Survival*, Vol. 35, No. 1, pp. 27–47.
Reynolds, V. (1980), 'Sociology and the Idea of Primordial Discrimination', *Ethnic and Racial Studies*, Vol. 3, No. 3, pp. 303–315.
Robertson, L. R. (1997), The Constructed Nature of Ethnopolitics', *International Politics*, Vol. 34, pp. 265–283.
Rothchild, D. and Groth, A. J. (1995), 'Pathological Dimensions of Domestic and International Ethnicity', *Political Science Quarterly*, Vol. 110, No. 1, pp. 69–82.
Scaritt, J. R. and Safran, W. (1983), 'The Relationship of Ethnicity to Modernization and Democracy: A Restatement of the Issue', *International Studies Notes of the International Studies Association*, Vol. 10, No. 2, pp. 16–21.
Schmitter, P. C. and Karl, T. L. (1991), 'What Democracy is ... and is Not', *Journal of Democracy*, Vol. 2, No. 3, pp. 75–88.
Sklar, R. (1967), 'Political Science and National Integration: A Radical Approach', *Journal of Modern African Studies*, Vol. 5, No. 1, pp. 1–11.
Sklar, R. (1979), 'The Nature of Class Domination in Africa', *Journal of Modern African Studies*, Vol. 17, No. 4, pp. 531–552.
Smith, A. (1981), 'War and Ethnicity: The Role of Warfare in the Cohesion and Self-image of Ethnic Groups', *Ethnic and Racial Studies*, Vol. 4, No. 4, pp. 375–397.
Spreitzer, E. and Snyder, E. E. (1975), 'Patterns of Variation Within and Between Ethnoreligious Groupings', *Ethnicity*, Vol. 2, No. 2, pp. 124–133.
Stanfield, J. H. (1995), 'Theories of Ethnicity', *American Behavioral Scientist*, Vol. 38, No. 3, pp. 389–390. The entire issue is dedicated to the question of ethnicity.
Stone, J. (1995), 'Race, Ethnicity, and the Weberian Legacy', *American Behavioral Scientist*, Vol. 38, No. 3, pp. 391–406.
Takougang, J. (1996), 'Multiparty Elections in Cameroon: Prospects for Democracy and Democratization', *Journal of Asian and African Studies*, Vol. 31, Nos. 1–2, pp. 52–65.
Udogu, E. Ike (1990), 'National Integration Attempts in Nigerian Politics, 1979–1984', *Canadian Review of Studies in Nationalism*, Vol. 17, Nos. 1–2, pp. 157–175.
Udogu, E. Ike (1994), 'The Allurement of Ethnonationalism in Nigerian Politics: The Contemporary Debate', *Journal of Asian and African Studies*, Vol. 29, Nos. 3–4, pp. 159–171.
Udogu, E. Ike (1995), 'The Military, Civil Society and the Issue of Democratic Governance: Toward Nigeria's Fourth Republic', *Journal of Developing Societies*, Vol. 11, No. 2, pp. 205–220.
Udogu, E. Ike (1999), 'The Issue of Ethnicity and Democratization in Africa: Toward the Millennium', *Journal of Black Studies*, Vol. 29, No. 6, pp. 790–808.
Uzodike, U. O. (1996), 'Democracy and Economic Reforms: Developing Underdeveloped

Economies', *Journal of Asian and African Studies*, Vol. 31, Nos. 1–2, pp. 21–38.
Van den Berge, P. (1983), 'Class, Race, and Ethnicity in Africa', *Ethnic and Racial Studies*, Vol. 6, No. 2, pp. 221–236.
Vaughan, Olufemi (1994), 'Communalism, Legitimation, and Party Politics at the Grassroots: The Case of the Yoruba', *International Journal of Politics, Culture, and Society*, Vol. 7, pp. 419–440.
Vaughan, Olufemi (1995), 'Assessing Grassroots Politics and Community Development in Nigeria, *African Affairs*, Vol. 94, No. 377, pp. 501–518.
Vincent, J. (1974), 'The Restructuring of Ethnicity', *Human Organization*, Vol. 33, No. 4, pp. 376–377.
Wallerstein, I. (1960), 'Ethnicity and National Integration in West Africa', *Cahiers d'Etudes Africaines*, Vol. 3, pp. 129–139.
Walters, T. (1995), 'Tutsi Social Identity in Contemporary Africa', *Journal of Modern African Studies*, Vol. 33, No. 2, pp. 343–347.
Weiner, M. (1992), 'Peoples and State in a New Ethnic Order?', *Third World Quarterly*, Vol. 13, No. 2, pp. 317–333.
Yanka, K. (1995), 'Displaced Academics and the Quest for a New World Academic Order', *Africa Today*, Vol. 47, No. 3, pp. 7–25.
Zack-Williams, A. B. (1985), 'Comments on the Manufacturing Sector in Sierra Leone', *Africa Development*, Vol. 10, No. 4, pp. 43–58.
Zack-Williams, A. B. (1995), 'Kamajors, "Sobel" and the Militariat: Civil Society and the Return of the Military in Sierra Leone Politics', *Review of African Political Economy*, Vol. 24, No. 73, pp. 373–380.

Index

Abacha, General Sani 6, 17, 61, 67, 82–6, 89
Abiola, M. K. O. 6, 81, 82, 83, 84
Abubaker, Abdulsalami 84, 86, 87–8, 92, 94
Abuja agreement 150, 163n1
accumulation by state 43, 60, 63, 64, 67, 71
ACRM *see* Anti-corruption Revolutionary Movement
Action Group (AG), Nigeria 81, 88
AD *see* Alliance for Democracy
Adisa, Abdulkarim 85
Afenifere 6, 84, 85, 86
AFRC *see* Armed Forces Revolutionary Council
African National Congress (ANC) 53
Africanists 9, 31, 127
Afrikaners 21
Agbakoba, Olisa 87
Agbese, P. O. 182
Ahidjo, Ahmadou 28, 177
Ake, Claude 21, 64, 65–7, 71–2, 73
Algeria
   autocracy 43
   post-independence problems 40
All Peoples' Congress (APC), Sierra Leone 26, 125, 131–2, 133–8, 144, 145
Alliance for Democracy (AD), Nigeria 19, 86–7, 163
ANC *see* African National Congress
Angola
   autocracy 43
   failed democratic transition 149
   military expenditure 51, 52
   peace agreements 150
   post-independence problems 40
   war 50
Anise, Ladun 20–1, 178

anthropology 38, 47, 127, 169, 170
Anti-corruption Revolutionary Movement (ACRM), Sierra Leone 131
Anyona, George 105, 110
apartheid 67
APC *see* All Peoples' Congress
Appiah, K. 172
Armed Forces Revolutionary Council (AFRC), Sierra Leone 125, 142, 145, 146
Asei, Nimi 93
autocrats 43
Awolowo, Chief Obafemi 21
Azikiwe, Dr Nnamdi 21

Babangida, General Ibrahim 61, 81, 89
Babatope, Ebino 17–18
Balewa, Sir Abubakar Tafawa 21
Bamiléké 29
Bangura, Yusuf 132, 142
Bankole-Bright, H. C. 128
Banton, Michael 45
Barber, Benjamin 45
Barre, Mohamed Siad 61
Barth, Fredrik 18
Bassas 29
Bell, Daniel 16
Benin
   autocracy 43
   post-independence problems 40
Berlin Conference (1884–5) 41, 46
Beti-Pahouin 29
Biafra 84
Bicesse Accord 150, 163n1
Binkolo Mafia 138
Biobaku, Saburi 86
Biwott, Nicholas 117
Biya, Paul 29, 61
Blyden, Edward 129

Bosnia, Western media depictions 173–4, 183n1
Botswana
  ethnic representations 118
  successful management of ethnicity 53
boundaries
  ethnic 14–15, 18–19, 20
    Cameroon 30
    Kenya 24–5
    Sierra Leone 26, 27
bourgeoisie 43, 66, 67, 68, 72, 75
  see also dominant elites
Brisibe, Aniemeseigha 93
Brownlie, Ian 38
Burundi
  ban on ethnic names 177
  ethnic conflict 53
  ethnic sentiments 45
  ethnic/tribe controversy 4
  failed democratic transition 149
  federalism 159
  genocide 158
  Kenya comparison 24
  military expenditure 50, 51, 52
  politics 27–8
  social/political competition 18
  socio-economic indicators 49
  state collapse 8, 149
  two ethnic bi-polarity 132
Buthelezi, Mangosuthu 18, 53

Cabral, Amilcar 71
Cameroon
  autocracy 43
  ethnic group behavior 4
  politics 28–30
  social/political competition 18
  state despotism 61–2
Cameroon People's Democratic Movement (CPDM) 29
Campbell, Aidan 126
capitalism
  Africa worse off under 65
  cause of state despotism 63
  colonialism 41
  Sierra Leone 126

Carew, G. M. 26
Cartwright, J. R. 128
Central African Republic
  autocracy 43
  post-independence problems 40
centralized ethnic systems 128, 143
Chikoko Movement 90–1
Choge, Kiptum 117
citizenship 119, 120
civil society 62, 67–8
civil war
  Liberia 67
  military expenditure 56n6
  Nigeria 6, 79, 88
  Sierra Leone 144–5
  Sudan 53, 162
class struggle
  ethnicity 71, 72
  liberal democracy 126–7
  state role 64, 65, 73
  see also social class
Clastres, Pierre 46–8, 53
coalition government 153, 154, 156–7, 162
COC see Council of Chiefs
Cohen, Abner 140, 141, 145
Cold War 2, 40, 44, 128, 149
collective action 94–5
colonialism 46–50, 71, 169–70
  African state formation 41–2
  cause of state despotism 63
  communal aspirations 81
  creation of ethnic conflicts 9, 70
  economics 4–5
  Kenya 101–2
  modernization 38
  political crises caused by 40
  Western justification of 177
  see also imperialism
Comaroff, J. 172
communism 128
competition
  ethnic 4, 18, 19, 20
    Cameroon 29, 30
    Kenya 24
    Rwanda-Burundi 28
    Sierra Leone 26

conflict-reduction strategies 149–66
Congo, Democratic Republic of
   autocracy 43
   ethnic sentiments 45
   post-independence problems 40
Connor, Walker 174
consociationalism 153–5, 156–9, 161–2
constitutions 75–6
   Ethiopia 6, 76
   Kenya 105–6, 114–15, 122
   Sierra Leone 128–9
constructivist paradigm 19
corruption
   Kenya 101, 102, 109, 112, 122
   Nigeria 79, 87
   Sierra Leone 144
   South Africa 53
   state power 42
Couloumbis, Theodore A. 20
Council of Chiefs (COC), Sierra Leone 139
CPDM *see* Cameroon People's Democratic Movement
Creoles
   Sierra Leone 25, 26, 131, 132
      decolonization 128–9
      free-masonry 140, 141, 145

Dahl, Robert 151
Davidson, Basil 9
debt, military expenditure relationship 50–3
decolonization 21, 41
   Nigeria 79, 80, 81
   Sierra Leone 128, 145
democracy 5, 30, 54, 75, 150–2, 161
   Cameroon 28, 29
   conflict reduction 150, 162
   consociationalism 153–5
   culture of 76
   ethnic block-voting 180
   failed transitions 149
   Kenya 111, 115–16
   lack of 40
   modernization theory 44
   Nigeria 6, 86, 95n6
   sovereignty 42

   see also democratization; liberal democracy
Democratic Party (DP), Kenya 114
democratization
   Kenya 115–16, 122
   Nigeria 94
   peace agreements 150
   Sierra Leone 26, 126
deracialization 48
destatization 59
development projects, Kenya 103
devolution 181
Diamond, Larry 2, 127–8
dispersed ethnic systems 128, 143
divide-and-rule
   colonial powers 70, 120
   Kenya 107
   state tactics 66
'divided societies' 174, 175
Diya, Oladipo 85
dominant elites 60, 63, 64, 71, 72, 74–5
   consociationalism 153, 157, 158
   democracy 152
   electoral incentives 163
   free-masonry 140, 141, 145
   independence 43
   Kenya 108–9, 112
   Nigeria 86
   resource appropriation 68
   Sierra Leone 126, 140, 141, 145
   see also bourgeoisie
domination of state 61–9
Doornbos, Martin 75, 76–7
Dorris, M. 169
double consciousness 170, 177, 183
Dubois, W. E. B. 170

ECA *see* United Nations, Economic Commission for Africa
ECOMOG *see* Economic Community of West African States Monitoring Group
economic aid 40
Economic Community of West African States Monitoring Group (ECOMOG) 125, 145
economic decline
   inability of state to respond 68–9

Kenya 101
Nigeria 81
Sierra Leone 130, 133–4, 145
economic issues
   Africanism 31
   colonial experience 4–5
   crises 68–9, 73
   development blocked by power struggles 66
   federalism 159–60
   modernization theory 43–4
   peasants 71–2
   post-independence problems 39, 40
   see also capitalism
Edo 92
Egbe Omo Yoruba 6, 84–5
Egi 90, 92
Ejobowah, John Boye 8, 149–66
Ekekwe, Eme 71, 72
Ekutay 8, 126, 135, 137, 138–45
Ekwueme, Alex 88
Elaigwu, J. I. 37
elections
   conflict reduction 31, 154, 155
   Kenya 23–4, 109–10, 111–12, 116
   Nigeria 81, 86–7
   Sierra Leone 133, 141
electoral incentives 154, 155, 160–1
emotionalism 17
employment
   Limbas 142–3
   Nigerian minorities 91, 92
enbourgeoisment 68
Equatorial Guinea, state despotism 61–2
Eritrea
   constitution 76
   independence struggle 46
   war with Ethiopia 149
Ethiopia
   constitution 6, 76
   ethnic conflict 46
   ethnic representations 118–19
   ethnic sentiments 45
   federalism 162
   military expenditure 50–1, 52
   Ogaden War 159
   socio-economic indicators 49

   war with Eritrea 149
ethnic cleansing
   Kenya 7, 23
   Rwanda-Burundi 27, 28
   Yugoslavia 149, 174
ethnic community 36
ethnic conflict 2, 8, 15, 30–1
   colonialism as cause of 70
   conflict-reduction strategies 149–66
   European encouragement of 35
   Kenya 109–10
   military expenditure 50–4
   nation-state definition 37
   perceived differences 36
   state stability 5
   Yugoslavia 127
   see also war
ethnic consciousness 1, 37, 70, 75, 77, 172
   decolonization 145
   global nature of 128
   group boundaries 15
   state system 5
ethnic federalism 8, 102, 118–20, 121, 160, 162
ethnic homogeneity 8, 53, 151
ethnic identity
   collapse of states 100
   instrumentalist perspective 45
   loyalty greater than towards state 69, 70, 73
   Northern Ireland 175
   primordialism 44
   representation 118–19
   Sierra Leone 25–6, 126
ethnic pluralism 76–7, 152, 174
ethnicity definition 13–16
ethnies 14, 47
ethno-regionalism 87–8
ethnonationalism 16, 18, 21, 100, 172, 180, 183
Europe
   colonialism 46–50
   ethnic community 36
   ethnic consciousness 5
   expansionism 35
   state formation 41

exclusiveness 15, 37
exploitation, state domination 66–7

Fabian, Johannes 169–70
Falana, Femi 87
Fanon, Frantz 48, 50
Fawehinmi, Gani 87
federalism 8, 31, 182
    conflict reduction 153, 154, 159–60, 162
    Kenya 118–20
    Nigeria 91, 159, 162
    see also ethnic federalism
Feronsola 143
FORD see Forum for the Restoration of Democracy
FORD-Asili 23, 24, 25, 110
FORD-Kenya 23, 24, 110
Forum for the Restoration of Democracy (FORD), Kenya 23–4, 109–10
Foulbe 29
free-masonry 140, 141, 145

Gambia, failed democratic transition 149
Gana, A. T. 59, 67
Ganguly, Rajat 100
Geertz, Clifford 17, 44
GEMA see Gikuyu Embu Meru Association
genocide
    possibility in Kenya 121
    Rwanda-Burundi 53, 121, 158
Ghana
    autocracy 43
    constitution 76
    military expenditure 51, 52
    post-independence problems 40
    university college 179
    world scrutiny of 177–8
Gikuyu Embu Meru Association (GEMA) 108
Githongo, J. 113
Glazer, N. 13
Glickman, Harvey 150
globalization 64, 65
Gottlieb, Gidon 1
governance 54

Gramsci, Antonio 61
grand coalition 154, 156–7, 162
Grinker, R. R. 169, 172–3
Grosby, Steven 18
Gross, Michael L. 19
Guinea-Bissau, autocracy 43
Gurr, Robert T. 2

Hall, R. L. 175
Handleman, Don 36
Harff, Barbara 2
Hausa-Fulani 21, 82, 83, 84–5, 157
Hechter, Michael 45
hegemony
    Sierra Leone 126, 132–3
    state domination 61, 62, 63
Herz, John 3
Horowitz, Donald 22, 46, 128, 164n4
    conflict reduction 9, 150, 154, 155, 159, 163
    inter-ethnic cooperation 143
Hozic, A. A. 169, 183
human rights 65, 66, 74, 76, 87, 182
Hutchinson, J. 1, 14, 36, 45
Hutu 27–8, 158, 159

Ibo 157
ideology
    Kenya 111
    tribalism 127
IFP see Inkatha Freedom Party
Igbo 4, 21, 82, 83–4, 87–8
Ihonvbere, Julius O. 5–6, 27–8, 59–78, 87
Ijaw 6, 29, 89–90, 91–2
Ijaw Youth Council (IYC) 89–90
IMF see International Monetary Fund
imperialism
    cause of state despotism 62–3
    ethnicity used to perpetuate 72
    see also colonialism
incentives for inter-ethnic cooperation 154, 155, 160–1
independence struggles 43, 116
industrialization 43
Inkatha Freedom Party (IFP) 18, 53
instrumentalist perspective 37, 45, 46

Nigeria 79–80, 81, 94
Rwanda-Burundi 27
Sierra Leone 25–6
intellectuals 107–8, 178–9, 182
International Legal perspective 38
International Monetary Fund (IMF) 22–3, 65, 137, 144
'irrelevant state' 60–1, 64, 67–8, 74, 75
Ismagilova, R. N. 2
Isoko 91, 92
Itsekeri 92
Ivory Coast, post-independence problems 40
IYC *see* Ijaw Youth Council

Jackson, Robert 41, 42
Johnson, D. Roosevelt 163n1
Joseph, Richard 142
Juxon-Smith, Andrew 131

Kabakka Yekka (KY) 158
Kabba, Ahmed Tejan 125, 142, 146
KADU *see* Kenya African Democratic Union
Kaiama Declaration 89, 90, 92
Kalaowei, Ebi 93
Kalenjin 23, 24, 110, 119, 120
    favored by Moi 107, 113
    Kenyatta regime 103
Kalu, Kelechi A. 4–5, 35–58
Kamajors 145, 146
Kamara, E. T. 137, 140
Kamara-Taylor, C. A. 138
Kamba 103, 110–11, 120
Kandeh, Jimmy D. 25, 133, 135
KANU *see* Kenya African National Union
Kapras 145
Karanja, Joseph 108
Kariuki, G. G. 106
Kenya 6–8, 22–5, 99–123
    autocracy 43
    economic aid 40
    ethnic sentiments 45
    ethnic/tribe controversy 4
    large number of ethnic groups 162
    military expenditure 51, 52
    post-independence problems 39–40
    socio-economic indicators 49
    state despotism 61–2
Kenya African Democratic Union (KADU) 102
Kenya African National Union (KANU) 24, 102, 107, 109, 110, 115
Kenya People's Union (KPU) 104
Kenyatta, Jomo 23, 102–5, 113
Kérékou, Mathieu 176–7
Kiai, Mugambi 116
Kibaki, Mwai 23, 25, 114, 117–18
    electoral politics 110, 111
    manipulation by Moi 106, 107, 108
Kieh, G. K. Jr. 168, 182
Kijana, Michael Wamalwa 110, 111
Kikuyu
    British stereotype 102
    elections 24, 25, 110, 111, 116
    ethnic federalism 119, 120
    ethnic/tribe controversy 4
    Kenyatta regime 102, 103, 104, 105–6
    Moi regime 107–8, 110, 111, 113, 114, 115
    violence against 7, 23, 117, 120
Kimenyi, Mwangi S. 54, 56n7
Kirdi 29
Kofele-Kale, N. 18
Kono Progressive Movement (KPM) 129
Koroma, Abdul K. 135
Koroma, S. I. 133, 135, 137, 138
KPM *see* Kono Progressive Movement
KPU *see* Kenya People's Union
Krasner, Stephen 38
Kuranko 143
Kuti, Beko 87
KY *see* Kabakka Yekka

Lake, David A. 30
language
    Ekutay 139
    ethnicity definition 15
    social formations 70
Lansana, Brigadier 131, 143
leadership, Kenya 25, 100–1, 102, 109, 113–14
Lemarchand, R. 158–9

Lenin, V. I. 38
Lewis, Arthur 8, 150–1, 152–3, 156, 161–2
Leys, Colin 112
liberal democracy 8, 44–5, 127, 150
   limitations 151–2
   Nigeria 79, 95n5
   reforms of 153
Liberia
   ethnic sentiments 45
   state collapse 53, 149
   Western trade with 67
Lijphart, Arend 9, 150, 153–4, 156, 157, 162
Limbas 8, 25, 26, 131, 146
   Ekutay 126, 138–9, 141, 142–3, 145
   ethnic hegemony 136
Linz, Juan 163, 164n4
Locke, John 151
Luhya 7, 23, 110, 113, 116, 120
Luo
   elections 24, 110, 111
   Kenyatta regime 104–5, 106
   Moi regime 106, 107, 110, 111, 116
   violence against 7, 23, 120

Maasai 120
Mafeje, Archie 127
Maina, Wachira 115
majimboism (ethnic federalism) 8, 102, 118–20, 121
Malaysia, coalition government breakdown 157–8
Mali, ethnic propaganda 177
Malinowski, Bronislaw 103
Mandingo 135
Manthai, Wangari 114
Margai, Albert 129, 130–1
Margai, Milton 128, 129–30, 132
Marx, Karl 38
Marxism 38, 39
Mathiu, Mutuma 99
Matiba, Kenneth 23, 25, 110
Mauritius, successful management of ethnicity 53
Mazrui, Ali 118–19, 172
Mbaku, J. M. 182

Mboya, Tom 7, 104–5
Mbriwa, Tamba 129
MDR *see* Movement for the Defense of the Republic
media
   Bosnian conflict 173–4, 183n1
   Western representation of African ethnicity 9, 167, 171, 173–4, 178, 181
Mende 8, 25–6, 129–30, 132, 135–7, 141–2
military expenditure 50–4
Mill, John Stuart 151
Minah, Francis 137–8
Mkandawire, Thandika 179
modernization theory 43–4
Moi, Daniel arap 7, 23, 24, 40, 61, 106–9
   critique of 100–1, 109
   electoral politics 110, 111, 112
   ethnic violence 117, 118
   presidential succession 113–15
Momoh, Joseph Saidu 125–6, 135, 136–8, 140, 143–4, 145
Monga, C. 168
Monynihan, D. P. 13
Moslems 29
MOSOP *see* Movement for the Survival of the Ogoni People
Movement for the Defense of the Republic (MDR), Cameroon 29
Movement for the Survival of the Ogoni People (MOSOP) 82, 89
Mozambique
   autocracy 43
   war 50
Mudimbe, V. Y. 176
Mugabe, Robert Gabriel 149
Muliro, Masinde 6–7, 105
Multi-Kamara, Ahmed 135
multinational corporations 5, 82, 89–94, 95n5
   see also transnational corporations
multiparty politics 22, 150
   Kenya 23, 109–10, 116, 117, 118
   Sierra Leone 126, 137
Muriuki, Gideon 101
Murungi, Kiraitu 111–12, 114

Mussolini, Benito 175–6
Musyimi, Mutava 120
Mutahi, W. 112
Mutai, Chelagat 105
Mwakenya 108
Mwangale, Elijah 113–14
Myers, G. 173–4

Nahum, Fasil 76
Nash, Manning 14–15
nation-building 39, 70, 102, 153, 177
nation-state 17, 20–1, 27, 36–7, 102
National Party of Nigeria (NPN) 157
National Peoples Party (NPP), Nigeria 157
National Reformation Council (NRC), Sierra Leone 131
National Union for Democracy and Progress (NUDP), Cameroon 29
nationalism 1, 2, 9, 21, 100, 178
Native Americans 169
Ndadaye, Melchoir 158
new social movements 80
Ngilu, Charity 110, 111
Nguema, N. 61
Niger, failed democratic transition 149
Nigeria 6, 79–97
   Alliance for Democracy victory 19
   autocracy 43
   broad range of elites 163
   class struggle 71
   coalition government breakdown 157
   ethnic sentiments 45
   ethnic/tribe controversy 4
   failure of political regimes 53
   federalism 91, 159, 162
   First Republic 21
   large number of ethnic groups 156
   Lewis constitutional model 161–2
   military expenditure 51, 52–3
   oil minorities 29, 82, 89–94, 182
   post-independence problems 40
   primordial attachments 18
   resources appropriated by state 68
   social/political competition 18
   socio-economic indicators 49
   state despotism 61–2, 73
   trade with United States 67
   tribal political discourse 179
Njonjo, Charles 106, 107
Nkrumah, K. 177–8, 179
Nnoli, Okwudiba 15, 30, 70, 72
Nordlinger, Eric 9, 150, 153, 156–7, 160, 162
Northern Ireland 175
NRC *see* National Reformation Council
NUDP *see* National Union for Democracy and Progress
Nyamoya, Albin 177
Nyong'o, Peter Anyang 108

OAU *see* Organization of African Unity
Obadare, E. 181
Obasanjo, Olusegun 161–2, 163
Obote, Milton 158
Ochieng, P. 117–18
Ocholla-Ayayo, A. B. C. 75
Odinga, Oginga 23, 24, 104–5, 106, 107, 110, 116
Odinga, Raila 107, 110, 111
Ofeimun, O. 180
Ogaden War (1977–78) 159
Ogbia 90, 92
Ogoni 6, 21, 68, 82, 89, 92, 93–4
oil multinationals 82, 89–94
Ojukwu, Odumegwu 83–4
Okumu, F. Wafula 6, 7, 99–123
Olanrewaju, Tunji 85
Olton, Roy 20
one-party politics
   Cameroon 28
   Kenya 22
   prevalence in African states 44
   Sierra Leone 125, 131, 133, 137, 141
Organization of African Unity (OAU) 65

Pan Niger Delta Conference 89
pan-Africanism 1, 9
Patterson, Orlando 16
peasants 71–2, 112
Peoples National Party (PNP), Sierra Leone 129
Plano, Jack 20
pluralism 76–7, 152, 174

PNP *see* Peoples National Party
political domination 61–2
Port Harcourt Resolution 89, 90
poverty
   Kenya 108, 112
   Sierra Leone 130
   state repression 68, 73, 74
power 48, 53, 79, 100
   see also domination of state
power sharing 30–1, 142, 152–3, 154, 158, 181–2
'primitive' societies 47–8, 53
primordialism 17, 18, 20, 43, 44, 46, 168
principle of derivation 88, 95n5
prisoner's dilemma models 54, 56n7
proportional representation 153, 154, 155, 156, 161, 162

racism 48, 172, 178
ranked ethnic systems 128
Rawls, John 151
Realists 38–9, 55n2
regional autonomy 31
religion, Northern Ireland 175
representation of ethnicity 167, 169–71, 172
repression 65, 66, 74, 92–4
resistance
   ethnic structures 79, 80
   Nigerian oil minorities 89–94
   Yoruba 83–7
resources
   Cameroon 29
   conflict over 15
   distribution of 45, 46
   ethnic competition theory 19
   federalism 160
   instrumentalist perspective 37
   political contestation over 16, 24–5
   principle of derivation 95n5
   resistance of Nigerian minorities 82, 89–94
   scarce 30, 35, 36, 45, 53
   state appropriation of 5–6, 68
Revolutionary United Front (RUF), Sierra Leone 125, 132, 144, 145, 146
Reynolds, Andrew 149

Robertson, L. R. 44
Rothchild, Donald 30
Rousseau, Jean-Jacques 151
RUF *see* Revolutionary United Front
rule of law 8, 65, 182
Rwanda
   ethnic sentiments 45
   ethnic/tribe controversy 4
   federalism 159
   genocide 53, 121, 158
   Kenya comparison 24
   military expenditure 50, 51, 52
   politics 27–8
   social/political competition 18
   socio-economic indicators 49
   state collapse 8, 149
   two ethnic bi-polarity 132
   Western media depictions 173–4

Saboat 120
Saitoti, George 108
Sankoh, Foday 125, 132, 137, 144
Saro-Wiwa, Ken Saro 82
Savimbi, Jonas 163n1
Schermerhorn, R. A. 14
SDF *see* Social Democratic Front
secessionism 2, 4, 45, 149
Seko, Mobutu Sese 40, 61, 177
self-determination 2, 91, 92, 153
Senegal, co-opting leaders 142
Seroney, Jean-Marie 105
Sheth, D. L. 37
Shikuku, Martin 105
Shils, Edward 17, 44
Shirikisho Party 110, 119
Shodipe, U. 181
Shona 4
Shonekan, Ernest 81
Sibathae 138
Sierra Leone 8, 25–7, 125–47
   ethnic group behavior 4
   failed democratic transition 149
   military expenditure 51, 52, 53
   peace agreements 150
   socio-economic indicators 49
   state collapse 8, 149

Sierra Leone Independence Movement
   (SLIM) 129
Sierra Leone Independence Progressive
   Movement (SLIPM) 129
Sierra Leone Peoples' Party (SLPP) 26,
   129, 130–1, 132, 143
single-party system *see* one-party
   politics
Sisk, Timothy 149
Sklar, Richard 30
SLIM *see* Sierra Leone Independence
   Movement
SLIPM *see* Sierra Leone Independence
   Progressive Movement
Slovo, Joe 161
SLPP *see* Sierra Leone Peoples' Party
Smart, John Karefa 131, 132
Smith, A. D. 1, 14, 36, 45
social class
   ethnicity relationship 71–2
   instrumentalist perspective 80
   Kenya 112
   limited independence of state from
      21, 64
   as main social determinant 127–8
   state repression 66
   see also class struggle; dominant
      elites
social closure 19, 20
   Cameroon 30
   Kenya 24
   Rwanda-Burundi 28
Social Democratic Front (SDF),
   Cameroon 29
social formations
   ethnic groups 15, 70
   European nation-state 36–7
   state role 59–60, 64
socialism 132
socio-economic indicators 49, 53–4
Somalia
   anarchy 121–2
   autocracy 43
   post-independence problems 40
   state collapse 8, 53, 149
   state despotism 61–2
Somalis 119, 159

South Africa
   Afrikaners 21
   constitution 76
   corruption 53
   democratic transformation 149
   ethnic/tribe controversy 4
   frontline states 50
   proportional representation 162
   rejection of ethnic federalism 160
   social/political competition 18
   state appropriation of resources 68
   trade during apartheid 67
   transitional constitution 157, 161
Southall, A. W. 170–1
sovereignty 38, 42
Soyinka, Wole 87, 179
Soyinka-Airewele, Peyi 9, 167–86
SSD *see* State Security Department
state 4, 5–6, 20–2, 59–78
   autocratic 43
   collapse of 3, 8, 149
   concept 36–7, 38–40
   decline of Kenyan 6–7, 100–1, 121–2
   formation of African 41–2
   hegemonic controls 150
   lack of loyalty towards 20, 63–4,
      73–4, 174
   legitimacy 4, 5, 20
   Nigeria 80
   'primitive' society lack of 47
   primordial attachments 17
   renouncement of 17
   resources 5–6, 45, 68, 71
   role 180–1
   Rwanda-Burundi 27
State Security Department (SSD), Sierra
   Leone 134
Statists 38
Steiner, C. B. 169, 172–3
Stevens, Siaka Probyn 8, 125, 126,
   131–3, 134–6, 144
   Ekutay 138, 141, 143
   tribal self-awareness 177
structural adjustment 29, 64, 134, 138,
   141
subordinate class 66, 71–2
Sudan

autocracy 43
centralization 162
civil war 53
ethnic sentiments 45
ethnic struggles 55n5
post-independence problems 40
social/political competition 18

Takougang, Joseph 28
Tamaboros 145
Tanzania, post-independence problems 40
Taras, Raymond C. 100
Taylor, Charles 67
Temne 8, 25–6, 131, 135–7, 141–2, 144
Toru-Ibe Forum 91
trade 67
transnational corporations 65, 71
  see also multinational corporations
tribalism 2, 4, 14, 118, 126, 127
  discourse of 168, 178, 179–80, 181, 183
  Kenya 99, 103, 108, 111, 114–15, 120
  state dismissal of 70
  Western conception of 169, 170, 171, 173, 175, 176
tribe
  Kenya 102
  terminological controversy 4, 13–14
  Western concept of 9, 47, 171, 172–3
Tsedu, Mathata 179–80
Turay, J. B. S. 140
Tutsi 4, 24, 27–8, 158, 159

Udogu, E. Ike 1–11, 13–34, 172
Uganda
  autocracy 43
  centralization 162
  coalition government breakdown 158
  constitution 76
  ethnic groups 156, 162
  failed democratic transition 149
  post-independence problems 39–40
Uganda Peoples Congress (UPC) 158
Union des Populations du Cameroun (UPC) 29

United Democratic Party, Sierra Leone 132
United Nations
  Cameroon sovereignty 29
  Economic Commission for Africa (ECA) 65
  peacekeeping operations 2
United Progressive Party (UPP), Sierra Leone 129
United States
  constitution 121
  racial cleavages 168
  trade with Nigeria 67
unranked ethnic systems 128
UPC see Uganda Peoples Congress; Union des Populations du Cameroun
UPP see United Progressive Party
Urhobo 90, 92
Uzodike, Ufo O. 30

Vaughan, Olufemi 6, 79–97
violence
  Kenya 7, 104, 116, 117–18, 120
  Nigerian state against oil minorities 92–3
  post-independence African leaders 50
  Sierra Leone 129, 133
  state 60, 61, 62, 65, 68, 74, 167
  Yoruba resistance 85
  see also ethnic conflict; genocide; war

Wallace-Johnson, I. T. A. 132
war
  colonial perception of Africans 47
  human cost of 50
  military expenditure 50–4
  Western depictions of Rwanda and Bosnia 173–4
  see also civil war; ethnic conflict; violence
Warigi, Gitau 118
Weber, Max 13, 19, 24, 38
Welsh, David 53
Were, Gideon 101
West Africa 21
Westphalian Treaty (1648) 5, 36, 38
Willis, Justin 101

Wolfe, James 20
World Bank 22–3, 65, 137

Yoruba 6, 19, 21, 81–2, 83–7, 92
Young, Crawford 15
Yugoslavia, former 127, 149, 174

Zack-Williams, Alfred B. 8, 125–47
Zaire
  economic aid 40
  ethnic groups 156–7, 162
  resources appropriated by state 68
  state collapse 149
  state despotism 61–2
Zambia, autocracy 43
Zartman, I. William 101, 159
Zimbabwe
  authoritarian rule 149
  autocracy 43
  ethnic/tribe controversy 4
  post-independence problems 40
Zulu 4, 18, 53, 149